Lecture Notes in Computer Science 6371

Commenced Publication in 1973
Founding and Former Series Editors:
Gerhard Goos, Juris Hartmanis, and J

Stefan Kowalewski   Marco Roveri (Eds.)

Formal Methods for Industrial Critical Systems

15th International Workshop, FMICS 2010
Antwerp, Belgium, September 20-21, 2010
Proceedings

 Springer

Volume Editors

Stefan Kowalewski
RWTH Aachen, Embedded Software Laboratory
Ahornstr. 55, 52074, Aachen, Germany
E-mail: kowalewski@embedded.rwth-aachen.de

Marco Roveri
Fondazione Bruno Kessler – IRST
Via Sommarive 18, 38123, Povo (Trento), Italy
E-mail: roveri@fbk.eu

Library of Congress Control Number: 2010934239

CR Subject Classification (1998): D.2.4, D.2, D.3, C.3, F.3, I.6

LNCS Sublibrary: SL 2 – Programming and Software Engineering

ISSN   0302-9743
ISBN-10   3-642-15897-8 Springer Berlin Heidelberg New York
ISBN-13   978-3-642-15897-1 Springer Berlin Heidelberg New York

springer.com

© Springer-Verlag Berlin Heidelberg 2010
Printed in Germany

Typesetting: Camera-ready by author, data conversion by Scientific Publishing Services, Chennai, India
Printed on acid-free paper   06/3180

Preface

This volume contains the papers presented at FMICS 2010, the 15th International Workshop on Formal Methods for Industrial Critical Systems, which was held on September 20-21, 2010, in Antwerp, Belgium. Previous workshops of the ERCIM working group on Formal Methods for Industrial Critical Systems were held in Oxford (March 1996), Cesena (July 1997), Amsterdam (May 1998), Trento (July 1999), Berlin (April 2000), Paris (July 2001), Malaga (July 2002), Trondheim (June 2003), Linz (September 2004), Lisbon (September 2005), Bonn (August 2006), Berlin (July 2007), L'Aquila (September 2008), and Eindhoven (November 2009).

The aim of the FMICS workshop series is to provide a forum for researchers who are interested in the development and application of formal methods in industry. In particular, these workshops bring together scientists and engineers who are active in the area of formal methods and are interested in exchanging their experiences in the industrial usage of these methods. These workshops also strive to promote research and development for the improvement of formal methods and tools for industrial applications.

The FMICS 2010 workshop was co-located with ASE 2010, the 25th IEEE/ACM International Conference on Automated Software Engineering, which offered a choice of events in the area in addition to the main conference. More information about ASE 2010 and the co-located events can be found on http://soft.vub.ac.be/ase2010/.

The topics chosen for FMICS 2010 included, but were not restricted to:

- Design, specification, code generation, and testing based on formal methods;
- Methods, techniques, and tools to support automated analysis, certification, debugging, learning, optimization, and transformation of complex, distributed, real-time systems, and embedded systems;
- Verification and validation methods that address shortcomings of existing methods with respect to their industrial applicability (e.g., scalability and usability issues);
- Tools for the development of formal design descriptions;
- Case studies and experience reports on industrial applications of formal methods, focusing on lessons learned or identification of new research directions;
- Impact of the adoption of formal methods on the development process and associated costs;
- Application of formal methods in standardization and industrial forums.

In response to the call for papers, 33 contributions were submitted from 16 different countries. The Program Committee selected 14 papers, basing this choice on their scientific quality, originality, and relevance to the workshop. Each paper was reviewed by at least four Program Committee members or external referees.

In addition to the regular papers, the workshop included four invited presentations by Aarti Gupta (NEC Labs, USA), Axel Simon (Technical University of Munich, Germany), Stephan Tobies (European Microsoft Innovation Center, Aachen, Germany), and Bert van Beek (Technical University of Eindhoven, The Netherlands).

Following a tradition established over the past few years, the European Association of Software Science and Technology (EASST) offered an award to the best FMICS paper. Further information about the FMICS working group and the next FMICS workshop can be found at: http://www.inrialpes.fr/vasy/fmics.

On behalf of the Program Committee, we would like to express our gratitude to all the authors who submitted papers and all external referees for their careful work in the reviewing process. Special thanks go to Jörg Brauer who supported the program chairs in many respects, and to Alessandro Fantechi, the coordinator of the ERCIM Working Group on Formal Methods for Industrial Critical Systems, for sharing his experiences. We are very grateful to the organizers of ASE 2010, who worked with enthusiasm in order to make this event possible. We are also grateful to Andrei Voronkov for making EasyChair available to us. Finally, we gratefully acknowledge the institutions which sponsored this event: Fondazione Bruno Kessler, RWTH Aachen University, ERCIM, EASST, European Microsoft Innovation Center, the research cluster Ultra High Speed Information and Communication Systems (UMIC), and AXXTEQ GmbH.

September 2010   Stefan Kowalewski
                                                                   Marco Roveri

Organization

Program Chairs

Stefan Kowalewski   RWTH Aachen University, Germany
Marco Roveri   FBK-irst, Italy

ERCIM FMICS Working Group Coordinator

Alessandro Fantechi   Università degli Studi di Firenze and
     ISTI-CNR, Italy

Program Committee

María Alpuente	Technical University of Valencia, Spain
Jörg Brauer	RWTH Aachen University, Germany
Luboš Brim	Masarykova Univerzita, Czech Republic
Dino Distefano	Queen Mary, University of London, UK
Wan Fokkink	Vrije Universiteit Amsterdam, The Netherlands
Hubert Garavel	INRIA Rhône-Alpes, France
Stefania Gnesi	ISTI-CNR, Italy
Aarti Gupta	NEC Labs, USA
Holger Hermanns	Universität des Saarlandes, Germany
Barbara Jobstmann	VERIMAG, France
Andy King	Portcullis Computer Security, UK
Daniel Kroening	Oxford University, UK
Thomas Kropf	Bosch, Germany
Diego Latella	CNR/IST Pisa, Italy
Thierry Lecomte	ClearSy, France
Radu Mateescu	INRIA Rhône-Alpes, France
Pedro Merino	Universidad de Málaga, Spain
Juan José Moreno-Navarro	Universidad Politécnica de Madrid, Spain
Francois Pilarski	Airbus, France
Andreas Podelski	University of Freiburg, Germany
Jaco van de Pol	Universiteit Twente, The Netherlands
Jakob Rehof	Technische Universität Dortmund, Germany
Thomas Santen	Microsoft (EMIC), Germany
Wilfried Steiner	TTTech, Austria

External Reviewers

Mauricio F. Alba-Castro	Technical University of Valencia, Spain
Jiri Barnat	Masarykova Univerzita, Czech Republic
Maurice H. ter Beek	CNR/IST, Italy
Clara Benac Earle	Universidad Politécnica de Madrid, Spain
Sebastian Biallas	RWTH Aachen University, Germany
Andrea Bracciali	Università de Pisa, Italy
Doina Bucur	Oxford University, UK
Manuel Carro Liñarez	Technical University of Valencia, Spain
Milan Češka	Brno University of Technology, Czech Republic
Jakub Chaloupka	Masarykova Univerzita, Czech Republic
Eva Darulova	EPFL, Switzerland
Alessandro Fantechi	Università degli Studi di Firenze and ISTI-CNR, Italy
Marco A. Feliú	Technical University of Valencia, Spain
Lars-Åke Fredlund	Universidad Politécnica de Madrid, Spain
Emilio Jesús Gallego Arias	Universidad Politécnica de Madrid, Spain
Rodolfo Gomez	University of Kent, UK
Nikos Gorogiannis	Queen Mary, University of London, UK
Daniele Grasso	General Electric Transportation Systems (GETS), Italy
Karin Greimel	Graz University of Technology, Austria
Andreas Griesmayer	VERIMAG, France
Radu Grigore	Queen Mary, University of London, UK
Alex Groce	Oregon State University, USA
Raúl Gutiérrez	Technical University of Valencia, Spain
Paul Hänsch	RWTH Aachen University, Germany
Ángel Herranz	Universidad Politécnica de Madrid, Spain
Alexander Kaiser	Oxford University, UK
Volker Kamin	RWTH Aachen University, Germany
Mark Kattenbelt	Oxford University, UK
Jeroen Ketema	Universiteit Twente, The Netherlands
Viktor Kuncak	EPFL, Switzerland
Frédéric Lang	INRIA Rhône-Alpes, France
Ralf Laue	Universität Leipzig, Germany
Julio Mariño	Universidad Politécnica de Madrid, Spain
Mieke Massink	CNR/IST Pisa, Italy
Franco Mazzanti	CNR/IST Pisa, Italy
Ralf Möller	Hamburg University of Technology, Germany
Nannan He	Oxford University, UK
Jacob Palczynski	RWTH Aachen University, Germany
Laura Panizo	Universidad de Málaga, Spain

Table of Contents

The Metrô Rio ATP Case Study

Alessio Ferrari[1], Daniele Grasso[2], Gianluca Magnani[2],
Alessandro Fantechi[2], and Matteo Tempestini[1]

[1] General Electric Transportation Systems (GETS), Firenze, Italy
[2] Universitá di Firenze, DSI, Firenze, Italy

Abstract. This paper reports on the Simulink/Stateflow based development of the on-board equipment of the Metrô Rio Automatic Train Protection system. Particular focus is given to the strategies followed to address formal weaknesses and certification issues of the adopted tool-suite. On the development side, constraints on the Simulink/Stateflow semantics have been introduced and design practices have been adopted to gradually achieve a formal model of the system. On the verification side, a two-phase approach based on model based testing and abstract interpretation has been followed to enforce functional correctness and runtime error freedom.

Quantitative results are presented to assess the overall strategy: the effort required by the design activities is balanced by the effectiveness of the verification tasks enabled by model based development and automatic code generation.

1 Introduction

Industrial applications of formal methods and model based development for railway signaling systems are discussed in many case studies. The Paris Metro [16], the SACEM system [17], and the San Juan metro [18] are past and recent examples of successful stories about the usage of these technologies in the railway domain. In this paper, we offer a further insight into the actual industrial usage of formal methods, describing the experience of a railway signaling company, namely the railway signaling division of General Electric Transportation Systems (GETS), in adopting formal specification and development techniques by means of Simulink/Stateflow for the development of the Metrô Rio Automatic Train Protection (ATP) system.

GETS was commissioned for the adaptation of its SSC ATP to Metrô Rio at the end of 2008. This was a time when the company was finishing its first large scale development project that made use of formal model based development with Simulink/Stateflow. Introducing this tool-suite within a safety-critical process is not a straightforward step: the lack of a formal semantics of the language and the absence of a certified code generator require strategies to be defined in order to have a sound and safe development. SSC - Metrô Rio provided the opportunity to improve and assess the process practices experimented in previous projects to address these issues. Indeed, GETS adopted the Simulink/Stateflow

S. Kowalewski and M. Roveri (Eds.): FMICS 2010, LNCS 6371, pp. 1–16, 2010.

platform first for the development of prototypes [9] and afterwards for requirements formalization and code generation [2]. Experimentation with the code generator led to the definition of an internal set of modeling rules in the form of an extension of the MAAB guidelines [6], a stable and widely accepted standard developed by automotive companies. With SSC - Metrô Rio, additional rules have been introduced to constrain the language to a semantically unambiguous set and a hierarchical derivation approach has been defined in order to gradually achieve a formal model of the system. Concerning verification of models and generated code, an enhancement of the two-phase approach presented in [13] has been adopted: control-flow and functional properties have been verified through model based testing, while static analysis by means of abstract interpretation has been used to check data-flow properties. The model based testing activity has been performed through a code validation framework that executes the same test cases both at model level and at code level, automatically verifying consistency of the test results for each model unit. This idea basically settles the problem of having a qualified code generator, since certification of conformity can be ensured each time the code is synthesized from a model.

The successful application of the presented process, witnessed by encouraging results in terms of cost reduction and safety assurance, has actually open the door to formal verification and we are currently exploring activities in this direction.

2   SSC Metrô Rio ATP System

The role of a metro signaling system is to protect trains by keeping vehicles a safe distance apart. Traditionally, the traffic along metro tracks is managed by dividing each track into segments called *block sections* or simply *blocks*, and ensuring each train not to enter a given block section unless the block is clear of other trains. Signals are placed at the beginning of each block to inform the drivers about the status of the section that they are entering. The meaning of each signal aspect can be broadly represented by three pieces of information (see Fig. 1):

Authorized speed: the speed that is permitted in the block that is being entered;
Target distance: the maximum distance that the train can move while still being
   protected;
Target speed: the maximum speed that the train is permitted to have over the
   target distance.

Automatic Train Protection (ATP) systems, such as the SSC Metrô Rio one, are typically embedded platforms that enforce the rules of signaling systems by adding an on-board automatic control over the speed limit allowed to trains along the track, thereby ensuring the safety of movement of the trains and consistent protection of the line traffic independent of train operator actions.

The SSC Metrô Rio system consists of wayside devices, composed by an encoder and a transponder, that respectively encode and transmit a telegram that contains the data to be processed by the carborne equipment. The wayside devices are positioned close to the actual signals, and the combination of encoder

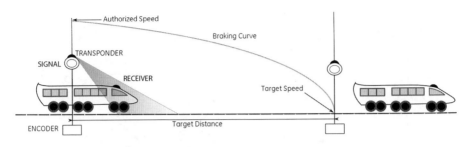

Fig. 1. Authorized speed, Target distance and Target speed

and transponder is commonly referred to as an *information point*. The carborne equipment receives the telegram data and performs the actual enforcement of train speed. Information managed by the carborne equipment concerns the approach speed and distance for signals, but also other information typical for a metro, such as the distance to the next platform and speed reduction due to particular conditions of the line. All of this information is managed by the system as concurrent targets: for each restriction, multiple braking curves are computed to determine the most restrictive speed. Interaction with the driver is primarily via a touch-screen panel which displays a speedometer with the current speed and the active speed limit, and provides a set of buttons and icons to let the driver control and monitor the system.

3 Process Overview

In this paper we focus on the approach followed for the development of the carborne equipment of the SSC Metrô Rio. The process adopted represents an application of model based practices to a V based life-cycle. Four phases are considered as the core of the system development: architecture, design, module verification and system integration/verification. Architecture and design activities concerning the project have been reported in a previous paper [15], while the verification steps represent an enhancement of the approach presented in [13].

Fig. 2 summarizes the overall process structure. Embedded in gray rounded boxes are the novel elements that have been introduced for this project. Starting from system requirements and using domain knowledge, a functional architecture in the form of a UML component diagram has been defined consisting of independent functional units. According to this decomposition, system requirements are partitioned into mutually exclusive sets of unit requirements to be apportioned to the functions. The UML architecture is then translated into a Simulink architecture and the unit requirements are formalized in terms of Stateflow finite-state automata. The software of an on-board equipment of an ATP system, such as the SSC - Metrô Rio product, is characterized by the extensive usage of control modes logic and message analysis algorithms. These are all features that can be properly represented through state machines, and hence through discrete Stateflow models. Due to this reason, in the context of the project,

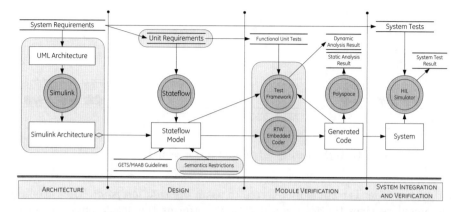

Fig. 2. Process Overview

only Stateflow has been adopted as specification language, while Simulink was only used as a simulation framework to allow interaction among Stateflow charts. Stateflow models have been designed using a safe subset of the language in order to ensure proper code synthesis. In previous projects already an extension of the MAAB guidelines was used, aimed at enhancing the readability, maintainability and structuring of the code, while with SSC Metrô Rio additional restrictions have been introduced to further constrain the Stateflow semantics to an unambiguous set of constructs. Concerning code generation, the company adopted the more customizable RTW Embedded Coder in place of Stateflow Coder: the transition was basically painless, since all the modeling rules developed for the previous tool resulted in being applicable also for the new one. Unit tests have been defined in the form of scenarios at Stateflow model level, using an internally developed framework that automatically executes the test suite on the Stateflow automaton and on the generated code to ensure functional coherence between model and software behaviour. The confidence on the correctness of the generated code is increased with the PolySpace tool for abstract interpretation, that completes the unit-level verification activities. Finally, system tests are performed on an ad-hoc train simulator with hardware in the loop.

4   Hierarchical Architecture Definition

When a large requirements set is involved in formal modeling, a well defined architecture of the model can help in clarifying which are the components of the system and how they are interconnected, bridging the gap between requirements definition and component design. When automatic code generation is adopted, the architecture of the model is reflected in the software: an effort has hence to be made to create formal models having a structure that makes sense also in terms of the architecture of the software system.

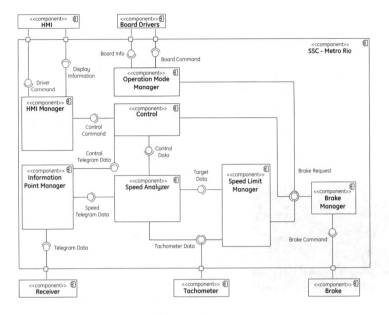

Fig. 3. Simplified component diagram

Though being powerful languages, Simulink and Stateflow are not suitable to represent the high-level architecture of a system and a more abstract approach was required in order to identify the semantic relationships between the software functional units to build up the conceptual architecture of the application. In the context of the project, we found useful to first represent the high-level software architecture through a UML component diagram (a simplified version is represented in Fig. 3). UML component diagrams focus on the interfaces and dependencies of the functional units. Each component is basically defined by a set of implemented interfaces, a set of required interfaces and a set of dependencies. In the diagram, the external components represent the software drivers that interface the system to external devices, such as the tachometer and the braking command device, while the internal components are the system functions (for a better insight refer to [15]).

In order to properly formalize this architecture through Simulink/Stateflow, the chosen strategy was to represent the system through a multiple-level hierarchical model (see Fig. 4). The different levels are intended for different development stages, from a more abstract to a more detailed view. A first level is defining the context, which means the interfaces with the environment in terms of input/output data. Starting from the component diagram, this level has been derived considering the boundary ports and mapping them into signals entering or exiting the Simulink blocks. This approach allowed us defining the borders of the software system, which can be treated as a black box completely defined by

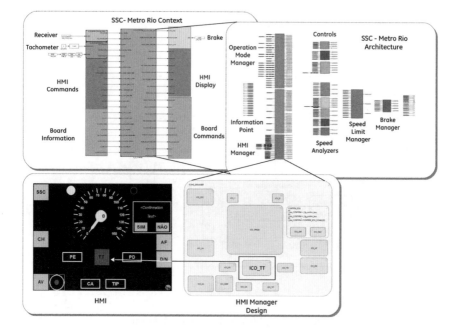

Fig. 4. The multiple level hierarchical model

its input/output signals. As part of this model we introduced other blocks simulating the actual interfaces (tachometer data, touch-screen buttons, telegram data, etc.), to perform interactive testing of the model.

A second level represents the internal software architecture in terms of interacting functional units modeled through Stateflow charts. For each one of the components of the original diagram, a Stateflow chart has been defined having the same input/output interfaces in terms of variables: each required interface becomes a set of input variables, while each implemented interface becomes a set of output variables. Note that no function is implemented through Simulink, used only as a simulation framework, and no block with continuous dynamics is used in our approach: any anlaysis problem that might be related to a hybrid semantics is therefore discarded.

A third level is actually the design level of the single Stateflow charts, each of them structured into parallel state machines formally modeling the system functional requirements. In order to derive such a formal model from the system requirements written in natural language, we first decomposed them into mutually exclusive sets of unit requirements, to identify the requirements apportioned to each single Stateflow chart. For example, consider the system functional requirement concerning the control over the unauthorized passing of a red signal (normally called Train Trip function): *When a red signal is passed without authorization, the system shall brake the train and the Train Trip icon (ICO_TT) shall blink on the display until the train come to a standstill.*

The requirement is decomposed as reported in Table 1.

Table 1. Unit requirements decomposition

	Requirement	Module
1	If an information point with authorized speed equals to zero is received, the system shall raise the Train Trip (TT) event	Information Point Manager
2	If the TT event is raised, the TT procedure shall be activated	Red Control
3	If the TT procedure is active, it shall remain active until the train is not standing	Red Control
4	If the TT procedure is active, the brake shall be activated	Brake Manager
5	If the TT procedure is active and ICO_TT is invisible, ICO_TT shall start blinking	HMI Manager

The first unit requirement is apportioned to the Information Point Manager, since this component is intended to interpret the telegram data and to forward events to the other functions. The second and third requirements are apportioned to the Red Control, which manages authorized and unauthorized passing of red signals. The fourth requirement is apportioned to the Brake Manager, that enforces any brake condition, and the fifth requirement is apportioned to the HMI Manager, controlling the interaction with the driver.

Fig. 5 shows the formal representation of the ICO_TT state machine, modeling the fifth requirement of Table 1, together with the corresponding generated code.

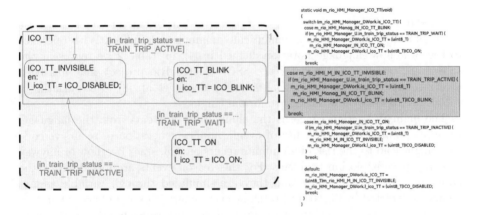

Fig. 5. Example of unit requirement formalization

5 Modeling Guidelines

Stateflow implements a variant of Harel's hierarchical statecharts [3], normally called charts according to the Stateflow taxonomy. The complex semantics of Stateflow is not formally based, though research has been performed to define an operational semantics [4] and a denotational semantics [5] for a Stateflow subset. Along with the development of the SSC - Metrô Rio project, in order to achieve more easily an unambiguous interpretation of Stateflow models, coherent with the automatically generated code, we further extended the MAAB guidelines

Table 2. Restricted Stateflow subset compared with the original language

Original set	Restricted subset
state s	state s
active state $s_a = \oslash_s \mid s$	active state $s_a = \oslash_s \mid s$
junction j	junction j
path $p = \oslash_p \mid s.p$	path $p = \oslash_p \mid s.p$
event e	$\oslash$
destination $d = p \mid j$	$\oslash$
action a	action sequence $a = \oslash_a \mid ba.a$ declarative action da basic action $ba = da \mid J$
condition c	condition c
transition $t = (e_t, c, a, d)$	state transition $t = (c, a, p)$, $c \neq \oslash$, $p \neq \oslash_p$ junction transition $tj = ((c \mid a), j)$ junction transition list $TJ = \oslash_{TJ} \mid tj.TJ$
transition list $T = \oslash_T \mid t.T$	transition list $T = \oslash_T \mid t.T$
composition $C = OR(s_a, p, T, SD) \mid AND(boolean, SD)$	composition $C = OR(s_a, p, T, SD) \mid AND(boolean, SD)$
state definition $sd = ((a, a, a), C, T_i, T_o, J)$	state definition $sd = ((a, a, a), C, T_i, T_o)$ where the conditions of the transitions in T_o are mutually exclusive
state definition list $SD = \{s_0 : sd_0; \ldots; s_n : sd_n\}$	state definition list $SD = \{s_0 : sd_0; \ldots; s_n : sd_n\}$
junction definition list $J = \{j_0 : T_0; \ldots; j_n : T_n\}$	junction definition list $J = \{j_0 : TJ_0; \ldots; j_n : TJ_n\}$

adopted in previous projects with a set of restrictions oriented to restrict the use of the Stateflow language to a semantically unambiguous subset. With reference to the Stateflow language notation defined in [4], in Table 2 we represent the subset of Stateflow adopted for the SSC - Metrô Rio project that has been identified following the approach shown by Scaife et al. [8] for translating a subset of Stateflow into the Lustre formal language.

The main restriction concerns the elimination of events from the language, since, as pointed out in [8], use of events implies generation of recursive code that might lead to the risk of an infinite recursion call, stack overflow or anyway to state-space explosion problems. For this reason events are forbidden by the adopted modeling guidelines and they are simulated through variable assignments as depicted in Fig. 6. In Stateflow every chart is executed according to a deterministic sequence (State A executes always before State B) and therefore

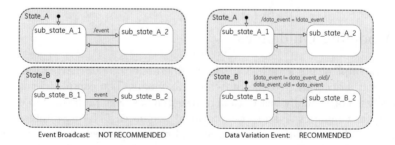

Fig. 6. Events can be avoided through proper variable assignments

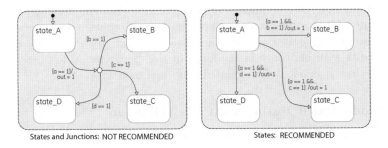

States and Junctions: NOT RECOMMENDED   States: RECOMMENDED

Fig. 7. State/Junctions transitions can be avoided through proper modeling solutions

any race condition is avoided. This approach preserves the sequential execution of the code, while allowing logical event implementation (each change on the variable value corresponds to an event).

Transitions have been distinguished between state transitions t and junction transition tj: it is not allowed to define transitions between states and junctions. These are objects that have a different operational semantics: at each simulation step, states belonging to a single OR composition are mutually exclusive, while more than one junction can be traversed during the same step. The behavior discrepancy between the two objects might bring to improper combined usage. One of the well known possible hazards is *backtracking without undo* [8], a problem consisting in the possibility of traversing a path made of junctions, possibly assigning values to variables, and afterwards backtracking without restoring variable values. Fig. 7 shows how an improper modeling can be correctly translated into an equivalent, yet safer, representation. The restriction concerning the state definition object, besides eliminating junction definition lists from states, requires the conditions over outgoing transitions to be mutually exclusive in order to avoid Stateflow to evaluate firing of transitions according to the *clockwise rule* [4]. This rule implies that transitions are ordered by their graphical appearance: the first transition is the one whose edge starts closest to the upper left corner of the source state, and the others follow clockwise. This implies that transitions naturally perceived as non-deterministic by the user, and interpreted as non-deterministic in other formal statechart languages such as Statemate, are actually deterministic. For this reason we require to make this determinism explicit by using mutually exclusive condition on guards of transitions outgoing from the same state.

6   Verification Approach

Traditionally GETS has used, as the main approach to verification of code units, white-box testing based on path coverage. This approach has revealed to be almost unfeasible due to the high structural complexity of the automatically generated code. A two phase verification process [13] was defined to address this shortcoming: the first phase implements model based testing to verify the functional requirements coverage, the second phase employs abstract interpretation

[12] to statically enforce runtime errors detection. For the application to the
Metrô Rio ATP the first phase has been improved to obtain an implicit validation of the code generator as well. The verification activity is completed by final
system tests with hardware in the loop. In this paper we do not describe this
last step since it is not strictly related to formal modeling.

6.1   Model Based Testing and Code Validation

Products traditionally developed by GETS, like any railway signaling application developed for Europe, shall comply with the CENELEC standards [1]. This
is a set of norms and methods to be used while implementing a product having
a determined safety-critical nature. The CENELEC EN 50128 considers two alternative strategies to assure the correctness of the tools that produce code that
is finally embedded in the product, such as compilers or automatic code genera-
tors: the first one requires the code generator to be validated, and the second one
is based on the so called *proven in use* property. However, both strategies could
not be applied for the adopted code generator: the validation of the generator is
unfeasible, since the source code is proprietary and no information is given about
its development process; the translator could anyway be considered as a *proven
in use* tool, since it is used by a certain number of industries that operates in
safety critical context. Furthermore, the creation of a specialized tool, and its
validation, is not in line with the company strategy, that contemplates a strong
usage of commercial tools.

The approach used in the context of the Metrô Rio project is inspired by
the one presented in [10], called Translation Validation: this approach is not
focused on the code generator itself, but on the inputs and the outputs of code
generation process and on their comparison. The validation of the generated
code is performed through two phases: the first one consists in running the same
extensive test suite, (defined starting from the modeled requirements, with a
100% requirements coverage), on the models (by simulation) as well as on the
generated code (by dynamic testing). In this phase a functional/black box testing
is performed, where both model and code are stimulated with the same inputs,
and their outputs are compared for equality. If there are differences between
the model outputs and the code outputs, they shall be assessed. A successful
outcome of this phase gives confidence that the model and the generated code
will show the same behaviour in response to the same stimuli.

However it is still necessary to demonstrate that unexpected and unwanted
behaviour has not been introduced during the translation process. The second
phase is carried out to address this question: after the execution of the tests,
the structural coverage percentage is measured on the models as well as on the
code, and the measures are compared. As stated in [10], if the code coverage obtained after test execution is less than the model coverage, then some unwanted
functionality might have been introduced by the translator. In order to perform
this evaluation, it is necessary to use comparable metrics for model and code
coverage [11]. In our case we chose to use decision coverage for the model and
branch coverage for the code. The choice of those metrics is due to the fact that

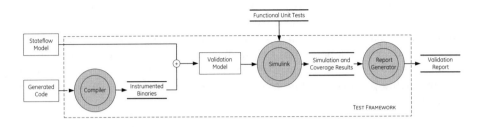

Fig. 8. 2M-TVF Test Framework

the CENELEC EN 50128 requires at least statements coverage; furthermore, since no continuos dynamic Simulink blocks are used in our modelling approach, the decision for those metrics is appropriate. A framework called *2M-TVF*, that stands for Matlab Model Translation Validation Framework, has been developed to perform the model based testing and the code validation process. The framework works under the Simulink environment, and in order to carry out the validation process, allows for the definition of a validation model that includes both the Matlab model to be tested and the related generated code, embedded in a Simulink block. The code is previously instrumented to permit the evaluation of the coverage after the tests execution, and then it is compiled and linked to obtain the executable. The definition of the test suite is a manual activity, and derives the tests from the models and the unit requirements defined during the design phase of the system development, according to the requirement coverage criterion. Automatic test generation techniques were not used due to the fact that they generally requires models with a higher level of abstraction than the ones we use to generate code. The time needed to devise the tests, by a domain expert, is of the same order of magnitude than the time needed to model the system.

2M-TVF is totally automated: starting from the system under test (SUT) and a reference to the test suites, the framework uses RTW Embedded Coder to generate the code for the SUT and then it creates the validation model. The tests are then used as input for the validation model, and a report is visualized after the execution of every test. The report contains information about the result of the comparison of the model and code outputs and a detailed section on the coverage metrics obtained on both model and code. A subsequent analysis of the report is needed to assess every mismatch between outputs or coverage values.

By implementing the approach on many applications that use the same generator, it is possible to achieve the *proven in use* property for the code generator and, at the same time, to validate the generated code of every single application.

6.2 Abstract Interpretation

Abstract Interpretation is a static analysis method that is able to infer dynamic properties of the code and to detect runtime errors and faulty states of the program without executing the code. The method defines an overapproximation of all the program reachable states, in order to check all the possible program runs. As one can infer from the theory, tools for abstract interpretation may lead to false positives caused by the analysis of runs possible in the overapproximation, but which do not belong to the real domain of the code. The tool chosen to perform abstract interpretation is PolySpace [14]. PolySpace works on C code and highlights possible runtime errors through the use of chromatic marks on the code:

- *green* if the statement can never lead to a runtime error;
- *orange* if the statement can produce an error;
- *red* if the statement leads to a runtime error in every analyzed runs;
- *grey* if the statement is not reachable.

Usually, the critical issue in using PolySpace is the mining of actual code errors from the high number of orange warnings caused by overapproximation. GETS has adopted a two step process (see Fig. 9) in order to significantly reduce the orange checks that have to be manually reviewed. With the first step the code is quickly verified using a large overapproximation set. In the second step a finer approximation set is applied using the information obtained from the previous step. The first step is useful to detect systematic runtime errors (red) and

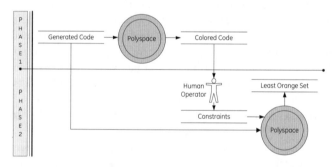

Fig. 9. Abstract Interpretation phase

unreachable statements (grey). Since no constraints are given in this analysis step, the set-up time spent is negligible. On the other hand results are not selective enough about the orange warnings, and, in order to define the constraints for the subsequent step, each orange has to be associated to the cause that could have produced it. An analyst with a minimum proficiency with the tool can easily evaluate the orange marks and quickly define the classes of causes they belong to, although in this step it is still difficult and time consuming to identify the oranges which are actually false positives. The identified classes give information sufficient to suggest input constraints to be given to the tool to restrict the analyzed abstract domain of the program. Examples of loose input constraints are related to interleaving of function calls and range of program variables. The tool generates an automatic call for each interface function of the module and initializes with full-range values the input parameters. Since the tool has not information about the correct order of invocation of the interface functions, it verifies all the possible interleaving of the generated calls. In Fig. 10 the four orange warnings, highlighted by the arrows, are caused by the function call generation performed by the tool. The input parameters are initialized with full-range values and consequently the tool detects that the pointers could be outside their bounds. The information obtained in the first step are capitalised to identify the part of the approximation that it is needed to refine. In the case of the Fig. 10, the definition of the values range for the input parameters initialized by the tool represents a constraint to add for the execution of the subsequent step. The second verification step, performed with restrictive settings, allows a finer approximation of the real domain of the program and a reduction of the number of false positives. The analyst can quickly check the small number of

```
/* Initial conditions for atomic system: '<Root>/m_rio_HMI_Manager' */
void m_rio_HMI_Manager_m_rio_HMI_Manager_Init(uint8_T *rty_0, uint8_T *rty_1,
  S_NORMAL_PAGE_CMD *rty_2, rtDW_m_rio_HMI_Manager_m_rio_HMI_Manager
  *localDW)
{
  /* Initialize code for chart: '<Root>/m_rio_HMI_Manager' */
  {
    localDW->is_HMI_MANAGER_MAIN_STATE = 0U;
    localDW->is_active_ALERT_EMERGENCY_BUZZER = 0U;

    (*rty_0) = 0U;
    (*rty_1) = 0U;
    (*rty_2).p_normal_ico_SSC = 0U;
    ........
  }
}
```

Fig. 10. Oranges caused by the automatic initialization of input function parameters

false positives and in the end is able to state that the code is free from runtime errors. It should be noticed that the use of two verification steps does not produce a high overhead. Our experience, as shown by the results given in the next section, confirms that the review performed on the first phase is simplified by the fact that the generated code is characterized by a limited number of classes of causes of orange warnings, while the results obtained with the second verification normally give a low number of warnings.

6.3 Results

The SSC Metrô Rio ATP system consists of 13 Stateflow models for a total amount of approximately 120K lines of code. For each Stateflow model, unit test cases have been manually provided according to the functional requirement coverage. The test suite consists of 238 test cases that cover 100% of functional requirements on the model. The test framework provides for executing the test cases, performed on the model, on the generated code. Table 3 compares the results of the verification activities on SSC Metrô Rio in terms of bugs found and time spent to detect and correct the bugs, with the results of these activities

Table 3. Bug detection and correction costs for comparable projects (modeling cost of approximately 4 man/months)

Project	#Modules	LOC	#Bugs	Man/H
SSC Metro Rio	13	120K	33	16
SSC BL1Plus	12	40K	114	105

on SSC BL1 product, a previous ATP project based on model based development where only the MAAB guidelines with proper restrictions were used. Although the new system has considerably increased the number of lines of code, the guidelines refinement led to a notable reduction of bugs while the well defined architecture derived from the novel design approach has allowed us to detect the errors in shorter time.

The first step of the PolySpace verification phase has detected no red errors, as shown in Fig. 11. Although many oranges have been detected, thanks to

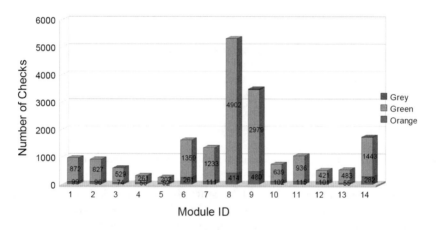

Fig. 11. Results of the first PolySpace verification step

the characteristics of the generated code, it has not been time expensive to classify these warnings according to the kind of approximation that supposedly produced them. Indeed, due to the disciplined use of modeling guidelines, the generated code has an high number of simple structures and has well-defined module interfaces, which has helped to confine the causes of orange marks to the two only classes, already mentioned, of wrong interleaving of function calls and automatic initialization of input function parameters.

The second step of the PolySpace phase has led to only few orange warnings, and most modules turn out to be entirely green. The results have been compared with the ones obtained on another previous project where PolySpace was first applied, but where modeling guidelines were less restrictive. As in the previous project, the oranges detected in the first step are approximately 15% of the total number of checks for each module, but the time spent to classify the oranges and

Table 4. Comparison of costs for classification and constraints definition

Project	#Modules	Oranges	Analyse (hours)	Constraints (hours)
SSC Metro Rio	13	2298	38	6
SSC BL3	21	1753	58	14

to determine the constraints for the second step have been considerably reduced thanks to the well defined structure of the generated code (Table 4).

7   Conclusion

In this paper we presented the formal model based process adopted by a railway signaling manufacturer for the development of the on-board equipment of the Metrô Rio ATP system. The approach is the result of a long-term effort in introducing formal methods in the development process of the company. According to our experience, the cost of formal modeling is 30% higher than manual coding. This workload increase is partly due to the fact that graphic editing is inherently slower than textual editing, and partly to the training cost required by the technological shift. Nevertherless, the case study shows that this greater effort is payed back by the cost reduction of the verification activities (about 70% in total, with respect to a manual coding based process) and by the increased confidence on the product safety and quality.

A missing element in the presented process is formal verification: indeed, although experiments have been conducted by means of Simulink Design Verifier, they have not yet secured a place for formal verification inside the production development process. The company is currently investigating the optimal strategies to introduce a formal verification phase in the development process, also in relation to the added value with respect to certification issues: the investigation will not consider only commercial solutions such as Simulink Design Verifier, but also open source solutions like NuSMV and SPIN.

References

1. European Committee for Electrotechnical Standardization: CENELEC EN 50128, Railway Applications - Software for Railway Control and Protection Systems (1997)
2. Ferrari, A., Fantechi, A., Bacherini, S., Zingoni, N.: Modeling Guidelines for Code Generation in the Railway Signaling Context. In: 1st NASA Formal Methods Symphosium (NFM), Moffet Field, California, U.S.A. (2009)
3. Harel, D.: Statecharts: A Visual Formalism for Complex Systems. Science of Computer Programming 8(3), 231–274 (1987)
4. Hamon, G., Rushby, J.: An operational semantics for stateflow. In: Wermelinger, M., Margaria-Steffen, T. (eds.) FASE 2004. LNCS, vol. 2984, pp. 229–243. Springer, Heidelberg (2004)
5. Hamon, G.: A denotational semantics for stateflow. In: 5th ACM Int. Conf. on Embedded Software, Jersey City, NJ, USA, pp. 164–172 (2005)

6. Mathworks Automotive Advisory Board (MAAB): Control Algorithm Modeling Guidelines Using Matlab, Simulink and Stateflow, Version 2.0 (2007), http://www.mathworks.com/industries/auto/maab.html

7. Sahbani, A., Pascal, J.C.: Simulation of hybrid systems using stateflow. In: Proceedings of the 14th European Simulation Multiconference on Simulation and Modelling: Enablers for a Better Quality of Life, pp. 271–275 (2000)

8. Scaife, N., et al.: Defining and translating a safe subset of simulink/stateflow into lustre. In: 4th ACM Int. Conf. on Embedded Software, Pisa, Italy, pp. 259–268 (2004)

9. Bacherini, S., Fantechi, A., Tempestini, M., Zingoni, N.: A Story about Formal Methods Adoption by a Railway Signaling Manufacturer. In: Misra, J., Nipkow, T., Sekerinski, E. (eds.) FM 2006. LNCS, vol. 4085, pp. 179–189. Springer, Heidelberg (2006)

10. Conrad, M.: Testing-based translation validation of generated code in the context of IEC 61508. In: Formal Methods in System Design, pp. 389–401. Springer, Heidelberg (2009)

11. Baresel, A., Conrad, M., Sadeghipour, S., Wegener, J.: The interplay between model coverage and code coverage. In: Proceedings of the 11th Eur. int. Conf. on Software Testing, Analysis and Review EuroSTAR'03, Amsterdam, Netherlands (2003)

12. Cousot, P., Cousot, R.: Abstract interpretation: A unified lattice model for static analysis of programs by construction or approximation of fixpoints. In: 4th ACM Symp. on Principles of Programming Languages (POPL), Los Angeles, California, pp. 238–252 (1977)

13. Grasso, D., Fantechi, A., Ferrari, A.: Model Based Testing and Abstract Interpretation in the Railway Signaling Context. In: 3rd International Conference on Software Testing, Verification and Validation (ICST), Paris, France, pp. 103–106 (2010)

14. Deutsch, A.: Static verification of dynamic properties. PolySpace White Paper (2004)

15. Ferrari, A., Fantechi, A., Papini, M., Grasso, D.: An industrial application of formal model based development: the Metrô Rio ATP case. In: 2nd International Workshop on Software Engineering for Resilient Systems, SERENE 2010 (2010)

16. Faivre, A., Benoit, P.: Safety critical software of meteor developed with the B formal method and vital coded processor. In: Proc. of WCRR'99, pp. 84–89 (1999)

17. Guiho, G., Hennebert, A.: SACEM Software Validation. In: 12th International Conference on Software Engineering, pp. 186–191 (1990)

18. Leuschel, M., et al.: Automated property verification for large scale B models. In: Cavalcanti, A., Dams, D.R. (eds.) FM 2009. LNCS, vol. 5850, pp. 810–814. Springer, Heidelberg (2009)

Practical Issues with Formal Specifications
Lessons Learned from an Industrial Case Study

Michael Altenhofen and Achim D. Brucker

SAP Research, Vincenz-Priessnitz-Str. 1, 76131 Karlsruhe, Germany
{michael.altenhofen,achim.brucker}@sap.com

Abstract. Many software companies still seem to be reluctant to use formal specifications in their development processes. Nevertheless, the trend towards implementing critical business applications in distributed environments makes such applications an attractive target for formal methods. Additionally, the rising complexity also increases the willingness of the development teams to apply formal techniques.

In this paper, we report on our experiences in formally specifying several core components of one of our commercially available products. While writing the formal specification, we experienced several issues that had a noticeable consequences on our work. While most of these issues can be attributed to the specific method and tools we have used, we do consider some of the problems as more general, impeding the practical application of formal methods, especially by non-experts, in large scale industrial development.

Keywords: ASM, industrial case study, formal specification.

1 Introduction

In this paper, we report on experiences we made with writing a formal specification for certain aspects of an application that had been designed and built by one of our product groups. Given the actual time and resource constraints, we did not attempt to write a full-fledged specification that would allow us to (semi-)automatically prove system properties, but rather opted for an *executable* specification that would help us gaining further insights into the behavior of the system via proper simulation runs. This both seemed feasible and desirable, especially since the target application has to operate in a cluster environment where testing and debugging is notoriously difficult.

Based on the experiences we had made in previous research [4], we decided to use abstract state machines (ASMs) [7] for our formalization. In more detail, we created a set of specifications where the refined version could eventually be executed in CoreASM [13]. Since CoreASM comes with built-in support for *literate specifications* (similar to literate programming [15]), we wrote a document that contained extensive documentation explaining the specification. The final version of that document accumulated to roughly 130 pages containing approximately 3 200 lines of CoreASM specification (code).

S. Kowalewski and M. Roveri (Eds.): FMICS 2010, LNCS 6371, pp. 17–32, 2010.

During the course of writing this specification we stumbled across several issues that had a noticeable influence on our work in general and the resulting specification in particular. While most of them can be clearly attributed to the method and tools we used, some of them seem to show more general problems that cannot be avoided by simply changing the underlying formal method. In this sense, we believe that our case study outlines several challenges that need to be tackled to foster the application of formal software specification methods in industrial product development environments.

The rest of the paper is organized as follows: In Sec. 2, we start with a short description of the application that we want to specify followed by an outline of the approach we have taken to eventually arrive at an executable formal specification. We then address the issues we have witnessed during the course of writing the specification in Sec. 3 and, finally, we conclude in Sec. 4.

2   Case Study: Distributed Object Management

In this section, we give an abstract description of the component we have specified formally. This component is part of an enterprise application that is built by one of our product development teams. Moreover, we briefly summarize the requirements that constrained the developers while designing and implementing the application.

2.1   The Problem: Consistent Distributed Object Management

In its essence, the application under consideration implements an event-condition-action *rule engine* [17], where events are represented as object state changes, conditions are formulated as expressions on object attributes, and actions lead to further changes in object states. To efficiently compute the actions that need to be executed on events, the engine uses a modified version of the Rete algorithm [14] that propagates object state *deltas* through Rete networks. The actual implementation is multi-threaded, so access and updates to objects need to be coordinated among a potentially large set of threads running concurrently.

If the engine runs in a non-distributed setting, i.e., a single application instance, optimistic locking provides exclusive read/write access to the different objects. The engine, however, may be deployed in a cluster variant, where multiple application instances are running on different *server nodes*. In this case, we need to consistently coordinate object access across these engine instances.

Although the overall cluster size may be fixed, the system exhibits dynamic behavior in that application instances may start or stop during the overall lifetime of the cluster. Thus, we need mechanisms to deal with variations in the cluster topology, especially in the case of unexpected changes due to application or cluster node failures.

2.2   The Solution: Object Ownership and Cluster Failover Management

The implemented system does not use a distributed locking protocol, but rather tries to coordinate object access among different instances by maintaining meta information, called *object ownership*, in a shared data structure.

The solution needs to guarantee *exclusive* object ownership, i.e., at most one application instance may work with an object at any point in time. Thus, any application instance that wants to access or modify an object needs to successfully acquire ownership for that object from its current owner. As scalability is an important property of the overall system, the data structure that keeps track of ownership information is not maintained by a central instance, but managed in a distributed manner: Each application instance is responsible for managing ownership information for a fixed subset of all objects and is called *authoritative indexer*[1] for this set of objects. Fig. 1a illustrates a scenario with three application instances A, B, and C: instance A is authoritative indexer for objects 1 and 2, B for objects 3 and 4, and C for objects 5 and 6. Objects do not need to be owned by their authoritative indexer. In our example, object 1 is owned by instance B, object 6 by instance A, while all other objects are unused.

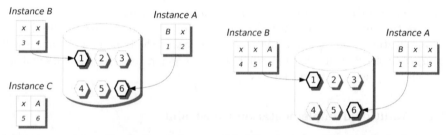

(a) Instance A is authoritative indexer for object 1 and 2, instance B for 3 and 4, and instance C for 5 and 6. Object 1 is owned by instance B, object 6 by instance A, while all other objects are unused.

(b) After instance C has left, instance A and B agree on a cluster of size 2, with A being authoritative indexer for objects 1 to 3, and instance B for objects 4 to 6. Instance B is informed that object 6 is owned by instance A.

Fig. 1. An example of a cluster distributed over several application instances

If an instance wants to acquire ownership for an object, it does so by always contacting the authoritative indexer of that object, not the current owner (if there is any). This approach has two advantages: first, the protocol requires at most two message exchanges; one from the requesting instance to the authoritative indexer and one from the authoritative indexer to the current owner. And

---

[1] Indexer refers to the fact that objects have unique identifiers that serve as an index into this data structure.

second, each cluster instance is able to compute all authoritative indexer by itself once it has learned the cluster topology after a successful join of the cluster.

If cluster topology changes, ownership and authoritative indexer information needs to be redistributed among all cluster members. Ownership information is propagated via a restructuring protocol that, upon successful completion, is supposed to ensure two (mutually independent) properties:

1. all participating instances will agree on the same view (i. e., size and topology) of the cluster, which allows each instance to locally compute *the same* authoritative indexer for any object.
2. each instance will know current ownership for its authoritative set of objects.

To illustrate this, recall our example in Fig. 1a. If instance C leaves the cluster, instance A and B will eventually agree on a new cluster of size 2, with A being authoritative indexer for objects 1, 2, and 3, and instance B for objects 4, 5, and 6. Furthermore, instance B has to be informed that object 6 is owned by instance A. So far, that information had been maintained by the leaving instance C. Fig. 1b illustrates the resulting cluster topology.

While each instance maintains its local view of the cluster, there is one dedicated *master* instance providing the current view of the cluster to new instances joining the cluster. Using a dedicated master avoids (cluster) discovery protocols, but requires explicit means for *master election*, including recovery mechanisms in case the current master instance may leave the cluster unexpectedly due to an application or server node failure. In those cases, the remaining instances will compete against each other regarding mastership and the failing parties will try to join the cluster in the usual way.

2.3   Additional Implementation Constraints

Application development, especially in large software companies, rarely happens in isolation. Overall, it has to obey various requirements and boundary conditions imposed by application frameworks and platforms and programming models that are already used. These constraints often have a noticeable effect on the resulting solution architecture. In this section, we briefly review those aspects that also had a significant impact on our formal specification work.

Avoid additional functionality by reusing existing frameworks. Rather than building dedicated functionality into the runtime environment, the development team was urged to implement functionality by reuse existing software frameworks and components as much as possible. While it is, e. g., desirable to have a central facility for storing cluster meta data, like information on the current cluster topology or on the current master instance, much like [11], the given cluster implementation does not foresee such mechanisms. Therefore, the team opted for *named* communication channels implemented using the Java Naming and Directory Interface (JNDI).

Minimize Central Knowledge while Avoiding Redundancy. Centralized knowledge requires additional synchronization among the cluster participants and increases the communication overhead among them. Furthermore, any form of centralized knowledge introduces bottlenecks and threatens system availability should the central instance stop working properly. A common practice to increase system availability is redundancy (e. g., via replication [12]), but such a feature is not part of the underlying runtime platform. Therefore the decision was made to solely rely on local meta information (i. e., object ownership) per instance which needs to be synchronized whenever the cluster topology changes (which is expected to happen rarely).

Global Synchronization via Locks. Whenever an operation requires synchronization among the instances in a cluster, the initiating party needs to enforce that by acquiring a global lock maintained by a central lock server (i. e., a central infrastructure component). Master election is an example for such an operation. In fact, there is no real election going on and no elaborated agreement protocol is used; instead, being able to become the master is just bound to the ability to acquire a global, exclusive *master lock* from the central lock server.

Synchronous Mode of Operation. Although the platform provides different means of communication for application instances running on a cluster, any protocol-related communication is implemented as synchronous remote method invocation (RMI) calls since that required less changes in the code base when moving from a stand-alone to a cluster-enabled version.

Continuous Operation during Restructuring. Obviously, the restructuring protocol for updating meta information on object ownership is one of the most critical parts of the overall solution. A defensive approach would probably try to block any other interfering operations (like object requests) during cluster restructuring until the system has reached a stable state again. But overall performance had been given higher priority leading to a significantly more complicated restructuring protocol.

2.4   Formal Specification

Ideally, we would have started with that formal specification, proven its correctness, and then iteratively refined it into executable code. Unfortunately, the real project settings were different and the development team had already designed and implemented a first version. Given that, we opted for a rather practical approach: our goal was to reverse-engineer the implementation into an executable specification that would allow us to simulate the system behavior in enough detail to detect any discrepancies between the desired and the implemented behavior. The initial plan was to focus on robustness of the protocol against communication failures. During our work, we followed a two-staged approach:

Table 1. An overview of the modules of the ASM specification

Module	Lines	Rules	Functions
Control ASM States	50	0	1
Cluster Master	161	12	10
Protocol Messages	138	0	25
Cluster Membership and Object Management	1 796	114	159
Object Requests	128	10	3
Cluster Environment (Notification)	328	19	31
Lock Management	141	7	19
Message Passing	362	12	56
Control Flow	88	10	5
Control State Handling	63	5	9
Total	3 255	189	318

1. We started with a high-level abstract specification on paper to capture the essence of the functional features. This abstract specification was used as our primary communication and discussion medium with the development team to clarify our understanding of the overall system architecture and behavior and to discuss remaining open issues.
2. Once that abstract specification had reached a critical mass, we began to manually refine it towards an executable specification. After that, we updated both versions in parallel while trying to keep the overall structure and naming conventions aligned. Although this does by no means replace any sort of formal proof of the correctness of our refinement, it eventually helped us correcting errors in the abstract specification that surfaced through simulation runs of the executable specification.

Given the dynamic nature of the application, we decided to model the system as an *asynchronous multi-agent ASM*. With this, we came fairly close to the implementation where the parallelism induced by multiple Java threads was mapped to a set of agents with dedicated functionality. As a positive side-effect, this also led to a more modular specification.

Within a time-period of six months, we spent 80 person days to write a multi-agent CoreASM specification that eventually consists of ten modules. Tab. 1 provides some details on the complexity of those modules. Out of these ten modules, the first four resemble the basic functionality outlined in Sec. 2.2. The fifth module, Object Requests, has been added to trigger random object access requests and thus simulate updates on ownership information. The next three modules provide functionality available via application frameworks (see Sec. 2.3), while the last two have been introduced to provide "syntactical sugar" when it comes to specifying complex control state machines. As the numbers show, we ended up with roughly 20% additional effort not providing core functionality, but is required to realistically model the implemented system behavior.

Table 2. The different agents per node and their number of control states

Agent	Control States
Object Requester	8
Object Request Processor	5
Node Failure Handling	22
Meta Data Management	15
Joining a Cluster	22
Leaving a Cluster	24

For each cluster node, we have six agents performing different tasks in the overall protocol and each agent is modeled as a control state ASM (see Tab. 2). Since some of the control states are shared between these agents, the overall number of distinct states is 79.

Specification 1.1 presents invariants (in CoreASM notation) which must hold whenever a cluster is considered in a stable state, i. e., no nodes are in the process of joining or leaving the cluster: As the names imply, we want to assert that, at any point in time, object ownership information is "in sync" and "valid" across the cluster. Synchronized information requires that, for each object, its authoritative indexer and its current owner share that view. Ownership information is considered valid if the current owner is still a member of the current cluster.

```
derived IndicesInSync =
  forall node in RunningNodes() holds IndexInSync(node)

derived IndicesAreValid =
  forall node in RunningNodes() holds IndexIsValid(node)

derived IndexInSync(node) =
  forall oid in [1..OID_MAX] holds SlotInSync(node, oid)

derived SlotInSync(node, oid) =
  node = authIndexer(oid, node) implies
    OWNER(OWNER(node, oid), oid) = OWNER(node, oid)

derived IndexIsValid(node) =
  forall oid in [1..OID_MAX] holds SlotIsValid(node, oid)

derived SlotIsValid(node, oid) =
  node = authIndexer(oid, node) implies
    OWNER(node, oid) memberof RunningNodes()
```

Specification 1.1. Cluster Protocol Invariants

2.5   Simulation Results

Given the specification above, a rough estimate shows that the state space required by a explicit state model checker is the range of 10^{50}. Thus, we rather went for simulating dedicated scenarios, instead explicit brute-force model checking.

As with any other distributed coordination protocol, it soon became clear that we needed to simulate protocol runs for exceptional cases, especially situations where nodes leave the cluster unintentionally. When we started our work, we thought we would need to spend most of our efforts into simulating message transmission errors. But after several talks with the development team it turned out that the system takes a fairly defensive approach for dealing with such errors: most of the time, a message transmission failure will lead to a node restart. Thus, we decided to focus on exploring the alternative paths with regard to cluster topology changes and failover handling.

As it turned out, the modularity of the specification came in very handy and we were able to factor out parts of the overall protocol complexity, like, e. g., object request handling. With this simplifications, we eventually ended up with a streamlined simulation scenario that revealed a bug in the initial implementation, not yet discovered by any standard testing procedures: While investigating the failover handling during changes of the cluster topology, we realized that the original failover protocol was based upon a faulty assumption, namely that notifications in the case of failure would be sent *immediately after a node failure*. As this notification is sent by the runtime environment and, thus, not controlled by the application, one can easily think of scenarios where this is not true. Just assume that the notification is delayed while a new node is starting up in parallel during that delay. Then, that node will become the master of a new cluster that would just consist of that one node. If the delayed notification is then passed on to the remaining nodes from the old cluster, they will try to become master, will all fail, and thus do nothing, assuming that the (unknown) winner will perform the outstanding restructuring. Since the new master is not aware of the old cluster, no repair will happen and we will end up with two independent clusters operating in parallel.

This undesired behavior can be reliably reproduced with the following abbreviated simulation scenario.[2] We start by setting up a cluster with two nodes. Furthermore, we specify a distinct id for a third node that will be started at a later stage and will become the new master of the new cluster.

```
if (scenarioPhase = 0) then {
  nodeList = ["N1", "N2"]
  newMasterNode = "N3"
    scenarioPhase = 1
}
```

---

[2] We have omitted some variable and rule declarations. The overall simulation script is 89 lines long.

Once these nodes are running, we know that the cluster has reached a stable state. We now disable node failure detection, by suspending the corresponding agents.

```
if (scenarioPhase = 1) then {
   if (AllNodesRunning()) then {
       SuspendNodeFailureHandlers()
       scenarioPhase := 2
       clusterIsStable := true
   }
}
```

After failure detection has been disabled, we forcefully shutdown the current master node.

```
if (scenarioPhase = 2) then {
   killedMaster := MasterNode()
   remove NodeID(MasterNode()) from nodeList
   SignalNodeShutdown(MasterNode(), true)
   scenarioPhase := 3
   clusterIsStable := false
}
```

As soon as the old master node is down, we start up the third node. Failure detection is still disabled, i.e., the remaining node in the old cluster is still not informed about the fact that the old master has left the cluster.

```
if (scenarioPhase = 3) then {
   if (NodeIsDown(killedMaster)) then {
     AddNode()
     add newMasterID to nodeList
     scenarioPhase := 4
   }
}
```

Once the new master has joined the cluster and there is a (new) master in that cluster, we resume the agents that will handle node failures.

```
if (scenarioPhase = 4) then {
   if (MasterNode() != undef
       and HasJoinedCluster(newMasterID)) then {
     ResumeElemLossHandlers()
     scenarioPhase := 5
   }
}
```

As a result of the previous step, the one remaining node of the old cluster will try to become master, but will fail (since the new node has taken over mastership). Assuming that another node from the old cluster has become master, it will do nothing. Once the remaining and the new master node have resumed

normal operation, we declare the cluster as stable again. But now the invariant
IndicesInSync does not hold anymore[3].

```
if (scenarioPhase = 5) then {
    if (AllNodesRunning()) then {
        clusterIsStable := true
        scenarioPhase := 6
    }
}
```

3 Lessons Learned

Although we have ultimately reached our goal, it turned out to be more difficult
than we expected. Some of the issues we have faced can clearly be attributed to
the method we have used, while other seem to reveal more general problems.

3.1 Method-Related Issues

Notation and Execution Semantics. As noted above, all protocol-related
communication is implemented as synchronous RMI calls, which means that
the calling thread will *block* until the answer has been received from the callee.
Translating this blocking behavior into ASM turned out to be difficult. At the
abstract level, we finally ended up with extending the standard semantics by
introducing an await construct (see [2] for details) and, moreover, provided
additional control state diagrams for further explanation.

Alas, this approach could not be taken for the executable specification since
that would have required substantial changes in the existing CoreASM runtime.
Instead, we transformed the corresponding rules and state diagrams from the
abstract specification into proper control state ASMs. To increase readability,
we ultimately developed a set of ASM macros that allowed us to use a more
concise notation, as the following example shows:

```
rule JoinCluster = {
    StepInto(@PrepareJoin, {startingUp, registerAtMaster})
    StepInto(@Rearrange, {arrangeCall})
    StepInto(@Commit, {rearrangeCompleted})
}
```

Here, the StepInto macro has the following semantics: If the control state
of the agent is a member of the state set specified in the second argument,
the *program* of that agent shall be overridden by the rule element specified in

---

[3] In the implementation, an authoritative indexer claims ownership for all unassigned
objects within its range. In our scenario, the new master—as the sole member of the
new cluster—will claim membership for all objects, which conflicts with ownership
information maintained by the old node.

the first argument. In other words, the first line in the example states that the agent should "step into" `PrepareJoin` if its control state is either `startingUp` or `registerAtMaster`.

Missing Scope for Locations. Although the ASM method provides a detailed classification scheme for functions and locations [7], we missed a way to restrict the scope or visibility of a location to an individual agent or a well-defined subset of agents. This feature would have allowed us to make constraints that exist in the implementation already visible (and checkable) at the specification level.

In Sec. 2.2, we outlined that the system requires "shared" information to operate correctly, but that implies that each application instance maintains its local copy of that information and any changes need to be propagated among the instances via proper message exchanges. Without having a way to attribute information as being "private" to an instance (similar to private fields in object-oriented languages), one could easily introduce errors in the specification by accidentally accessing such private information in other contexts.

Missing Tool Support for Refinements. As the name suggests, abstract specifications should provide a high-level view capturing the essential functionality of a system. We took the freedom to "abstract away" implementation related issues during the initial phase of our work. Compared to that, the executable specification had to spell out all the details that we had left out in the abstract specification. That constitutes a large refinement and should have probably been broken up into several steps. Unfortunately, none of the tool sets that were available to us does provide any support for controlled refinements.

Faced with that problem, we again took a rather pragmatic approach: we tried to establish a strong linkage on the syntactical level by staying as close as possible to the naming conventions and signatures introduced in the abstract specification although we could have used a more concise notation in some cases. There are, e. g., abstract rules which are parametrized with a *node* referring to the application server node which will process a request. In the executable specification, we do have functions that establish a unique relationship between an agent and such a server node. Given that relationship, the node parameter in the CoreASM rule signature is redundant, but has been retained to keep the rule signatures synchronized.

Reusable Specification Modules. When writing our specification, we often encountered situations in which we needed to specify common concepts (e. g., asynchronous communication channels) that, with respect to our target, we would classify as "infrastructure." Based on our experiences with programming languages that are equipped with large, thoroughly tested libraries of common data structures and algorithms, we often felt the need for similar libraries of well-proven, generic specifications of common software engineering artifacts. Consequently, we tried to make our specification as re-usable as possible; still, we cannot claim that our specification can be easily reused in other contexts than our own. We believe that is partially due to our own lack of experience in writing modular ASM specification and partially due to the lack of generic modules in ASM. Finally, while systems like Isabelle [18] or Coq [6] provide a large variety of re-usable libraries formalizing mathematical concepts, we still see a lack of similar libraries for data-structures, algorithms, and high-level components (e.g., of-the-shelf middleware components). Besides being the basis for further formalization work, such libraries of standard components and algorithms could also serve as means for learning how to write good specifications. Thus, we would especially encourage initiatives collecting and maintaining formal specifications for software artifacts, similar to "The Archive of Formal Proofs" (`http://afp.sourceforge.net`) for Isabelle.

3.2   Tool- and Process-Related Issues

While the topics above can be attributed to the specific method we have chosen, we also see deficits when it comes to development tools and processes used and established in industrial environments.

Insufficient Support for Literate Specifications. Within our work, we have experimented with the literate specification feature in CoreASM: We embedded the executable specification into a document written in OpenOffice.org (`http://www.openoffice.org`) which should allow us to use the full power of a modern desktop publishing system to improve the comprehensiveness of the formal part with diagrams, cross-references, etc. The CoreASM runtime engine is able to extract the specification part from such a document and directly execute it.

While this loose coupling seems flexible and elegant at first sight, it has proven inferior in both usability and efficiency: On one hand, an editing environment that is unaware of the specification language syntax lacks many of the sophisticated features, like syntax highlighting, auto-completion, etc., found in modern, integrated development environments, such as Eclipse (`http://www.eclipse.org`). On the other hand, having no real feedback loop between the editing front-end and the runtime back-end unnecessarily prolongs the round trip for error corrections in comparison to state-of-the-art development tools. In hindsight, we would prefer a tight integration into existing tool environments over such loosely coupled tool chains.

Although there are first examples of tools that strive for better integration into existing environments, e.g., the Rodin platform (`http://www.event-b.org/platform.html`) for Event-B [1], support for literate specifications still seems to be lacking behind. We still see a tendency to follow the tradition to treat a formal specification as part of an (academic) *publication*. In Rodin, e.g., there is no easy way to export a machine specification other than exporting it to LaTeX (via a separate plug-in). But for large-scale application development, we need a way to make a formal specification a *living document* within the overall development life-cycle.

Debugging Support. When writing specifications one often has to cope with situations similar to programming. Like programs, specifications may have bugs, and finding these bugs may require a deeper inspection of what is going on. While simulation support primarily asks for ways to steer execution runs and have a way to observe the externally visible state changes, debugging support would extend this towards the possibility to fully explore the state of the specification execution.[4] Such a fine-grained specification animation helps, on the one hand, in convincing oneself (and, in our case, also the developers) that the formal specification captures the informal requirements and, on the other hand, it allows for finding the inconsistencies ("bugs") in the specification in an early stage.

For example, we envision support for executing deterministically specified traces within the animation environment while being able to set breakpoints for examining the system state (e. g., variables, messages sent). As a first step in that direction, our experiences in simulating ASM runs in CoreASM resulted in the development of a scripting language for CoreASM that is discussed elsewhere [3]. Overall, this scripting language allows for deterministically provoking the bug described in Sec. 2.5 by performing the following steps automatically:

1. Start a cluster with two nodes and wait until it has reached a stable state.
2. Disable node failure notification.
3. Stop the master node.
4. Once the master node is done, start a new node.
5. Once that new node has finished building the new cluster, enable node failure notification.

In our experience, such "scripted" traces are also very helpful in communicating with the developer of the analyzed product.

Combining Formal and Semi-formal Development Processes. Whereas formal methods are far from being deeply integrated into our software development process, semi-formal methods, e. g., in the form of UML or BPMN are used routinely. Therefore, these already existing, semi-formal specifications should be reused in a tool-supported way. This could be done either by providing formal methods tool for these languages and integrating them into model-driven development processes (e. g., similar to [9,8]) or by generating specifications in the formal language of choice. Such generated specifications could describe, on the one hand, the environment, and on the other could serve as the basis for a formal high-level system specification.

Lack of Commercially Applicable Tools. While being a completely non-technical issue, we experience amazingly often the situation in which the software license of a tool prevented its use—even for case-studies. Either, while being available for download, the tools did not have any licensing information (which, at the end, forbids their use) or because the use in a commercial environment is excluded explicitly in the license terms (and, furthermore, no option for obtaining a commercial license is provided). Thus we would like to encourage tool

---

[4] Lacking that feature in CoreASM, we fell back to the "traditional" way of debugging by augmenting the specification with logging statements. In the final version, roughly 10% of the whole specification are dedicated to produce meaningful execution traces.

developers to state their intended license terms clearly. In our experience, this is especially important to advertise the use of formal methods in environments that are not able (either due to a lack of resources or expertise) to develop their own tools. For example, today's (rare) use of formal methods at SAP is too diverse to suggest a concrete formal toolchain (and specification language) to our product groups. Thus, we would like to use formal tools from external vendors, similar to our uses of development tools (e. g., for Java development) from external vendors. Consequently, we see a higher chance to educate our product groups in using SAT or SMT solvers[5] for specific problems than writing formal specification of whole software components.

4   Conclusion

Fully automated tools, that apply formal methods without the need for an explicit specification (neither of the underlying software system or of the properties to be analyzed), e. g., Polyspace (http://www.mathworks.com/products/polyspace/) or Coverty (http://www.coverty.com/), can be used by non-experts in formal methods [19]. Similar experiences are reported for automated tools that only require light-weight specifications (e. g., based on pre-, postconditions and invariants) on the level of source code annotations that enjoy a deep integration into the development life-cycle, e. g., [5].

In our experience, the use of formal specifications, within an industrial software development process for business software, using languages like ASM [7], B [1], or Z [20], is still a challenge. While we do not see a fundamental problem in requiring an expert for the (potential) interactive analysis (e. g., verifying system properties), non-experts should be able to document, write, type-check, and animate (execute) formal specifications and the system properties that should be verified during an analysis. Overall, to achieve this goal, the specification and animation environment needs to be integrated into modern software development tool chains used in industry. Moreover, as software is usually developed in, potentially distributed teams, support for a collaborative writing of specifications seems to be a necessity. This is in particular true if existing software development teams work closely together with formal methods experts.

Overall, we see in particular four areas for future research: First, the integration of collaboration techniques, e. g., wikis[6], into environments for writing specifications would allow for turning formal specifications from nicely formatted (academic) papers into living documents. While there are first experiments in integrating interactive theorem provers into a semantic wiki for generating formally checked pages [16], we still see this only as a first step. Collaborative

---

[5] At SAP, using SAT solvers, at least for prototypes, seems to be an accepted development approach. Nevertheless, due to technological and licensing issues it is still unclear if a solution based on a SAT solver will make its way into shipped products or if, during production, they might be replaced by a customized analysis algorithm.

[6] There is another interesting aspect to this: wikis have successfully proven that a simplified notation can significantly extend the user base.

scenarios with distributed teams (of developers and formal method experts) may require sophisticated life-cycle and versioning support that would allow teams to develop, refine and test several specification variants in parallel.

Second, software changes over time and the same should be true for its accompanying documentation and formal specification. Therefore, a tool-supported process that (automatically) ensures consistency and traceability among all dependent artifacts is, in our opinion, a central cornerstone of the successful application of formal specifications in the mainstream software industry.

Third, we would like to stress once again the importance of a library mechanism allowing for both the structuring of specifications and, more importantly, the reuse of already analyzed specifications. Similar to the component libraries available for programming language, such libraries need to be easily available within the regular tool chain (e. g., similar to the handling of Java libraries in Eclipse), reusable, covering a wide application area (ranging from data structures, over algorithms and protocols, to high-level specifications of large components, e. g., middleware), and, last but not least, available to the public.

Finally, we see a potential for integrating test case generation techniques (e. g., similar to [10]) into specification and animation environments. This would allow for both the generation of test cases on the level of the specification and the generation of test cases on the specification level. While the former allow for validating that the implementation–including the environment it is executed in—is a refinement of the specification, the latter can be used for guiding the animation of the specification.

Acknowledgments. We would like to thank Egon Börger, who helped in writing the abstract specification, and Roozbeh Farahbod, who provided substantial support to us in successfully using CoreASM.

The work described here was partly supported by the EU research project ICT 214158 DEPLOY (Industrial deployment of system engineering methods providing high dependability and productivity)[7]. The authors are responsible for the content of this publication.

References

1. Abrial, J.R.: Modeling in Event-B: System and Software Design. Cambridge University Press, New York (2009)
2. Altenhofen, M., Börger, E.: Concurrent abstract state machines and $+CAL$ programs. In: Recent Trends in Algebraic Development Techniques, pp. 1–17. Springer, Heidelberg (2009) doi 10.1007/978-3-642-03429-9_1
3. Altenhofen, M., Farahbod, R.: Bârun: A scripting language for coreasm. In: Frappier, M., Glässer, U., Khurshid, S., Laleau, R., Reeves, S. (eds.) ASM 2010. LNCS, vol. 5977, pp. 47–60. Springer, Heidelberg (2010) doi 10.1007/978-3-642-11811-1_5
4. Altenhofen, M., Friesen, A., Lemcke, J.: ASMs in service oriented architectures. Journal of Universal Computer Science 14(12), 2034–2058 (2008)

---

[7] http://www.deploy-project.eu/

5. Barnett, M., Leino, K.R.M., Schulte, W.: The Spec♯ programming system: An overview. In: Barthe, G., Burdy, L., Huisman, M., Lanet, J.L., Muntean, T. (eds.) Construction and Analysis of Safe, Secure, and Interoperable Smart Devices (CASSIS), pp. 49–69 doi 10.1007/b105030

6. Bertot, Y., Castéran, P.: Interactive Theorem Proving and Program Development. In: Coq'Art: The Calculus of Inductive Constructions. Springer, Heidelberg (2004)

7. Börger, E., Stärk, R.F.: Abstract State Machines: A Method for High-Level System Design and Analysis. Springer, Heidelberg (2003)

8. Brucker, A.D., Doser, J., Wolff, B.: An mda framework supporting ocl. Electronic Communications of the EASST 5 (2006)

9. Brucker, A.D., Wolff, B.: HOL OCL – A Formal Proof Environment for UML/OCL. In: Fiadeiro, J., Inverardi, P. (eds.) FASE 2008. LNCS, vol. 4961, pp. 97–100. Springer, Heidelberg (2008) doi 10.1007/978-3-540-78743-3_8

10. Brucker, A.D., Wolff, B.: Hol testgen: an interactive test-case generation framework. In: Chechik, M., Wirsing, M. (eds.) FASE 2009. LNCS, vol. 5503, pp. 417–420. Springer, Heidelberg (2009) doi 10.1007/978-3-642-00593-0_28

11. Burrows, M.: The chubby lock service for loosely-coupled distributed systems. In: OSDI '06: Proceedings of the 7th Symposium on Operating Systems Design and Implementation, pp. 335–350. USENIX Association, Berkeley (2006)

12. DeCandia, G., Hastorun, D., Jampani, M., Kakulapati, G., Lakshman, A., Pilchin, A., Sivasubramanian, S., Vosshall, P., Vogels, W.: Dynamo: Amazon's highly available key-value store. ACM SIGOPS Operating Systems Review 41(6), 205–220 (2007) doi 10.1145/1323293.1294281

13. Farahbod, R., Gervasi, V., Glässer, U.: CoreASM: An extensible ASM execution engine. Fundamenta Informaticae 77(1-2), 71–103 (2007)

14. Forgy, C.L.: Rete: A fast algorithm for the many patterns/many objects match problem. Artificial Intelligence 19(1), 17–37 (1982) doi:10.1016/0004-3702(82)90020-0

15. Knuth, D.E.: Literate programming. The Computer Journal 27(2), 97–111 (1984) doi 10.1093/comjnl/27.2.97

16. Lange, C., McLaughlin, S., Rabe, F.: Flyspeck in a semantic Wiki. In: Lange, C., Schaffert, S., Skaf-Molli, H., Völkel, M. (eds.) SemWiki. CEUR Workshop Proceedings, vol. 360. CEUR-WS.org (2008)

17. McCarthy, D., Dayal, U.: The architecture of an active database management system. In: SIGMOD '89: Proceedings of the 1989 ACM SIGMOD International Conference on Management of Data, pp. 215–224. ACM Press, New York (1989) doi 10.1145/67544.66946

18. Nipkow, T., Paulson, L.C., Wenzel, M.: Isabelle/HOL—A Proof Assistant for Higher-Order Logic. In: Nipkow, T., Paulson, L.C., Wenzel, M.T. (eds.) Isabelle/HOL. LNCS, vol. 2283. Springer, Heidelberg (2002) doi 10.1007/3-540-45949-9

19. Venet, A.: A practical approach to formal software verification by static analysis. Ada Lett. XXVIII(1), 92–95 (2008) doi 10.1145/1387830.1387836

20. Woodcock, J., Davies, J.: Using Z: Specification, Refinement, and Proof. Prentice Hall International Series in Computer Science. Prentice Hall, Englewood Cliffs (1996)

Formal Analysis of BPMN Models Using Event-B

Jeremy W. Bryans[1] and Wei Wei[2]

[1] School of Computing Science, Newcastle University, United Kingdom
Jeremy.Bryans@ncl.ac.uk
[2] SAP Research CEC Darmstadt, SAP AG, Bleichstr. 8, 64283 Darmstadt, Germany
wei01.wei@sap.com

Abstract. The use of business process models has gone far beyond documentation purposes. In the development of business applications, they can play the role of an artifact on which high level properties can be verified and design errors can be revealed in an effort to reduce overhead at later software development and diagnosis stages. This paper demonstrates how formal verification may add value to the specification, design and development of business process models in an industrial setting. The analysis of these models is achieved via an algorithmic translation from the de-facto standard business process modeling language BPMN to Event-B, a widely used formal language supported by the Rodin platform which offers a range of simulation and verification technologies.

Keywords: business process modelling, verification, BPMN, Event-B.

1 Introduction

Complex, large-scale business information systems are critical to the successful operation of many businesses, and SAP is a leading provider of such systems. Business process modeling has become increasingly important to the development of enterprise software applications [13]. Nowadays, business applications are usually built by integrating a broad range of highly configurable software components and services, which can be rapidly tailored to satisfy different and constantly changing business needs. Business process models are used to describe such integration scenarios and their work flows, facilitating an intuitive common understanding of the business logic between customers and developers. In addition to their use as documentation, business process models can also be simulated, analyzed and verified to reveal design errors at an early stage in software development. This promises to enhance the efficiency of reaching high-quality software solutions and can save substantial implementation and diagnosis costs which would otherwise be incurred at later development phases.

We wish to use formal methods to improve the quality of business process models within a software design process, and also aim to reduce the extra burden that formal methods induce on designers and developers. Within the context of the DEPLOY project[1], we choose the Event-B modeling formalism [1] and the

---

[1] www.deploy-project.eu

S. Kowalewski and M. Roveri (Eds.): FMICS 2010, LNCS 6371, pp. 33–49, 2010.

Rodin platform [2] in our pursuit of these goals. The choice is also encouraged by our past successful experiences of using Event-B for describing and analyzing business applications [5,6]. Event-B offers many indispensable features for analyzing business process models such as the ability to model data. The Rodin platform is empowered by a large number of plug-ins providing various analysis capabilities like specialized provers, model checking, and simulation.

This paper examines our recent work on the formal analysis of business process models using Event-B and Rodin, and discusses the impact of the analysis results on software design and development. We also investigate the potential to largely automate these analyses in order to pave the way for future industrial deployment. We designed an algorithmic translation from BPMN, the de-facto standard business process modeling language, to Event-B. The translation covers most of the commonly used BPMN features, also including features newly introduced in the proposed draft of the second version of the language [15]. We also make the Event-B translation structurally faithful to the original BPMN model, which not only improves readability, but also enhances provability and analyzability.

Outline. In Section 2 we briefly introduce BPMN and Event-B, and in Section 3 sketch our translation from BPMN to Event-B. Sections 4 and 5 describe two case studies to illustrate how formal analysis is performed on the Event-B translations of BPMN models, and also discuss the possibility of automating these analysis procedures. Related work is discussed in Section 6, before we conclude in Section 7 with a discussion of our next steps. Due to space constraints, we have moved some of the Event-B code and discussion into appendices.

2   Background

BPMN. We introduce the Business Process Modeling Notation (BPNM) elements we use in this paper. We only show syntactic compositions here. The semantics of syntactic elements will be discussed later when we explain how they are translated.

A typical BPMN model consists of one or more *pools*, each representing a collaboration partner (such as FACTORY and WORKER in Figure 1). Each pool usually contains a top process. A *process* contains flow objects and the connections between them. Flow objects include *events*, *gateways* and *activities*. Events either throw or catch triggers and are represented as circles containing a marker indicating the kind of trigger. Gateways converge or diverge control flows and are represented as diamonds. An *activity* can be either an atomic *task* or a composite *sub-process* that contains an inner process. An activity can be a loop. Activities are graphically represented as rounded rectangles. A process may contain data items as process instance attributes. There are also data stores that are process-independent and globally accessible.

Two pools communicate with each other mainly by exchanging messages, which may carry data fields. Message flows are represented as directed dotted lines connecting two pools. BPMN does not dictate how the message exchange mechanism works. In this paper, we assume that messages may not be lost, duplicated, or altered but may arrive in any order. Furthermore, BPMN provides the concept of correlation to identify the proper recipient of a message.

An important concept of BPMN is activity compensation that usually happens when the effect of an activity is no longer desired and needs to be reversed. We will discuss compensation in greater length in Section 3.6. A complete description of all BPMN features can be found in [15].

Event-B and Rodin. An Event-B model consists of *contexts* and *machines*. The contexts describe the static elements of the model, whereas the machines specify the dynamic behavior of the model. Each machine may contain *variables* that model persistent state data, *invariants* that restrict the valid content of variables, and guarded *events* that describe functionality of the machine in terms of actions defined over the state variables. Typically, a model consists of a chain of Event-B machines, each of which (apart from the first) is linked to its predecessor by a refinement relation expressed in terms of a gluing invariant between the two machines. In a refinement relation, we refer to the successor machine and its components as *concrete* and the predecessor and its components as *abstract*. A concrete event refines an abstract event if the guards of the concrete event imply the guards of the abstract event and the abstract actions simulate the concrete ones with respect to the gluing invariant. Machines and refinement steps give rise to proof obligations that ensure internal consistency of individual machines (e.g. well-definedness and feasibility of events) and behavior preservation across refinement steps. A typical Event-B model has an extremely simple initial machine, with detail added in a controlled way through refinement steps. These steps are usually small to reduce the size and complexity of the generated proof obligations and the associated burden on the automatic provers. We make substantial use of refinement in our translation from BPMN to Event-B. A detailed account of the Event-B language can be found in [1].

Rodin is an open, extensible toolset for modelling and verification of Event-B models. A model editing interface is provided for constructing Event-B machines and refinement steps. Proof obligations are automatically generated and discharged (as far as possible automatically) by proof tools built into the platform. In the event of an obligation not being automatically discharged, an interface for manual proof guidance can used.

3   Translating BPMN to Event-B

BPMN is specified using natural and graphic languages, and comes with no rigorous semantics defined. Therefore, there are a lot of ambiguities in BPMN that had to be clarified when we designed the translation into Event-B. These clarifications are according to the specific needs of our use cases, so by no means do they offer the only proper solutions – other semantic variants can be chosen.

The translation covers most of the commonly used BPMN features including comprehensive modeling of control flows, data modeling, compensation, message based communication, error and exception handling, sub-processes, looping and multi-instance activities. The uncovered BPMN features are most notably choreography and conversations as well as some types of flow objects, including call activities, transactions, conditional events and complex gateways. Some of these missing features are rarely used in practice and add significant complexity to the model. Other missing features such as transactions have very vague descriptions in the official BPMN specification and are difficult to interpret.

Our translation was guided by three principles. First, the Event-B translation should be **structurally faithful** to the original BPMN model so that anyone with knowledge of the original model can easily understand the translation. Also, any analysis result that we may obtain from the Event-B translation can be easily mapped back to the original model. Second, the translation should be designed to improve **provability**, i.e. it should result in the automatic discharge of as many proof obligations as possible. Finally, we are interested in verifying properties for systems that allow **multiple instances** of same processes.

We are unable to give a detailed description of how each BPMN element is translated. We therefore select a few important BPMN features and explain the intuition of their translation.

3.1   The Structure of the Translation

We take the model in Figure 1 as an example to show how its Event-B translation is structured (Figure 2). This model describes the management of shift work within a factory: A worker assigned to a shift becomes unavailable, and the manager has to find a replacement from the pool of available workers. The status of each worker is maintained in a database. In this scenario, an attempt is made to automatically choose a replacement. A request is sent to an available worker, who has a fixed length of time to reply. If he accepts, he is assigned to the shift and the database is updated. Otherwise, the process may be repeated up to a maximum of five times. If, after five attempts, a replacement has not been found, a manager steps in to allocate a worker to the shift directly.

The contexts in the Event-B translation contain common definitions such as process life cycle states as well as abstract constants and carrier sets that represent process instances, message instances, data types, and so on. The translations of processes and their communication are gradually added to a series of refining machines: The machine at the first level contains nothing but the control flow information of the Factory process. In particular, it has neither data information nor the internal detail of the sub-process schedule. The machine at the second level preserves or refines all information in the first machine, and adds also the data flow information of Factory. Details of schedule and WORKER are added similarly into later refinements. In the end, the communication between the two top processes is added into the last machine.

The above structure preserves the hierarchical structure of the original model through refinements: the information of a sub-process (e.g., schedule) is always added into machines at higher refinement levels than that of the container process (e.g., FACTORY). Our structure also achieves separation of concerns, which is very

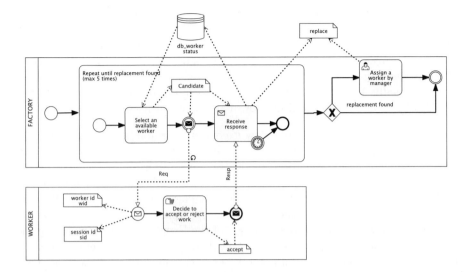

Fig. 1. The shift worker scheduling model

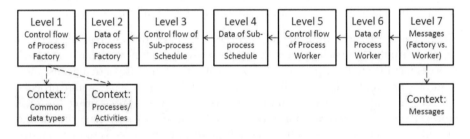

Fig. 2. The structure of the Event-B translation of Figure 1

beneficial for automated provers: A property about the control flow of process Factory can be expressed and proved at the first refinement level since it needs no information from later levels. This means a smaller hypothesis space for automated provers to search.

3.2   Processes

We allow multiple instances of a process. We use an abstract carrier set to represent all possible instances of each process (e.g. PROC_FACTORY_INSTANCES) in contexts. The machines contain variables recording existing process instances (e.g. instances_Factory); recording the life cycle state of each existing instance (e.g. state_Factory) and, in case of a sub-process, recording the parent of each sub-process instance (e.g. parent_inner_schedule); and recording which activity instance (outer instance) results in the creation of a sub-process instance (e.g. outer_inner_schedule).

Control flow. Our interpretation of sequential and parallel executions of flow objects uses tokens. For each sequence flow, we define a function that maps each process instance to the number of tokens in this particular process instance. Tokens are initialized when a new process instance is created by a start event: all outgoing sequence flows from the start event receive a certain number of tokens (usually 1), and all other flows receive no tokens. Each flow object is guarded by a condition stipulating how many tokens it needs to start execution.

Control flow convergence. With a few exceptions like join gateways, a flow object with multiple incoming flows needs only one of the incoming flows to carry enough tokens to start execution. In this case, we use as many Event-B events to represent the flow object as the number of incoming flows: each event describes the situation in which the tokens on the corresponding incoming flow are consumed. This is because otherwise we must express disjunctive choices and updates of tokens in the guard and action of the Event-B event representing the flow object. Automated provers often struggle to deal with disjunctions because they lead to case splitting and a potential explosion in the size of the proof tree. A example of the translation of control flow convergence can be found in Appendix A. On the contrary, a join gateway requires all incoming flows to carry enough tokens to start execution. Then, it is enough to have one Event-B event to represent the gateway, which consumes tokens from all incoming flows.

Data. There are three kinds of data: process attributes, data stores, and activity inputs/outputs. For each process attribute, we define a function that maps each process instance to the runtime value of the attribute in that particular instance. A data store is globally accessible and does not belong to a particular process. Therefore, unlike process attributes, the data structure representing the data store involves no process information. Finally, activities may have input and output parameters. BPMN allows activities to have multiple sets of inputs or outputs. However in our translation we stipulate that any flow object or subprocess has at most one input set and one output set. We also do not explicitly represent inputs and outputs, since the runtime values of inputs/outputs are decided by process attributes or data stores.

3.3   Events Triggers

An event either throws or catches a certain kind of triggers. The BPMN specification provides no information of trigger structures and how triggers are processed, stored, and discarded. In our understanding, each kind of triggers has its specific processing mechanism. For instance, the trigger of a message receiving event occurs when a desired message becomes available, and it persists until the message is consumed. On the contrary, the trigger of a conditional event occurs when a certain condition is fulfilled. However, if the conditional event is not ready to be triggered, e.g, it has no incoming tokens, then the trigger immediately disappears. Based on the above discussion, we have no explicit and unified representation for all kinds of triggers. Instead, we model the trigger behavior implicitly in their executional contexts.

3.4   Messages

Message buffers are implemented simply as sets since message order information is absent. For each type of message, we introduce two variables to record (1) the set of already sent messages of the type and (2) the set of messages still in the buffer (i.e., not yet received). Note that the buffer is shared by all process instances that may send or receive this type of messages. Sending a message is simply to add the message into both the buffer and the set of already sent messages, while receiving a message is to remove it from the buffer. Message fields are defined as functions that map each message instance to the concrete value of the corresponding field in that message.

Some message fields may contain correlation information that identifies the intended receiver which contains matching correlation information. In the model in Figure 1, session identifiers (sid) are used as correlation information. Each response message contains an sid field, which can be received only by a process instance with a matching sid as its process attribute. A request message is used to create a new WORKER instance. Therefore, a new request message should contain a new sid. Further detail on the translation of correlation-based message exchanges is available in [7].

3.5   Sub-processes

In BPMN, a sub-process can be either collapsed or expanded, with the internal structure of the sub-process either hidden or revealed respectively. These two appearances find their analogies in the refinement hierarchy of the Event-B translation: The sub-process is first specified without internal detail when the control flow of its containing process is added. The internal detail of the sub-process is specified at later refinement levels.

For a looping sub-process, each execution creates a single *outer* instance, which acts as a container for multiple inner instances. The execution of an inner instance corresponds to a single loop iteration. Further detail on the translation of the "collapsed view" of the loop sub-process in the FACTORY process in Figure 1 can be found in [7].

The translation of the "expanded view" is shown below. At this level we add the outer instance attribute loop counter, and also introduce an auxiliary variable next to control the creation of the next inner instance. In our example, the loop condition is tested before each iteration, and therefore we initialize next to *false* to enforce the checking of the loop condition before any inner instance is created. Note that in the following code we leave out all guards and actions inherited from abstract events.

```
MACHINE   Level_03_Sub_schedule_CF
VARIABLES
    ......
    at_outer_schedule_loopcounter
    au_outer_schedule_next

    ......
EVENTS
Event   act_Factory_schedule_activate  ≙
refines  act_Factory_schedule_activate
```

any

    pid

    $child$

where

    ... : ......

then

    ... : ......

    act5 : $au\_outer\_schedule\_next(child) := FALSE$

    act6 : $at\_outer\_schedule\_loopcounter(child) := 0$

end

Event $act\_Factory\_schedule\_complete \;\widehat{=}$

refines $act\_Factory\_schedule\_complete$

any

    pid

    $child$

    $inners$

where

    ... : ......

    grd6 : $inners = dom(outer\_inner\_schedule \rhd \{child\})$

    grd7 : $ran(inners \lhd state\_inner\_schedule) \subseteq \{completed\}$

    grd8 : $at\_outer\_schedule\_loopcounter(child) \geq max\_retry$

then

    act1 : $state\_outer\_schedule(child) := completed$

    act2 : $tk\_Factory\_schedule\_gate(pid) := tk\_Factory\_schedule\_gate(pid) + 1$

end

Event $act\_Factory\_schedule\_next \;\widehat{=}$

any

    pid

    $child$

    $inners$

where

    ... : ......

    grd6 : $inners = dom(outer\_inner\_schedule \rhd \{child\})$

    grd7 : $ran(inners \lhd state\_inner\_schedule) \subseteq \{completed\}$

    grd8 : $at\_outer\_schedule\_loopcounter(child) < max\_retry$

then

    act1 : $au\_outer\_schedule\_next(child) := TRUE$

end

Event $evt\_schedule\_start \;\widehat{=}$

any

    pid

    $parent$

    $outer$

where

    ... : ......

    grd8 : $au\_outer\_schedule\_next(outer) = TRUE$

then

    ... : ......

    act10 : $au\_outer\_schedule\_next(outer) := FALSE$

    act11 : $at\_outer\_schedule\_loopcounter(outer) := at\_outer\_schedule\_loopcounter(outer) + 1$

end

END

3.6 Compensation

Compensation starts with the execution of a compensation throwing event. Each
throw event has a scope, and only activities within this scope can be compensated. An activity is within the scope of a compensation throw event if (1) the
activity is contained in the same process as the event; or (2) the event is contained in a compensation event sub-process of the process that contains the
activity.

Usually, a compensation throw event contains a reference to the activity to be
compensated. However, it is left open in the official BPMN document whether
all completed instances of the activity inside the scope will be compensated, or
only the last instance is to be compensated. In our translation, all completed

instances are compensated. An activity can be compensated only after being completed. If a compensation trigger is thrown when an activity instance is still active, the compensation handler of the activity instance is not triggered and, in this translation, will never be triggered unless another compensation trigger is thrown again in the future.

The following code shows how the **shipping** activity in Figure 3 is compensated. **au_Retailer_shipcomp_insts** records the activity instances which need to be compensated, and **au_Retailer_shipcomp_sync** is used to wait for the completion of the involved compensations before passing tokens to outgoing flows.

MACHINE   Level_04_Retailer_Data
VARIABLES
......
    au_Retailer_shipcomp_sync
    au_Retailer_shipcomp_insts
......
EVENTS
Event $evt\_Retailer\_shipcomp\_activate \; \widehat{=}$
extends $evt\_Retailer\_shipcomp\_activate$
    any
        pid
        to_comp
    where
        grd1 : $pid \in instances\_Retailer$
        grd2 : $state\_Retailer(pid) = active$
        grd3 : $tk\_Retailer\_gate\_shipcomp(pid) > 0$
        grd4 : $au\_Retailer\_shipcomp\_sync(pid) = FALSE$
        grd5 : $to\_comp \subseteq instances\_ship$
        grd6 : $to\_comp = dom(parent\_ship \rhd \{pid\}) \cap dom(state\_ship \rhd \{completed\})$
    then
        act1 : $tk\_Retailer\_gate\_shipcomp(pid) := tk\_Retailer\_gate\_shipcomp(pid) - 1$
        act2 : $au\_Retailer\_shipcomp\_sync(pid) := TRUE$
        act3 : $au\_Retailer\_shipcomp\_insts(pid) := to\_comp$
    end
Event $evt\_Retailer\_shipcomp\_complete \; \widehat{=}$
extends $evt\_Retailer\_shipcomp\_complete$
    any
        pid
    where
        grd1 : $pid \in instances\_Retailer$
        grd2 : $state\_Retailer(pid) = active$
        grd3 : $au\_Retailer\_shipcomp\_sync(pid) = TRUE$
        grd4 : $ran(au\_Retailer\_shipcomp\_insts(pid) \lhd state\_ship) \subseteq \{compensated\}$
    then
        act1 : $au\_Retailer\_shipcomp\_sync(pid) := FALSE$
        act2 : $tk\_Retailer\_shipcomp\_chargecomp(pid):=tk\_Retailer\_shipcomp\_chargecomp(pid)+1$
        act3 : $au\_Retailer\_shipcomp\_insts(pid) := \varnothing$
    end
Event $act\_Retailer\_shipcomp \; \widehat{=}$
refines $act\_Retailer\_shipcomp$
    any
        pid
        $child$
    where
        grd1 : $pid \in instances\_Retailer$
        grd2 : $child \in instances\_ship$
        grd3 : $state\_ship(child) = completed$
        grd4 : $parent\_ship(child) = pid$
        grd5 : $child \in au\_Retailer\_shipcomp\_insts(pid)$
    then
        act1 : $state\_ship(child) := compensated$
        act2 : $db\_order\_status(at\_Retailer\_order(pid)) := returned$
    end
END

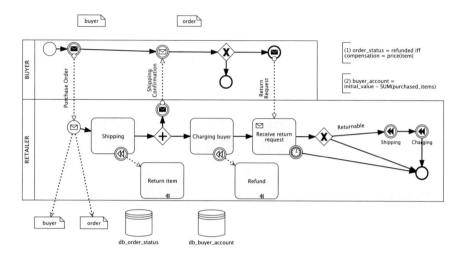

Fig. 3. A BPMN model for an online retailer

4   Consistency of Business Processes

We can use the Rodin toolset to examine the generated Event-B models for
properties such as deadlock and livelock. In this section we show how we may gain
further confidence in the correctness of the BPMN model by stating and proving
application-level properties as invariants within the Event-B model. We use the
online retailer model in Figure 3 as an example. The BPMN contains two extra
annotations in the top right corner. These are extra application-level consistency
conditions on the BPMN model. We anticipate these conditions to be defined
by the developer and treated by the implementor as further constraints on the
model. We show how we take account of them within the Event-B translation.

The online retailer model starts with the buyer, at which point a new instance
of the process is generated. The buyer sends a purchase order to the retailer,
which contains order and buyer information. The retailer ships the requested
item, and the buyer is then charged. If, within a specified time period, the
buyer asks to return the item, and the retailer chooses to accept the return,
then both the shipping and charging activities must be compensated – shipping
by the return of the item and charging by sending a refund to the buyer. The
consistency of the information maintained about the order status and the buyer
account must be maintained by this process.

The BPMN compensation event passes control to an associated compensating
activity (**Return item** and **Refund** in our example.) The purpose of the compensating activity is to "undo" an earlier part of the workflow. A precise specification
of the behaviour of this activity is usually left to a later stage in the development
process.

The text annotations we investigate here, such as (1) and (2) in Figure 3, give
the BPMN developer the opportunity to provide a more precise specification of

required properties of this subsequent development. Text annotation (1) in states that the order status is refunded if and only if the compensation paid is equal to the price of the item. Translating annotation (1) extends the Event-B refinement hierarchy with a new machine containing a new variable *compensation* and an additional invariant. The variable records the compensation paid in each instance of the retailer process. The consistency invariant introduced is formalized as

$$\forall pid \cdot pid \in instances\_Retailer \Rightarrow$$
$$(db\_order\_status(at\_Retailer\_order(pid)) = refunded \Leftrightarrow$$
$$(compensation(pid) = price(at\_Retailer\_order(pid))))$$

where the order is marked as *refunded* only when the compensation paid is equal to the price of the goods ordered. The event generated from the refund activity is also extended to record the compensation paid on that order. The new event is shown below with `act4` as the additional action.

Event $act\_Retailer\_chargecomp \, \widehat{=}$
extends $act\_Retailer\_chargecomp$
   any
       pid
       $child$
   where
       grd1 : $pid \in instances\_Retailer$
       grd2 : $child \in instances\_charge$
       grd3 : $state\_charge(child) = completed$
       grd4 : $parent\_charge(child) = pid$
       grd5 : $child \in au\_Retailer\_chargecomp\_insts(pid)$
   then
       act1 : $state\_charge(child) := compensated$
       act2 : $db\_buyer\_account(at\_Retailer\_buyer(pid)) := db\_buyer\_account(at\_Retailer\_buyer(pid)) +$
           $price(at\_Retailer\_order(pid))$
       act3 : $db\_order\_status(at\_Retailer\_order(pid)) := refunded$
       act4 : $compensation(pid) := price(at\_Retailer\_order(pid))$
   end

The second annotation in Figure 3 is a property over all instances of processes. The value in the account of any buyer should be the initial value of the account less any purchased items. Translating annotation (2) again adds a new machine to the model, which includes the invariant

$$\forall b \cdot (b \in BUYERS \Rightarrow$$
$$(db\_buyer\_account(b) = initial\_buyer\_account(b) -$$
$$Sum(ran(dom(at\_Buyer\_buyer \rhd \{b\}) \lhd at\_Buyer\_order)$$
$$\cap$$
$$dom(db\_order\_status \rhd \{charged, returned\}))))$$

in which the clause $ran(dom(at\_Buyer\_buyer \rhd \{b\}) \lhd at\_Buyer\_order)$ identifies all orders placed by buyer b. This is restricted to orders with status *charged* or *returned* by the clause $dom(db\_order\_status \rhd \{charged, returned\})$. Order status *returned* identifies those orders which have been returned but not yet refunded, and therefore still need to be included in our invariant.

Proofs. The first property results in 28 proof obligations, of which 16 are automatically discharged. The other proof obligations require expert human intervention. The second property is considerably more complex and therefore results in

582 proof obligations, of which 300 are automatically discharged. The proving of both properties requires the discovery and use of auxiliary invariants as lemmas. For the second property, a total number of 88 additional invariants are added. Currently, we need to manually discover these lemmas. However, we observe that 30 lemmas express relations between token quantities on different sequence flows, e.g., if the incoming flow of `Charging buyer` has tokens then the incoming flow of `Shipping` cannot have tokens. Such information can be obtained by an automated static analysis on the control flow of the model. Therefore, it is possible to automatically discover these 30 lemmas. In future work we will also investigate the possibility of discovering other kinds of lemmas. Furthermore, we observe a highly repeated pattern in the proofs that involves case splitting to distinguish process instances. Such patterns can be implemented as proof strategies customized for proving a certain class of invariants.

5   Enhancement of Processes Models Using Patterns

When a property is violated by a model, it is possible that the model contains undesired behavior which can be removed by further constraining the model via refinement steps. We may directly perform such steps on the Event-B translation of the model in order to verify whether such refinement steps are valid, before making changes to the original model. Moreover, refinements in Event-B can be done automatically using patterns.

Event-B patterns [3,11,12,8] are a means of expressing reusable modeling structures and managing effort by promoting proof re-use. In this example, we use the type of pattern presented in [11], which provides a controlled way of extending an Event-B development with a pre-validated refinement step. Since the refinement step between the abstract and the concrete pattern machines has been proved in advance, any application of the pattern results in a new, fully-proved, refinement step. The approach is automated as a plug-in for the Rodin platform ([10]). In the example we present below, a pattern is used to correct a previously discovered omission in a specification.

We use the shift worker scheduling process in Figure 1 as an example. The process depicted in Figure 1 contains a timing-related fault[2], which can lead to an inconsistency in the data maintained by the business process. It is caused by the use of the timeout at the point where worker responses are received. It arises when a request is sent to a potential worker but no reply is received within the allotted time. Another request is therefore sent to another available candidate. He may accept and be assigned to the shift, after which an accept message is received from the first worker. Now the first worker thinks he is the replacement, but in fact the second has been chosen. We discovered this error using the Rodin model checker *ProB*: we added an invariant expressing the property that at most one worker accepts the shift at any given time. ProB found an erroneous execution within a short time.

---

[2] Note that the shift worker scheduling process is a simplified version of a BPMN workflow proposal, and not a part of any real world system.

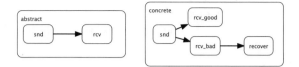

Fig. 4. Structure of the timed error recovery pattern

When translated into Event-B, the flaw present in the described scenario can be corrected using the timed error recovery pattern, shown in Figure 4 and presented in full in [6]. It is designed to be applied to any model in which late messages are not properly processed. When applied, a further refinement level is added to the Event-B development. This new level contains the error recovery behavior which ensures adequate processing of any late messages.

The concrete machine in the pattern separates normal and recovery behavior by distinguishing the receipt of messages before and after the deadline and handling these two cases separately. Late responses are followed with a compensation event, which may be further refined depending on the way in which recovery is implemented.

Applying the pattern requires the identification of the activities in the workflow where the timer is set and the (on time or late) replies are received. These activities are then matched with the sending and receiving events in the pattern abstract machine (snd and rcv in the abstract machine in Figure 4). The pattern variables must also be matched to the appropriate variables within the development.

In the Shift Worker Scheduling model in Figure 1, the timer is set at the task `Select an available worker`. The `Receive response` action is the point at which messages are received. The application of the pattern introduces a new event corresponding to rcv_bad (the arrival of late replies) and given below.

Event $act\_schedule\_response\_late \mathrel{\widehat{=}}$
    any
        pat_m
    where
        grd1 : $pat\_m \in q\_rcv$
        grd2 : $tt(pat\_m) < now$
    then
        act1 : $q\_rcv := q\_rcv \setminus \{pat\_m\}$
        act2 : $q\_comp := q\_comp \cup \{pat\_m\}$
        act3 : $timercvd := timercvd \cup \{pat\_m \mapsto now\}$
    end

In this event, pat_m is the message and q_rcv and q_comp are the messages queued for reception and compensation respectively. The second guard requires that the current time (now) is later that the target arrival time of the message ($tt(pat\_m)$). On arrival, the message moves to the queue for compensation and the time at which it is received is recorded.

The recover event refines the rcv event. As well as retaining all the functionality of rcv, it places the compensated message in the database of consistent messages. The precise nature of the compensation activity required will vary according to the particular activity it is compensating, so the recover event acts as a placeholder for a fuller description of compensation within the workflow, which may be added (perhaps by the application of a more specific pattern) in further refinements.

The ability to automatically add pre-validated refinement steps to generated Event-B models can be used to support BPMN development. In our example, the refinement step made to the Event-B translation can be re-constructed in the original model by introducing a parallel thread to detect and react to late messages. Such reconstruction can be achieved either through a reverse translation procedure from Event-B back to BPMN, or by building up a repository of BPMN refinement patterns corresponding to Event-B patterns. We will explore both possibilities in future work.

6   Related Work

Unlike our work presented in this paper, existing work in this area is largely concentrated on an examination of BPMN control flow, and does not consider data modeling. Most of them also consider only a small fraction of the BPMN language, and put many restrictions on models that can be analyzed. [9] uses Petri nets to formalize and analyze BPMN control flows while abstracting from data information. The approach requires 1-safeness (i.e., having at most one token on any sequence flow) in order to analyze exception handling for sub-processes. On the contrary, we wish to be able to model multiple processes instances. [17] also uses Petri nets to treat transactions and compensations, and also limits his treatment to pure control-flow aspects of models. [20] focuses on the control flow aspects of BPMN in a mapping to the formal workflow language YAWL. [18] formalizes a subset of BPMN in CSP but does not consider features such as compensations and correlation. It is also unclear how data is modeled. The recent work to be published in [4] gives a precise and well-structured semantics of BPMN using Abstract State Machines. This is, to our knowledge, the largest coverage of BPMN besides ours. In [16] a subset of BPMN is translated into the process algebra COWS in order to exploit the stochastic extensions to perform quantitative reasoning on BPMN processes. In [19] the authors present a relative timed semantics for BPMN using CSP. This approach concentrates on the correctness of control flow. In [14] the authors outline a framework for the verification of business processes suggesting the use of TLA+ as well as Petri nets.

7   Conclusions and Further Work

We have presented our work on the formal analysis of business process models through a translation into Event-B. The translation can be fully automated and covers a large set of BPMN features. In particular, we consider the modeling of both control flow and data flow. We showed how properties can be verified by the help of automated provers in the Rodin platform, and also showed how Event-B patterns can be used to support the correction of design errors.

Subsequent work on this topic will be driven by our long-term goal: to allow the BPMN developer to benefit from the improved analytic power of formal methods (and in particular Event-B) while adding minimal extra complexity to the design process. As an initial step, we expect to implement the presented translation as a plug-in to the Rodin toolkit.

The two proofs of possibility presented in Sections 4 and 5 point to two different enhancements to the BPMN development method which we could aim to support. The first, of adding annotations to BPMN, will require a definition of the annotation language and a formalization and implementation of the rules to translate these annotations to Event-B. The second, of using patterns to transform the generated Event-B models, would benefit from the definition of the inverse translation from Event-B to BPMN. Note that this is not the same as a *general* Event-B to BPMN translation, as we would be able to impose relatively strong conditions on the structure (and indeed syntax) of source Event-B models in this translation. We could also develop a library of BPMN transformations together with their Event B patterns, and offer developers a choice from this library in response to identified problems.

Both these approaches suffer from the high number of proof obligations which must be manually discharged. We will therefore work on the automatic discovery of auxiliary lemmas to assist in the proof task. Furthermore, we plan to design and implement various proof strategies tailored for specific classes of proof obligations in order to increase the number of automatically discharged proofs.

Finally, we expect to explore the use of model-checking as a means of providing rapid feedback to the developer on the reason for a failed proof. The challenge here is to provide feedback in a way meaningful to the developer.

Acknowledgments

We are grateful to the anonymous reviewers for their valuable comments and to Deploy project colleagues for their continuing fruitful collaboration. This work has been supported by the EC FP7 Integrated Project *Deploy* and the EPSRC grant *TrAmS* (EP/E035329/1).

References

1. Abrial, J.-R.: Modeling in Event-B: System and Software Engineering. Cambridge University Press, Cambridge (2010)
2. Abrial, J.-R., Butler, M., Hallerstede, S., Voisin, L.: An open extensible tool environment for Event-B. In: Liu, Z., He, J. (eds.) ICFEM 2006. LNCS, vol. 4260, pp. 588–605. Springer, Heidelberg (2006)

3. Ball, E., Butler, M.: Event-b patterns for specifying fault-tolerance in multi-agent interaction. LNCS, vol. 5454, pp. 104–129. Springer, Heidelberg (2009)
4. Börger, E., Sörensen, O.: BPMN Core Modeling Concepts. Inheritance-Based Execution Semantics. In: Handbook of database technology. Springer, Heidelberg (to appear, 2010)
5. Bryans, J.W., Fitzgerald, J.S., Romanovsky, A., Roth, A.: Formal modelling and analysis of business information applications with fault tolerant middleware. In: Proc. of ICECCS 2009, pp. 68–77. IEEE Computer Society, Los Alamitos (June 2009)
6. Bryans, J.W., Fitzgerald, J.S., Romanovsky, A., Roth, A.: Patterns for modelling time and consistency in business information systems. In: Proc. of IECCS 2010, pp. 105–114. IEEE Computer Society, Los Alamitos (2010)
7. Bryans, J.W., Wei, W.: Formal Analysis of BPMN models using Event-B. Technical Report CS-TR 1201, School of Computing Science, Newcastle University (May 2010)
8. Cansell, D., Méry, D., Rehm, J.: Time constraint patterns for event B development. In: Julliand, J., Kouchnarenko, O. (eds.) B 2007. LNCS, vol. 4355, pp. 140–154. Springer, Heidelberg (2006)
9. Dijkman, R.M., Dumas, M., Ouyang, C.: Formal semantics and analysis of BPMN process models using Petri nets, http://eprints.qut.edu.au/7115/01/7115.pdf
10. Fürst, A.: Design patterns in Event-B and their tool support. Master's thesis, ETH Zürich (2009)
11. Hoang, T.S., Fürst, A., Abrial, J.-R.: Event-B Patterns and Their Tool Support. In: Proc. of SEFM 2009, pp. 210–219. IEEE Computer Society, Los Alamitos (2009)
12. Iliasov, A.: Design Components. PhD thesis, Newcastle University (2008)
13. Kätker, S., Patig, S.: Model-driven development of service-oriented business application systems. In: Wirtschaftsinformatik (1), vol. 246, pp. 171–180. Österreichische Computer Gesellschaft (2009), books@ocg.at
14. Masalagiu, C., Chin, W.-N., Andrei, Ș., Alaiba, V.: A rigorous methodology for specification and verification of business processes. Formal Aspects of Computing 21(5), 495–510 (2009)
15. OMG. Business process model and notation (BPMN), FTF beta 1 for version 2.0, http://www.omg.org/spec/BPMN/2.0/Beta1/PDF/
16. Prandi, D., Quaglia, P., Zannone, N.: Formal analysis of BPMN via a translation into COWS. In: Lea, D., Zavattaro, G. (eds.) COORDINATION 2008. LNCS, vol. 5052, pp. 249–263. Springer, Heidelberg (2008)
17. Takemura, T.: Formal semantics and verification of BPMN transaction and compensation. In: Proc. of APSCC 2008, pp. 284–290. IEEE, Los Alamitos (2008)
18. Wong, P.Y.H., Gibbons, J.: A process semantics for BPMN. In: Liu, S., Maibaum, T., Araki, K. (eds.) ICFEM 2008. LNCS, vol. 5256, pp. 355–374. Springer, Heidelberg (2008)
19. Wong, P.Y.H., Gibbons, J.: A Relative Timed Semantics for BPMN. Electronic Notes in Theoretical Computer Science 229(2), 59–75 (2009)
20. Ye, J.-H., Sun, S.-X., Wen, L., Song, W.: Transformation of BPMN to YAWL. In: CSSE (2), pp. 354–359. IEEE Computer Society, Los Alamitos (2008)

A Translation of Control Flows

The following shows how the end event[3] in the FACTORY process in Figure 1 are translated. This end event has two incoming flows. Every tk_Factory_xx_xx is a token function that maps each Factory instance to the number of tokens on the respective flow. The end event can be executed only if the containing Factory instance is still active. This is reflected by the guard grd2 in each Event-B event.

MACHINE Level_01_Factory_CF
SEES Data_Types, Processes
VARIABLES
......
    tk_Factory_schedule_gate
    tk_Factory_gate_assign
    tk_Factory_gate_end
    tk_Factory_assign_end

INVARIANTS
  ... : ......
    inv4 : $tk\_Factory\_schedule\_gate \in instances\_Factory \rightarrow \mathbb{N}$
  ... : ......
EVENTS
Event $evt\_Factory\_end\_in1 \,\widehat{=}\,$
    any
        pid
    where
        grd1 : $pid \in instances\_Factory$
        grd2 : $state\_Factory(pid) = active$
        grd3 : $tk\_Factory\_assign\_end(pid) > 0$
    then
        act1 : $tk\_Factory\_assign\_end(pid) := tk\_Factory\_assign\_end(pid) - 1$
    end
Event $evt\_Factory\_end\_in2 \,\widehat{=}\,$
    any
        pid
    where
        grd1 : $pid \in instances\_Factory$
        grd2 : $state\_Factory(pid) = active$
        grd3 : $tk\_Factory\_gate\_end(pid) > 0$
    then
        act1 : $tk\_Factory\_gate\_end(pid) := tk\_Factory\_gate\_end(pid) - 1$
    end
END ... ...

---

[3] An end event is a sink for tokens, i.e., it only consumes tokens without generating any. Reaching an end event does not necessarily imply the completion of process execution.

Developing Mode-Rich Satellite Software by Refinement in Event B

Alexei Iliasov[1], Elena Troubitsyna[2], Linas Laibinis[2], Alexander Romanovsky[1], Kimmo Varpaaniemi[3], Dubravka Ilic[3], and Timo Latvala[3]

[1] Newcastle University, UK
[2] Åbo Akademi University, Finland
[3] Space Systems Finland
{alexei.iliasov,alexander.romanovsky}@ncl.ac.uk
{linas.laibinis,elena.troubitsyna}@abo.fi
{Dubravka.Ilic,Timo.Latvala,Kimmo.Varpaaniemi}@ssf.fi

Abstract. To ensure dependability of on-board satellite systems, the designers should, in particular, guarantee correct implementation of the mode transition scheme, i.e., ensure that the states of the system components are consistent with the global system mode. However, there is still a lack of scalable approaches to formal verification of correctness of complex mode transitions. In this paper we present a formal development of an Attitude and Orbit Control System (AOCS) undertaken within the ICT DEPLOY project. AOCS is a complex mode-rich system, which has an intricate mode-transition scheme. We show that refinement in Event B provides the engineers with a scalable formal technique that enables both development of mode-rich systems and proof-based verification of their mode consistency.

1 Introduction

Currently the use of formal methods in the industrial practice is getting a new momentum. For instance, in the EU FP7 Integrated Project Deploy [13] the project partners work on advancing methods and tools for refinement based-development and verification. The goal of the project is to enable deployment of these techniques in the industrial practice. Recently, Space Systems Finland in cooperation with the academic partners has undertaken a formal development of the Attitude and Orbit Control System within the Event B framework. In this paper we present this development and discuss the lessons learnt.

The Attitude and Orbit Control System (AOCS) [6] is a generic component of satellite onboard software. The main purpose of AOCS is to achieve and maintain optimal attitude of a satellite. While achieving it, the system components and the overall system correspondingly go through several stages, called *operational modes*. These modes are mutually exclusive sets of the system behaviour [9,14], and form a useful structuring concept that facilitates design of dependable systems in various domains. AOCS is a typical example of a mode-rich system with a complex mode transition scheme. There are two distinctive characteristics that make AOCS development and verification challenging. The first one is

S. Kowalewski and M. Roveri (Eds.): FMICS 2010, LNCS 6371, pp. 50–66, 2010.

long running (i.e., non-instantaneous) mode transitions that are caused by slow dynamics of the involved electro-mechanical components. The second characteristic is an integration of error recovery with mode transition scheme, i.e., error recovery is implemented as rollbacking to certain degraded modes. Together, these two features may lead to cascading mode transitions, i.e., the situations when a system transition to one mode is preempted by a transition to another (degraded) mode due to failure occurrence(s). It has been noted that testing and model checking of the systems with such cascading mode transitions is difficult and suffers from poor scalability [18].

In this paper we demonstrate how to employ a correct-by-construction development approach to circumvent this problem. We use the Event B framework [2,16] (extended with modularisation capabilities [11]) as our modelling language. The Rodin platform [20] and its modularisation plug-in [17] provide us with an automated modelling and verification environment. We define a generic module interface for mode-rich components and demonstrate how to create different mode-managing AOCS components by instantiating the generic module. We develop the system in a layered fashion, i.e., by gradually unfolding system architectural layers while proving consistency between mode transitions on adjacent layers. This approach allows us to cope with complexity of AOCS.

We argue that the AOCS development presented in this paper is a successful experiment in formal refinement-based development of a complex industrial size system. Hence we believe that Event B extended with modularisation facilities shows good potential for the use in the industrial practice.

2   Event B

We start by briefly describing our development framework. The Event B formalism [2,16] is an extension of the B Method [1], a state-based formal approach that promotes the correct-by-construction development paradigm and formal verification by theorem proving. Event B enables modelling of event-based (reactive) systems by incorporating the ideas of the Action Systems formalism [3] into the B Method. Event B is actively used within the FP7 ICT project DEPLOY to develop dependable systems from various domains.

2.1   Modelling and Refinement in Event B

The Event B development starts from creating a formal system specification.

A simple Event B specification has the following general form:

```
MACHINE AM
SEES Context
VARIABLES v
INVARIANT Inv
EVENTS
 INITIALISATION  =  ...
 E₁  =  ...
  ...
 Eₙ  =  ...
END
```

Such a specification encapsulates a local state (program variables) and provides operations on the state. The operations (called *events*) can be defined as

ANY vl **WHERE** g **THEN** S **END**

where vl is a list of new local variables (parameters), the guard g is a state predicate, and the action S is a statement (assignment). In case when vl is empty, the event syntax becomes **WHEN** g **THEN** S **END**. If g is always true, the syntax can be further simplified to **BEGIN** S **END**. The guard g defines the conditions for the statement to be executed, i.e., when the event is *enabled*.

The statement S can be either a deterministic assignment to the variables or a non-deterministic assignment from a given set or according to a given post-condition. One way to denote a non-deterministic assignment is $v :\in Set$, where Set is an non-empty set (or type) of possible values that can be assigned to v.

The **INVARIANT** clause contains the properties of the system (expressed as state predicates) that should be preserved during system execution. The data types and constants needed for modelling the system are defined in a separate component called Context.

To check consistency of an Event B machine, we should verify two properties: event feasibility and invariant preservation. Formally, for each event e,

$$Inv(v) \wedge g_e(v) \ \Rightarrow \ \exists v'.\ BA_e(v, v')$$

$$Inv(v) \wedge g_e(v) \wedge BA_e(v, v') \ \Rightarrow \ Inv(v')$$

where BA_e is a before-after predicate relating the variable values before and after the event e. The semantic for each concrete B statement is given in the form of a predefined before-after predicate.

The main development methodology of Event B is refinement – the process of transforming an abstract specification by gradually introducing implementation details while preserving correctness. Refinement allows us to reduce non-determinism present in an abstract model. It can also introduce new variables and events. The connection between the newly introduced variables and the abstract variables that they replace is formally defined in the invariant of the refined model. For a refinement step to be valid, every possible execution of the refined machine must correspond to some execution of the abstract machine.

The consistency of Event B models as well as correctness of refinement steps should be formally demonstrated by discharging *proof obligations*. The Rodin platform [20], a tool supporting Event B, automatically generates the required proof obligations and attempts to automatically prove them. Sometimes it requires user assistance by invoking its interactive prover. However, in general the tool achieves high level of automation (usually over 80%) in proving.

2.2   Modelling Modular Systems in Event B

Recently the Event B language and tool support have been extended with a possibility to define modules [11,17] – components containing groups of callable operations. Modules can have their own (external and internal) state and the invariant properties. The important characteristic of modules is that they can be developed separately and, when needed, composed with the main system.

A module description consists of two parts – *module interface* and *module body*. Let M be a module. A module interface MI is a separate Event B component. It allows the user of module M to invoke its operations and observe the external variables of M without having to inspect the module implementation details. MI consists of external module variables w, constants c, and sets s, the external module invariant M_Inv(c, s, w), and a collection of module operations, characterised by their pre- and postconditions, as shown below.

```
INTERFACE MI  =
    SEES MI_Context
    VARIABLES w
    INVARIANT M_Inv(c, s, w)
    OPERATIONS
        res ← op₁ =
            ANY par
            PRE M_Guard₁(c, s, par, w)
            POST M_Post₁(c, s, par, w, w', res')
            END
... END
```

Fig. 1. Interface Component

The primed variables in the operation postcondition stand for the final variable values after operation execution. If some primed variables are not mentioned, this means that the corresponding variables are unchanged by an operation.

A module development always starts with the design of an interface. After an interface is defined, it cannot be altered in any manner. This ensures correct relationships between a module interface and its body. A module body is an Event B machine, which implements each interface operation by a separate group of Event B events. Additional proof obligations guarantee that each event group faithfully implement the corresponding pre- and postconditions.

When the module M is "included" into another Event B machine, the including machine can invoke the operations of M and read the external variables of M. To make a specification of a module generic, in MI_Context we can define some constants and sets (types) as parameters. The properties over these sets and constants define the constraints to be verified when the module is instantiated.

Module instantiation allows us to create several instances of the same module. Different instances of a module operate on disjoint state spaces. Via different instantiation of generic parameters the designers can easily accommodate the required variations when developing components with similar functionality. Hence module instantiation provides us with a powerful mechanism for reuse.

In the next section we demonstrate the use of Event B extended with modularisation capabilities in the development of AOCS.

3 Attitude and Orbit Control System

The Attitude and Orbit Control System (AOCS) is a generic component of satellite onboard software, the main function of which is to control the attitude and

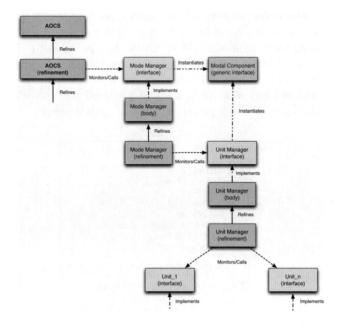

Fig. 2. AOCS Development Hierachy

the orbit of a satellite. Due to a tendency of a satellite to change its orientation because of disturbances of the environment, the attitude needs to be continuously monitored and adjusted. An optimal attitude is required to support the needs of payload instruments and to fulfill the mission of the satellite.

In general, the behaviour of AOCS is cyclic. At each iteration the sensors provide the control algorithms with various measurements. They are used to generate the commands to the actuators that adjust the positioning of the spacecraft to ensure correct pointing of the payload instrument. AOCS consists of seven physical units: four sensors, two actuators and the payload instrument.

We formally develop the AOCS system as follows. Our initial specification models the overall system in an abstract way. The following refinements introduce implementation details in a structured manner, by unfolding system components and gradually delegating part of system functionality to them. Moreover, we identify a generic template for such components in the form of a generic module interface. Actual components will be introduced by instantiating this template, thus formally decomposing the overall system in a structured and well-defined way. The general development structure is presented in Figure 2.

On the architectural level, such a refinement strategy corresponds to gradual unfolding of system layers. The control logic of the system components residing on different layers is expressed in the terms of operational modes and their transitions. One of the main objectives of the AOCS formal development is ensure mode consistency of different layer components. The case study presented below is based on our previous work on formalisation of mode-rich systems [12].

3.1 Abstract Model

The purpose of the system is to position a satellite so that scientific instruments are oriented towards a particular region of Earth. At the most abstract level, we capture this as a succession of two atomic steps: the preparation step, orienting the satellite, and the activation step, initiating the instrument operation. Each step is associated with a boolean flag. The system is in the preparation stage when $pr = FALSE$, is in the activation stage when $pr = TRUE \land act = FALSE$ and, finally, it has activated the instrument when $act = TRUE$.

Whenever a non-recoverable error occurs ($err = TRUE$), the system enters a permanently disabled state (until the underlying hardware platform is reset). It is possible for the preparation step to be interrupted by a recoverable error. In such a situation, the preparation is restarted. In this abstract model this is depicted by a non-deterministic assignment $pr :\in BOOL$.

```
MACHINE aocs
    VARIABLES pr, act, err
    INVARIANT
        pr ∈ BOOL ∧ act ∈ BOOL ∧ err ∈ BOOL
        pr = FALSE ⇒ act = FALSE
        err = TRUE ⇒ pr = FALSE ∧ act = FALSE
    INITIALISATION
        pr, act, err := FALSE, FALSE, FALSE
    EVENTS
        preparation  =   WHEN err = FALSE ∧ pr = FALSE THEN pr :∈ BOOL END
        activation   =   WHEN
                             err = FALSE ∧ pr = TRUE ∧ act = FALSE
                         THEN
                             act := TRUE
                         END
        recovery     =   WHEN err = FALSE THEN pr, act := FALSE, FALSE END
        error        =   BEGIN err, pr, act := TRUE, FALSE, FALSE END
END
```

The model at this stage is just a simple state transition system. This is done to portray the high-level properties of the system in clear and concise terms.

At some point, the *AOCS* development is decomposed into two independent strands. One focuses on unfolding of the functionality abstracted by the *preparation* event. The other deals with activation of the scientific instruments by expanding the *activity* event of the abstract model. To obtain two independent developments, we show how to refine a machine into the composition of a refined machine and a module. The composition with a module, while being a part of the refinement process, is also a formal proof of a model decomposition. As a result, we decompose the overall AOCS specification into a top level component (a refinement of the *aocs* machine) and a subsystem in charge of the initialisation and control of the positioning hardware. The subsystem is responsible for the positioning of the satellite and the execution of necessary corrective actions.

3.2 Modal Component

To single out the preparation subsystem into a separate development, we start by defining a module interface specifying the contract between the subsystem

```
INTERFACE ModalComponent
    VARIABLES last, prev, next, error
    SEES ModalContext
    INVARIANT
        inv1 :  last ∈ MODE ∧ next ∈ MODE ∧ prev ∈ MODE ∧ error ∈ ERROR
        inv2 :  next = prev ⟹ next = last
        inv3 :  next ≠ prev ⇒ next ↦ prev ∈ ORDER ∨ prev ↦ next ∈ ORDER
        inv4 :  {last ↦ prev, last ↦ next} ⊆ ORDER ∪ ORDER⁻¹
    INITIALISATION
        last, prev, next := InitMode, InitMode, InitMode
        error := NoError
    OPERATIONS
        r ← ToMode        =   ANY m PRE
                                  error = NoError ∧ m ∈ MODE
                                  m ≠ next ∧ m ↦ next ∈ ORDER ∪ ORDER⁻¹
                              POST
                                  r′ = last  ∧  prev′ = next  ∧  next′ = m
                              END
        r ← ResetError    =   PRE error ≠ NoError POST r′ = last  ∧  error′ = NoError END
        r ← Mode_Advance  =   PRE
                                  next = prev ∧ error = NoError
                              POST
                                  r′ = last  ∧  error′ ∈ ERROR  ∧  prev ↦ next′ ∈ ORDER
                              END
        r ← Continuation  =   PRE
                                  next ≠ prev ∧ error = NoError
                              POST
                                  r′ = last′  ∧  error′ ∈ ERROR ∧
                                  last′ ↦ next ∈ ORDER ∪ ORDER⁻¹∧
                                  ((last′ ≠ next ∧ prev′ = prev) ∨ (last′ = next ∧ prev′ = last′))
                              END
END
```

Fig. 3. Generic Modal Component Interface

and the environment. Let us note that derivations of this generic interface will be used several times to structure the development into subsystems.

Our structuring strategy is to identify subsystems that are components of a cyclic control system. As any control system, it observes environment changes and controls the actuators. The control logic, though, is fragmented. Each such fragment deals with a specific class of environment and subsystem conditions. In our previous research, we have proposed to apply the notion of operational modes in the formal development of such systems [12]. The essential idea is that a mode-rich control system evolves in two dimensions: as a conventional control system and as a mode transition system.

A mode can be seen as an encapsulation of a piece of the control logic. Hence, a mode transition is a change in the set of control laws. In such class of systems, it is typical to have a mode comparing relation such that a 'better' mode satisfies stronger constraints. While attending to its sensor/control/actuator duties, a mode-rich control system also tries to progress towards a more advanced mode. In the process of this it may encounter adverse environment conditions and switch to a more basic (i.e., degraded) mode.

In this section we give the definition of a generic module interface (see Figure 3) for mode-rich control systems. It is essentially a template that we will use several times in our development. The interface declares four variables. The detected component errors are modelled by the variable *error*. The remaining three variables characterize the mode transitioning part of the component:

- *last* signifies the last successfully reached mode;
- *next* signifies the target mode a component is currently in transition to;
- *prev* signifies the previous mode that a component was in transition to (though it has not necessarily reached it).

These variables describe the actual mode of a component and also the mode transition dynamics. Based on their values, an environment is able to tell whether the component has settled in a stable mode ($last = prev \wedge next = prev$), is working towards a more advanced mode ($last = prev \wedge prev \mapsto next \in \text{ORDER}$), or is degrading its mode due to error recovery ($prev \mapsto next \in \text{ORDER}^{-1}$).

The operation ToMode can be called by an upper layer component to set a new target mode. The operation ResetError is to clear the raised error flag when the detected error is being handled. Finally, the operations Preparation and Continuation model the component behaviour when it receives the control while being correspondingly in a stable or a mode transitional state.

The interface constants MODE, InitMode, ORDER, ERROR, NoError, which are defined in a separate context component, contribute to abstract characterization of the mode logic. MODE is a set of possible modes of a component, ORDER is a relation containing all the allowed mode transitions, InitMode is a predefined initial mode, ERROR is a set of component errors, and NoError is a special value denoting the absence of errors.

CONTEXT ModalContext
    CONSTANTS MODE, InitMode, ORDER, ERROR, NoError
    AXIOMS

axm1 : InitMode $\in$ MODE
axm2 : ORDER $\in$ MODE $\leftrightarrow$ MODE
axm3 : id $\subseteq$ ORDER

axm4 : ORDER $\cap$ ORDER^{-1} $\subseteq$ id
axm5 : ORDER; ORDER $\subseteq$ ORDER
axm6 : NoError $\in$ ERROR
axm7 : ERROR $\setminus$ NoError $\neq \varnothing$

END

---

where id is an identity relation and ";" stands for relational composition.

The relation ORDER also defines a partial order on modes ($axm3$, $axm4$, and $axm5$ express, correspondingly, the reflexivity, antisymmetry and transitivity properties). For any two modes, it states whether the modes are comparable and, if they are, which one of them is closer to the top mode.

3.3 Mode Manager Interface

The new subsystem introduced in the development is called Mode Manager. It is a control system with its own set of modes and an internal mode transition scenario. The Mode Manager interface is the product of extending (instantiating) the generic module interface.

> INTERFACE ModeManager EXTENDS ModalComponent
> SEES ModeManagerContext

More specifically, the set of modes and the mode ordering relation are given concrete definitions at the interface level. The following is the definition of the Mode Manager context.

> CONTEXT ModeManagerContext
> ...
> AXIOMS
> iaxm1 : $MODE = \{OFF, STANDBY, SAFE, NOMINAL, PREPARATION, SCIENCE\}$
> iaxm2 : $Scenario = \{OFF \mapsto STANDBY, STANDBY \mapsto SAFE, SAFE \mapsto NOMINAL,$
> $NOMINAL \mapsto PREPARATION, PREPARATION \mapsto SCIENCE\}$
> iaxm3 : $ORDER = closure(Scenario)$
> iaxm4 : $OFF = InitMode$
> iaxm5 : $partition(ERROR, RecovErrors, UnrecovErrors, \{NoError\})$
> iaxm6 : $RecovErrors \neq \oslash \wedge UnrecovErrors \neq \oslash$

In the above, *Scenario* defines the sequence of steps needed to bring the system to the mode where the scientific payload instrument is ready to perform its tasks. This sequence consists of the following modes: *OFF* - the satellite is in this mode right after system (re)booting; *STANDBY* - this mode is maintained until the separation from the launcher; *SAFE* - a stable attitude is acquired, which allows the coarse pointing control; *NOMINAL* - the satellite is trying to reach the fine pointing control, which is needed to use the payload instrument; *PREPARATION* - the payload instrument is getting ready; *SCIENCE* - the payload instrument is ready to perform its tasks. The mission goal is to reach this mode and stay in it as long as it is needed.

Let us note that *Scenario* is merely a helper construct used to constrain the ORDER relation. Specifically, ORDER is defined as relational closure of *Scenario*. Moreover, the abstract set *ERROR* is now partitioned into the disjoint parts *RecovErrors*, *UnrecovErrors*, and the predefined constant *NoError*.

First Refinement. To integrate Mode Manager with the main development, the (instantiated) Mode Manager interface is included into a refinement of the abstract *aocs* machine. The refined machine *aocs1* imports the module *ModeManager* and thus has the read access to the module interface variables. The first step in decomposition refinement is to link the *aocs1* state with that of the imported module. In our case, the link is quite strong. In fact, we are able to replace the abstract variable *pr* with an expression on the module variables.

> REFINEMENT aocs1
> REFINES aocs
> USES ModeManager
> INVARIANT
> inv1 : $error \notin UnrecovErrors \Rightarrow err = FALSE$
> inv2 : $pr = TRUE \Leftrightarrow (next = last \wedge last = SCIENCE)$
> ...

In the model fragment above, $inv1$ expresses the connection between global and local errors. Intuitively, it means that the Mode Manager component is currently the only source of errors (though some errors may be tolerated). $inv2$ expresses a connection between the mode logic of Mode Manager and the state of preparedness of the abstract model. Here we simply state that the preparation is complete once Mode Manager has reached the *SCIENCE* mode.

The second step of decomposition is the integration of the Mode Manager operations into the functionality of the top-level component. The abstract event *preparation* is refined into a pair of events.

mode_advance REF *preparation*	=	WHEN	
			$error = \text{NoError} \wedge last \neq \text{SCIENCE}$
			$last = prev$
		THEN	
			Mode_Advance
		END	
intermediate REF *preparation*	=	WHEN	
			$error = \text{NoError} \wedge last \neq \text{SCIENCE}$
			$last \neq prev$
		THEN	
			Continuation
		END	

Here Mode_Advance and Continuation use a shortcut notation for an operation call where the return value is ignored. Both events refine *preparation* and use subsystem operations to advance the model state. The events try to accomplish the same goal – reach the mode SCIENCE. The first one is enabled when Mode Manager is in a stable mode, while the second addresses the case when a mode transition is on its way. These events do not assign to the *aocs* variables and thus this part of the system functionality is completely delegated to Mode Manager.

The other group of events deals with error conditions. Mode Manager distinguishes unrecoverable and recoverable errors. Sometimes, the system would simply remove an error, treating it as recoverable one. This is an abstraction of the error handling activity at this level. In other cases, to recover from an error, it may be necessary to reconfigure Mode Manager. This happens when there is a malfunction in some hardware unit and, as a result, the unit must be switched off to put the system into a healthy state. Since the failed unit is no longer available, the Mode Manager mode is downgraded to the one where the system does not need the failed unit. Since the system is cyclic, once the error is cleared, the preparation would restart and attempt to switch on the failed unit.

recovery	=	ANY m WHERE	
			$m \mapsto next \in \text{ORDER}^{-1}$
			$error \in \text{RecovErrors}$
		THEN	
			ResetError
			ToMode(m)
			$act := FALSE$
		END	
error	=	WHEN $error \in \text{UnrecovErrors}$ THEN $err, act := TRUE, FALSE$ END	

3.4   Mode Manager

Let us now consider the Mode Manager development. It starts with an Event B machine implementing the Mode Manager interface. For each interface operation, there is one event group realising the operation. Some groups events are *final* designating the group exit point – the terminal events returning the control to the calling environment. An event that is not final must pass control to another event in the same event group. The following is an excerpt from the abstract machine of the Mode Manager development.

MACHINE MMBody
    IMPLEMENTS ModeManager
    . . .
    GROUP Continuation BEGIN
        FINAL adv_skip   =   WHEN $next \neq prev$ THEN $error :\in$ ERROR END
        FINAL adv_partial =   ANY m WHERE
                                $next \neq prev$
                                $m \in$ MODE $\wedge m \neq next$
                                $m \mapsto next \in$ ORDER $\cup$ ORDER^{-1}
                            THEN
                                $last := m \parallel error :\in$ ERROR
                            END
        FINAL adv_comp   =   WHEN
                                $next \neq prev$
                            THEN
                                $error :\in$ ERROR $\parallel last := next \parallel prev := next$
                            END
    ... END

The **Continuation** operation is realised by a group containing three events. The event *adv_skip* models the behaviour when no mode change happens during the call. This is needed to model mode transitions that take substantial time and thus are spread over several control cycles. A transition to some intermediate mode is modelled by *adv_partial*. Intermediate modes are observed when a component is progressing to some mode that is not reachable directly from the current mode. Finally, *adv_comp* specifies when the system successfully reached the target mode (and thus arrived to a stable state).

Mode Manager does not directly control the satellite hardware. Instead it relies on a special subsystem, called Unit Manager. The purpose of Unit Manager is to abstract the specifics of a hardware configuration and provide a simple common control interface to the hardware. We approach Unit Manager design as another instance of a mode-rich control system.

Unit Manager Interface. The Unit Manager interface is a specialisation of the generic interface defined in Figure 3. Like Mode Manager, it defines its own set of modes and a mode transition scenario.

INTERFACE UnitManager EXTENDS ModalComponent
    SEES UnitManagerContext

The Unit Manager modes define the positioning algorithms and are closely related to the set of hardware units involved in computing the positioning commands. The modes NAV_EARTH and NAV_SUN use crude algorithms based on the input from the Earth and Sun sensors. NAV_ADV and NAV_FINE use the GPS unit to compute the satellite position in respect to the Earth surface. The mode NAV_INSTR is the final target mode meaning that the scientific instrument hardware is enabled.

```
CONTEXT UnitManagerContext
   ...
   AXIOMS
      uaxm1 :  MODE = {OFF, NAV_EARTH, NAV_SUN, NAV_ADV,
                        NAV_FINE, NAV_INSTR}
      uaxm2 :  Scenario = {OFF ↦ NAV_EARTH, OFF ↦ NAV_SUN,
                        NAV_EARTH ↦ NAV_ADV, NAV_SUN ↦ NAV_ADV,
                        NAV_ADV ↦ NAV_FINE, NAV_FINE ↦ NAV_INSTR}
   END
```

Unit Manager Integration. After a number of refinement steps, the Mode Manager development is decomposed to separate the Unit Manager development. The link between the two developments is quite tight. Mode Manager relies on Unit Manager in most of its operations as Mode Manager does not have a direct access to the controlled hardware. The required mode consistency between these components is defined as a a relation linking the modes of Mode Manager and Unit Manager. Moreover, the added invariant properties (in the Mode Manager model) guarantee that the modes of two components are always in agreement with each other. A model excerpt specifying this is given in Figure 4.

The mode mapping relation is defined as the constant *um_mode* under the *USES* clause. To avoid name clashes, the Unit Manager module is instantiated with the prefix *um*. Consequently, all the names imported from the module appear with the prefix.

The gluing invariants, *gi*1, ..., *g*4, define the correspondence between the Mode Manager and Unit Manager modes and errors. All the events of Mode Manager must maintain this correspondence. As a result, an update of the Unit Manager mode often necessitates an update of the Mode Manager mode.

The Unit Manager development, in its turn, is split into the main control part and a number of subsystems modelling individual hardware units. Each such subsystem follows the same modelling pattern and starts with a version of the generic Modal Component interface. However, unlike Mode Manager and Unit Manager, the hardware units are not a part of the control logic we are developing. Collectively, the units define the environment of the system and thus are only characterised by their interfaces.

3.5   Unit Interface

The hardware unit subsystems differ by their set of modes and mode transition rules. Each one also define its own set of error conditions. Instead of defining

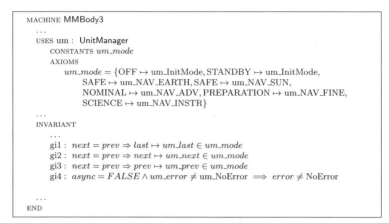

Fig. 4. Unit Manager Integration

an extended interface for each individual unit we use a single parameterised interface. Consequently, unit modes and mode transitions are specified at the point of module integration.

```
INTERFACE UnitComponent EXTENDS ModalComponent
   PARAMETERS MODE, InitMode, ORDER, ERROR, NoError
```

In the specific hardware configuration that we are modelling there are six hardware units. To construct a faithful model close to the executable program, we explicitly introduce each unit subsystem by importing the (correspondingly instantiated) generic module interface.

4   Lessons Learnt

The AOCS system described here is a modified (due to confidentiality reasons) version of a realistic AOCS. The real system was developed by Space Systems Finland some time ago using traditional development approaches. The company has observed that verification of the AOCS mode transitions via testing was quite difficult and time consuming. This has prompted the idea of experimenting with a formal AOCS development to ensure correctness of mode transitions.

The initial attempt [21] to formally develop a system was rather unsuccessful. This modelling was significantly influenced by the code that was developed for the real AOCS. It started from modelling the overall control cycle that consisted of a sequence of events abstractly modelling the entire system structure and functionality – the mode manager, the unit manager and fault tolerance mechanisms. Then, in the further refinement steps, we had to introduce a large number of variables and events (modelling program counters and procedure calls) to continue representing interdependencies between the system components and functions. Moreover, at the time of this development, Event B was still lacking modularisation support. As a result, fairly soon the developed monolithic model became unreadable for the developers and unmanageable for the Rodin platform. We concluded that further development would be quite problematic.

Apart from some technical issues that had to be resolved in the Rodin platform, we have learnt the following main lessons:

- Extensive support for modularisation is absolutely necessary to enable scalable formal development of complex industrial systems in Event B;
- The development should support architectural-level modelling and allow us to express logical interdependencies between different level components;
- It is important to maintain readability of models.

This second development attempt [10] was preceded by a preparatory work that aimed at alleviating discovered problems. We have developed a modularisation plug-in [17] implementing the modularisation extension for Event B that we have proposed previously [11]. Moreover, while formalizing reasoning about mode-rich systems [12], we developed a pattern for specifying mode-managing components. However, probably most importantly, before starting the development as such, we drafted a refinement strategy. Our strategy was to build the system model in a hierarchical layered fashion via instantiation of generic modules. This approach indeed demonstrated its viability.

The second development attempt – the one which is described in this paper – achieved the desired goal. We succeeded in building a detailed AOCS model and verified (by proofs) that it correctly implements the desired mode transition scheme. The development was performed in a structured way, where the levels of abstraction corresponded to the architectural layers. While performing a refinement step, we unfolded the architectural layers and established the consistency of mode transitions between adjacent layers as a part of refinement verification. The specifications of components were produced as a result of instantiating the generic module interface that is common for mode managing components on different layers of abstractions.

Refinement by instantiating the generic components significantly simplified the development and proof activity. As a result, we have alleviated the problem of manipulating large monolithic models. The produced models of modules (components) are much smaller. They are also easier to understand and verify. The overall system model is also rather compact and can be easily maintained because it includes only references to the components visible state and interface.

In our development we have made a smooth transition from the architectural modelling to modelling the detailed behaviour of each particular component. The properties of generic module parameters determine the constraints on concrete data structures that should be proved during module instantiation. Our mechanism of module instantiation and then subsequent development (refinement) of a module ensures that these constraints are satisfied by module implementation.

The layered development has also facilitated modelling and verification of the system fault tolerance mechanisms. The hierarchical architecture allowed us to distribute the responsibilities of error handling across the different layers, which resulted in a well-structured implementation of the fault tolerance mechanisms.

The main lessons that we have learnt from this development are the following

- It is important to have a strategy of the development - a certain refinement plan that is drafted before the real development commences;
- It is beneficial to refrain from modelling major design decisions in the initial specification since it can significantly complicate the later development;
- Modularisation support is paramount in modelling large scale systems;
- Without a mature tool support a formal development of industrial systems is infeasible.

5   Related Work

Formal validation of the mode logic and, in particular, fault tolerance mechanisms of satellite software has been undertaken by Rugina et al [18]. They have investigated different combinations of simulation and model checking. In general, simulation does not allow the designers to check all execution paths, while model checking often runs into the state explosion problem. To cope with these problems, the authors had to experiment with combination of these techniques as well as heavily rely on abstractions. Our approach is free from these problems. First, it allows the developers to systematically design the system and formally check mode consistency within the same framework. Second, it enables exhaustive check of the system behaviour, yet avoiding the state explosion problem.

The mode-rich systems have been studied to investigate the problem of mode confusion and automation surprises. These studies conducted retrospective analysis of mode-rich systems to spot the discrepancies between the actual system mode logic and the user mental picture of the mode logic. Most of the approaches relied on model-checking [4,9,19], while [5] relied on theorem proving in PVS. Our approach focuses on designing fully automatic systems and ensuring their mode consistency. Unlike [9], in our approach we also emphasize the complex relationships between system fault tolerance and the mode logic.

In our previous work [7], we have studied a problem of specifying mode-rich systems from the contract-based rely-guarantee perspective. These ideas have been further applied for fault tolerance modes [15]. According to this approach, a mode-centric specification of the system neither defines how the system operates in some specific mode nor how mode transitions occur. It rather imposes restrictions on concrete implementations. In this paper we have demonstrated how to combine reasoning about the system mode logic and its functioning.

6   Conclusions

In this paper we described formal development of the AOCS system by refinement in Event B. The attempted case study has shown that the Event B framework and the supporting RODIN platform have promising scalability. Our approach facilitated creating a clean system architecture and also allowed us to make a smooth transition from the architectural-level system modelling to specification and refinement of each particular component. Moreover, refinement-based development techniques coped well with modelling the complex mode transition scheme and verification of its correctness.

Verification of all possible mode transitions (including complex cascading effects) was done by proofs and did not require any simplifications. Currently that level of assurance cannot be delivered neither by model-checking, simulation or testing alone nor by combination of these techniques. The proposed modularisation and stepwise development style allowed us to keep manual proof efforts at a reasonable level (about 17 percent of proofs had to be carried out interactively). Hence formal verification by theorem proving has become more accessible for industry practitioners.

In the presented work we aimed at not merely experimenting with modelling a particular industrial-size system in Event B, but rather at creating a generic solution facilitating development of AOCS-like systems. Indeed, our approach to modelling mode-rich components using generic instantiation supports both reuse and composition. Such reuse is safe, since while developing a component by refinement we formally ensure its conformance to the instantiated specification of its interface. Moreover, it becomes manageable to verify composition of components whose state and behaviour are succinctly and formally modelled.

Our work can be seen as a step towards creating a formal approaches for model-driven development and establishing the reference architecture for the space sector – the two recent initiatives of European Space Agency [8]. As a future work it would be interesting to connect our approach to the languages specifically dedicated to architectural modelling. Moreover, it would be useful to continue experimenting with formal modelling of various types of architectures of mode-rich systems as well as address the problem of ensuring mode consistency in the presence of dynamic reconfiguration.

Acknowledgments

This work is supported by the FP7 ICT DEPLOY Project and the EPSRC/UK TrAmS platform grant. We also wish to thank the anonymous reviewers for their very valuable comments and suggestions.

References

1. Abrial, J.-R.: The B-Book. Cambridge University Press, Cambridge (1996)
2. Abrial, J.-R.: Modelling in Event-B. Cambridge University Press, Cambridge (2010)
3. Back, R., Sere, K.: Superposition refinement of reactive systems. Formal Aspects of Computing 8(3), 1–23 (1996)
4. Buth, B.: Analysing mode confusion: An approach using fdr2. In: Heisel, M., Liggesmeyer, P., Wittmann, S. (eds.) SAFECOMP 2004. LNCS, vol. 3219, pp. 101–114. Springer, Heidelberg (2004)

5. Butler, R.W.: An introduction to requirements capture using PVS: Specification of a simple autopilot. Technical report, NASA TM-110255 (May 1996)
6. DEPLOY Deliverable D20 – Report on Pilot Deployment in the Space Sector. FP7 ICT DEPLOY Project (January 2010), http://www.deploy-project.eu/
7. Dotti, F., Iliasov, A., Ribeiro, L., Romanovsky, A.: Modal Systems: Specification, Refinement and Realisation. In: Breitman, K., Cavalcanti, A. (eds.) ICFEM 2009. LNCS, vol. 5885, pp. 601–619. Springer, Heidelberg (2009)
8. European Cooperation for Space Standardization. Software general requirements ECSS-E-ST-40C (2009)
9. Heimdahl, M., Leveson, N.: Completeness and Consistency in Hierarchical State-Based Requirements. IEEE Transactions on Software Engineering 22(6), 363–377 (1996)
10. Iliasov, A., Laibinis, L., Troubitsyna, E.: An Event-B model of the Attitude and Orbit Control System, DEPLOY Publication Repository (2010), http://deploy-eprints.ecs.soton.ac.uk/
11. Iliasov, A., Troubitsyna, E., Laibinis, L., Romanovsky, A., Varpaaniemi, K., Ilic, D., Latvala, T.: Supporting Reuse in Event B Development: Modularisation Approach. In: Frappier, M., Glässer, U., Khurshid, S., Laleau, R., Reeves, S. (eds.) ABZ 2010. LNCS, vol. 5977, pp. 174–188. Springer, Heidelberg (2010)
12. Iliasov, A., Troubitsyna, E., Laibinis, L., Romanovsky, A., Varpaaniemi, K., Väisänen, P., Ilic, D., Latvala, T.: Verifying Mode Consistency for On-Board Satellite Software. In: SAFECOMP 2010, LNCS. Springer, Heidelberg (2010)
13. Industrial deployment of system engineering methods providing high dependability and productivity (DEPLOY). IST FP7 project, http://www.deploy-project.eu/
14. Leveson, N., Pinnel, L.D., Sandys, S.D., Koga, S., Reese, J.D.: Analyzing Software Specifications for Mode Confusion Potential. In: Johnson, C.W. (ed.) Proceedings of Workshop on Human Error and System Development, Glasgow, Scotland, pp. 132–146 (March 1997)
15. Lopatkin, I., Iliasov, A., Romanovsky, A.: On fault tolerance reuse during refinement. In: Proc. of 2nd International Workshop on Software Engineering for Resilient Systems (April 2010)
16. Rigorous Open Development Environment for Complex Systems (RODIN). Deliverable D7, Event B Language, http://rodin.cs.ncl.ac.uk/
17. RODIN modularisation plug-in. Documentation, http://wiki.event-b.org/index.php/Modularisation_Plug-in
18. Rugina, A.E., Blanquart, J.P., Soumagne, R.: Validating failure detection isolation and recovery strategies using timed automata. In: Proc. of 12th European Workshop on Dependable Computing, EWDC 2009, Toulouse (2009)
19. Rushby, J.: Using model checking to help discover mode confusion and other automation suprises. In: Reliability Engineering and System Safety, vol. 75, pp. 167–177 (2002)
20. The RODIN platform, http://rodin-b-sharp.sourceforge.net/
21. Varpaaniemi, K.: Event-B Project DepSatSpec015Model000. DEPLOY Publication Repository (January 2010), http://deploy-eprints.ecs.soton.ac.uk/168

Automatic Error Correction of Java Programs

Christian Kern[*] and Javier Esparza

Technische Universität München
{kernch,esparza}@in.tum.de

Abstract. We present a technique for automatically detecting and correcting software bugs. The programmer is required to define a catalog of *hotspots*, syntactic constructs she considered to be error prone (e.g. i < N), together with suitable *alternatives* (e.g. i < (N + 1) and i < (N - 1)). Given a faulty program, search techniques are then applied to find a combination of alternatives yielding a correct program. The technique is implemented on top of the Java Pathfinder Framework.

1 Introduction

It has been estimated that 50% to 75% of the cost of software development is spent on debugging [8]. While many tools for detecting bugs and reporting error traces exist, the problem of automatically localizing and fixing the bug is far less understood, and constitutes an active research field.

When debugging, programmers often look for "hotspots" in the program where bugs are likely to occur, and check if a change in the code may correct the bug. A typical example of hotspots are comparisons of integer expressions, which are likely to lead to "off-by-one" errors, like typing x < 0 instead of x <= 0, or for (int i = 0; i < N; i++) instead of for (int i = 0; i < N+1; i++). We propose to automatize this approach. Instead of manually searching for hotspots, programmers just define a catalog of syntactic constructs, like for instance EXPRESSION1 < EXPRESSION2, and for each of them a set of possible alternatives, like, for instance, EXPRESSION1 <= EXPRESSION2. Furthermore, they specify a set of test inputs, for instance by fixing the range of input variables. A tool can then in principle generate all possible variants of the program generated by the alternatives, and test each of them on the test inputs, until some variant passes all the tests. However, realizing such a tool and making it efficient is a challenging task, and the subject of this paper.

A naive way of testing all variants on all test inputs is to sequentially test each variant on all inputs. However, this approach is highly inefficient. The first contribution of the paper is a better algorithm: given a program P, we first generate a meta-program P_m that can simulate all the variants of P obtained by independently selecting alternatives at the hotspots, and then run P_m in a certain way on the set of test inputs, excluding variants along the way. The second contribution is an implementation of this approach on top of the Java

---

[*] The author was supported by the DFG Graduiertenkolleg 1480 (PUMA).

S. Kowalewski and M. Roveri (Eds.): FMICS 2010, LNCS 6371, pp. 67–81, 2010.

Pathfinder (JPF) model checker. In fact, the state exploration algorithm of JPF turns out to exactly meet the needs of our technique.

Related Work. Bug localization (sometimes called bug interpretation) and bug fixing have been intensely studied in the last years. Several proposals for bug localization are based on the idea of capturing differences between error traces and successful traces of a program. Cleve and Zeller [4] compare the intermediate program states of error and successful traces, apply Delta Debugging [15] to find a minimal set of variables transforming a successful run into a failing run, and search for a program transition responsible for this transformation. Ball et al. [1] search for transitions occurring in multiple error traces but no successful trace. Their approach is implemented in the SLAM Toolkit [2], and similar techniques [7] have also found its way into the Java Pathfinder [12] model checker. Groce et al. [6] propose a notion of distance between traces, generate a closest pair containing a successful and an error trace using CBMC [3], and localize the bug using the differences between them. Tarantula [10] visualizes differences between successful and error traces: program statements are colored according to the ratio between how often they are visited by successful traces, and how often by failure traces.

Further proposals for bug localization only use information from error traces. Wang et al. [13] determine a causality-chain inducing the error by applying an algorithm for computing preconditions to an error trace. Griesmayer et al. [5] consider systems with several components, and propose an iterative procedure that considers one error trace at a time, and uses it to narrow down the set of components that can be responsible for the fault.

A common advantage of all these approaches with respect to our proposal is the absence of assumptions about the cause of the bug, compared to our assumption that bugs are located at hotspots. However, the absence of assumptions also makes automatic repair problematic, and in fact none of the approaches above explicitly studies it.

The two approaches closest to our work present proposals for automatically localizing *and* fixing bugs. Weimer et. al [14] assume the bug can be fixed by deleting, inserting or swapping instructions in the source code. They use genetic algorithms to generate program variants, which are then sequentially tested. Instead of applying genetic algorithms, we generate one single meta-program embedding all variants, and explore it using search techniques. We suspect that this approach is more adequate for bugs requiring to change the code at several places; however, a detailed comparison is problematic, because genetic algorithms can be tuned according to a wide range of parameters, and is beyond the scope of this paper. Jobstman et al. [9,11] reduce program repair to finding a winning strategy in a game, and present impressive benchmarks, albeit mostly in the hardware area. Our approach can be seen as a special case of their technique that can be implemented on top of JPF with reasonable effort, allowing to profit from all the algorithmic expertise embodied in it.

Structure. The paper is structured as follows. Section 2 shows how to identify hotspots and propose alternatives. Section 3 describes our search technique; more precisely, Section 3.1, briefly introduces the Java Pathfinder model checker; Section 3.2 describes the metaprogram; Section 3.3 introduces the search strategy; and Section 3.4 describes an efficient data structure especially designed for the strategy. Finally, Section 4 presents experimental results, and Section 5 contains conclusions.

2   Selecting Hotspots and Alternatives

We use syntactic analysis to search for *hotspots*, code locations where a bug could have been injected. Formally, a hotspot is just a subtree in the parse tree of the program. Our implementation is based on the Java Compiler API[1]. We explain our approach by means of an example. Listing 1.1 shows part of a sorting algorithm in Java. The heuristic in this example extracts all binary expressions combined with the less-then comparator; i.e. all expressions of the form EXPRESSION1 < EXPRESSION2. For these two lines of code, three expressions of this form are found (①-③).

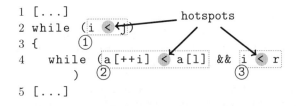

Listing 1.1. Heuristically selected hotspots

For each hotspot a *changeset entry* collects a set of possible alternatives, plus the original code. A *changeset* collects all changeset entries for a program.

$$CS = \{ ① \to \{ i < j, i > j \}, ② \to \{ a[++i] < a[l], a[++i] > a[l] \}$$
$$③ \to \{ i < r, i > r \}\}$$

Fig. 1. Example changeset

For instance, for the hotspots in Listing 1.1, we consider a heuristic that suggests EXPRESSION1 > EXPRESSION2 as alternative to EXPRESSION1 < EXPRESSION2. This results in the changeset displayed in Figure 1, i.e., a set containing a changeset entry for each hotspot.

We extract a templated program with one template for each hotspot, see Listing 1.2. A *program variant* is the result of replacing each template by one of the elements in its corresponding changeset entry.

---

[1] http://java.sun.com/javase/6/docs/jdk/api/javac/tree/index.html

```
1 [...]
2 while ((1))
3 {
4    while ((2) && (3));
5 [...]
```

Listing 1.2. Templated program

2.1 Conflicting Hotspots

Two hotspots are *conflicting* if one of them is a subtree of the other. For instance, in Listing 1.3, hotspots (1) and (3) are conflicting, but (1) and (4) are not. When heuristics produce conflicting hotspots, we use Algorithm 1 to generate a changeset entry for the outermost hotspot, and use it for producing program variants.

```
1 [...]
2 int m =  (a + b) < (c + (d + a))
3 [...]
```

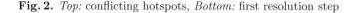

Listing 1.3. Conflicting heuristics

$$CS_c = \{ (1) \rightarrow \{ a + b, a - b \}, (2) \rightarrow \{ c + (d + a), c - (d + a) \},$$
$$(3) \rightarrow \{ (a + b) < (c + (d + a)), (a + b) > (c + (d + a)) \},$$
$$(4) \rightarrow \{ d + a, d - a \}\}$$

$$CS_1 = \{ (1) \rightarrow \{ a + b, a - b \},$$
$$(2) \rightarrow \{ c + (d + a), c - (d + a), c + (d - a), c - (d - a) \},$$
$$(3) \rightarrow \{ (a + b) < (c + (d + a)), (a + b) > (c + (d + a)) \}\}$$

Fig. 2. *Top:* conflicting hotspots, *Bottom:* first resolution step

The algorithm constructs a forest F with hotspots as nodes. If (b) is a subtree of (a) in the parse tree of the program, we add to F the edge ((a), (b)), and remove all transitive edges from the graph. We then generate a new changeset entry for each root of the forest by means of an iterative procedure. Given an edge (v_1, v_2) and elements e_1, e_2 of the changeset entries of v_1 and v_2, we denote by $e_1[e_2]$ the result of substituting e_2 for the code of v_2 in e_1. The procedure picks an edge (v_1, v_2) such that v_2 is a leaf, and replaces v_1's changeset entry by $Merge(v_1, v_2) := \{e_1[e_2] \mid e_1 \in Che_1, e_2 \in Che_2\}$, where Che_1, Che_2 are the changeset entries of v_1 and v_2, respectively; then the procedure removes v_2 from the graph, removes the changeset entry of v_2 from the changeset, and iterates.

Consider for example the source code part in Listing 1.3 with the changeset of Figure 2/Top. The algorithm constructs the conflict graph $G = (V, E)$ with the set of edges $E = \{((3),(1)), ((3),(2)), ((2),(4))\}$ and the set of vertices $V = [(1)-(4)]$. Changeset entry (4) is a leaf, and so its changeset entry is merged with the changeset entry of ②. The result is shown in Figure 2/Bottom. After repeating this procedure as long as possible, we get a merged changeset entry for program location ③.

Algorithm 1. ConflictResolution

---

input : Set of conflicting hotspots H_c
output: Resolved set of changeset entries R
begin
    $V \longleftarrow H_c$
    $E \longleftarrow \emptyset$
    Directed Graph $G = (V, E)$
    for $v1 \in V$ **do**
        for $v2 \in V$ **do**
            if $ProgramLocation(v1) \subset ProgramLocation(v2)$ **then**
                $E \longleftarrow E \cup (v1, v2)$

    $RemoveAllTransitiveEdges(G)$
    while $\exists\, (v1, v2) \in E$ **with** $v2$ *has no outgoing edges* **do**
        $v1 \longleftarrow Merge(v1, v2)$
        $E \longleftarrow E \setminus \{(v1, v2)\}$
        $V \longleftarrow V \setminus v2$
    return *changeset entries of remaining vertices* V
end

---

3   Search

We have described heuristics for identifying "error prone" program locations (hotspots) in a faulty program and suggesting alternatives. The heuristics return a changeset containing a changeset entry (a set of alternatives) for each hotspot. Now we show how to use the changeset to derive a corrected program. We generate test inputs, search the space of program variants obtained by a combination of changeset code replacements, and select those variants satisfying the specification for all test inputs. The correctness of this set of variants can then be further examined using some model checker. Since our implementation is based on the Java Pathfinder (JPF) model checker, we first discuss its search strategy.

3.1   Java Pathfinder

The JPF model checker is an explicit state model checker. Conceptually, JPF is a virtual machine that can simulate all possible runs of a program. Its input is a program P in Java Bytecode. Various techniques, e.g., state compression and partial order reduction, are applied to keep the state space small. The state space of P is exhaustively explored using various search techniques. In this work, we focus on JPF's depth-first search, shown in Algorithms 2 and 3.

Algorithm 2. Java Pathfinder

---

input : Program P
output: Is P correct?
begin
> $s \longleftarrow$ **new** choice_point stack
> **while** *true* **do**
>> /* Program is executed until non-det. choice is possible or an
>> end state is reached   */
>> executeProgram(P)
>> **if** *endState* **then**
>>> **if** *endState is errorState* **then** **return** *false*
>>> **else if** *!Backtrack(s)* **then** **return** *true*
>>
>> **else**   /* Non-deterministic point in execution */
>>> *choice_point* $\longleftarrow$ **new** choice_point
>>> *choice_point*.doNextChoice()
>>> s.push(*choice_point*)

end

Non-determinism is introduced either indirectly, e.g., when selecting the next thread that executes an action, or directly, as statements in the source code under test. The program is executed until a non-deterministic choice is possible or the execution terminates. For each non-deterministic point in the execution, a choice_point is created on top of the choice_point stack, storing the different possibilities to continue the execution, those that have already been explored, and the current program state. The execution is continued using depth-first search, i.e., the first choice not marked as explored is executed and marked as explored. If an error state is reached, a program failure and an error trace is returned. If an end state is reached without errors, the search backtracks to the first choice_point in the choice point stack having at least one unexplored choice. The program state of this choice_point is restored, and the execution continues with the unexplored choice. If no backtracking is possible, the program is declared correct.

3.2 Searchable Meta Program

We construct a meta-program P_m. Given P_m as input, JPF explores each program variant of P for a given changeset on each test input. Observe that all the steps described next for modifying the original source code are carried out automatically.

Test inputs are introduced with help of non-deterministic choices in the source code under test. Consider for instance the code in Listing 1.4, where the method Verify.getInt(a,b) returns a value in the range $[a, b]$, chosen non-deterministically. When the JPF model checker runs on this code, it creates choice points and explores all possible arrays a[] of size 1-5 and values array entries 0-50 (a reasonable range of test inputs for sorting algorithms).

Algorithm 3. Backtrack

---

input : A reference to `choice_point` stack s.
output: Was backtracking possible?
begin

> **while** *true* **do**
>
>> **if** *s.empty()* **then**
>>> **return** false
>>
>> *choice_point* ⟵ s.pop()
>> **if** *choice_point has more choices* **then**
>>> restore_state(*choice_point*)
>>> *choice_point*.doNextChoice()
>>> s.push(*choice_point*)
>>> **return** true

end

Program variants are explored in a similar way. Recall that a changeset is a set of changeset entries, each of them consisting of a set of alternatives for a single program code location. We force JPF to explore each alternative in its depth-first search procedure. For that, we introduce an additional function `Explore.getChoice(size, ident)` that also returns a value. This function is very similar to the one used for generating test inputs. JPF explores the values within the range $[0, \text{size}-1]$. However, during the execution of the program under test, a `choice_point` is only created when no `choice_point` with the identifier `ident` exists in the choice point stack, i.e., only the first time this function gets called in a path of the execution with this identifier. In all subsequent calls, the current choice of the already existing `choice_point` in the choice point stack is looked up and returned.

```
1 int[] a = new int[Verify.getInt(1,5)];
2 for(int i=0; i!=a.length; ++i)
3 a[i] = Verify.getInt(0,50);
```

Listing 1.4. Test input generator

For each changeset entry, we create an `Explore` function at its associated program location with an unique identifier `ident`, and set the parameter `size` to the number of alternatives of the changeset entry. The value returned by `Explore` determines the program alternative of the changeset entry to be executed next. This is the motivation for only allowing one `choice_point` for each identifier, created in one run of the program. Otherwise, e.g., because of recursive calls, all variants of a changeset entry could be exhaustively explored again. We use the "?:" operator[2] to execute the specific program variant. Its simplified syntax is:

CONDITION ? EXPRESSION : EXPRESSION

---

[2] http://java.sun.com/docs/books/jls/third_edition/html/expressions.html# 15.25

If CONDITION evaluates to true (resp. false), the first (resp. second) expression is evaluated and its result is returned. This conditional operator is applied recursively. Consider for example the expression

$$j==1 \ ? \ EXPR\_1 \ : \ j==2 \ ? \ EXPR\_2 \ : \ j==3 \ ? \ EXPR\_3 \ : \ EXPR\_0.$$

If variable j has value n with $n \in [0-3]$, then EXPR_<n> gets evaluated. For every changeset entry, we replace the expression at the respective program location by such a conditional expression. We use the return value of the Explore function as choice for a code alternative of each program variant. Listing 1.5 shows the code segment we obtain for the example in Listing 1.1 and the changeset in Figure 1.

```
1 [...]
2 while ( Explore.getChoice(2, id1) == 1 ?
3            i < j : i > j )
4 {
5   while ( Explore.getChoice(2, id2) == 1 ?
6              a[++i] < a[l] : a[++i] > a[l] &&
7           Explore.getChoice(2, id3) == 1 ?
8              i < r : i > r )
9 [...]
```

Listing 1.5. Searchable meta program

Observe that in this approach alternatives and hotspots must necessarily be Java Expressions.

In summary, using Explore and Verify we transform the original program into a metaprogram P_m. On input P_m, the JPF model checker explores the behaviour of each program variant derivable from the changeset on each generated test input.

3.3   Search Strategy

We discuss how to efficiently search for a correct program using the meta program P_m introduced in the last section. We modify JPF's depth-first search strategy so that it *backtracks* instead of terminating when it finds an error, thus forcing a complete exploration of all test inputs and program variants.

We use a search tree to visualize the depth-first search (see Figure 3). Nodes are either choice points, on which we branch, or end states, where we start to backtrack. There are two different types of choice point nodes: those generating test inputs (TC-points, displayed as dashed nodes — "-_-"), and those where we choose different program variants (PC-points, displayed as dotted nodes — "........"). Each program execution path ends up in a leaf (gray node). Two possible end states are possible: "✓"— the execution terminated without an error and "⨎"— the execution terminated with an error. An error is induced by one of the following events:

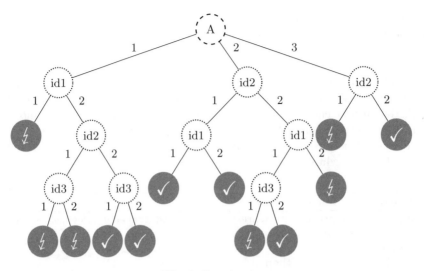

Fig. 3. Search tree

- An uncaught exception occurs.
- The execution takes too long — this is necessary, because infinite executions are possible and JPF cannot detect them. We therefore restrict the amount of instructions for each path of the execution.
- The specification is violated.
- The program exits, but the defined end state of the program has not been reached.

A *program decision* is a tuple $\langle$PC-point, choice$\rangle$, like for example $\langle$id1, 2$\rangle$. A *decision trace* is a set of program decisions where each PC-point occurs at most once. The *size* of a trace is the number of tuples it contains. Each (partial) path in the search yields such a decision trace. A *complete decision trace* T_c contains a program decision for every defined PC-point, i.e., a decision for each changeset entry. It characterizes a simulated program variant $P(T_c)$ within the meta-program P_m. We search for a complete trace T_c such that $P(T_c)$ satisfies the specification on every test input.

Assume an end state is reached by depth-first search. If it is an error state, then its decision trace *cannot be* a subset of any complete trace T_c^1 such that $P(T_c^1)$ is the correct program, because $P(T_c^1)$ fails at least on one test input. If it is a success state, then its decision trace is a *candidate trace*: it could be a subset of a complete trace T_c^2 such that $P(T_c^2)$ is a correct program on all test inputs. This motivates storing two sets of decision traces during the search: a set containing the candidate traces (*good traces*), and another one containing the traces reaching an error state (*bad traces*).

Whenever an end state is reached during the depth-first search, Algorithm 4 is executed. If the end state is a success state and its decision trace does not contain a bad trace as subset, we add it to the set of good traces. If the end state is an error state, the extracted error trace can be shortened if there exists a PC-point in the search path towards the error, such that every successor of this node leads to an error state. This information is made available when a PC-point was completely explored. Therefore, whenever we hit an error state that is an end state, we do not add its trace to the set of bad traces, instead we mark the actual choice of the above PC-point as bad. When a PC-point was completely visited, we check if all its choices are marked as bad. If this is the case, we again mark the current choice of the PC-point above as bad. If there exists no such node above, we cannot find a correction. If not all choices are marked as bad, the decision traces of successors that induce an error state are stored as bad traces. This procedure is shown in Algorithm 5.

Algorithm 4. FinalStateReached

    input: Final state f, reference to a set of good traces g, reference to a set
            of bad traces b.
    begin
        if f *is* errorState **then**
            BackTrackToProgramChoicePoint()
            choice_point.markCurrentChoiceBad()
        else
            $d_c \longleftarrow$ extractDecisionTrace()
            if $\forall\ d_b \in b$: d_b *does not contradict* d_c **then**
                g.add(d_c)
    end

Consider for example the search in Figure 3. The path <A,1>-<id1,2>-<id2,1>-<id3,1> reaches an error state, and choice 1 in id3 is marked as bad. <A,1>-<id1,2>-<id2,1>-<id3,2> also reaches an error state, so now the choices 1 and 2 in id3 are marked as bad. When backtracking, since all choices of id3 are bad, we propagate this to id2, marking its choice 1 as bad. After id2 is completely explored, not all its choices are marked as bad, and so we add the decision trace {<id1,2>,<id2,1>} to the set of bad decision traces.

After a bad decision trace is added, the set of good traces is updated, so that all decision traces containing the new bad decision trace are removed. If all successor choices are marked bad and we have completely explored all choices of the top-most PC-point, no correct candidate decision trace for a test input is found, therefore, we cannot derive a correct program and return failure.

During the search, the set of bad traces is used to prune the search space. Whenever we are about to visit a path whose decision trace contains as subset a decision trace from the set of bad traces, we skip this path, because we cannot find a good decision trace in it.

Consider again the search in Figure 3. Since the path <A,1>-<id1,1> is erroneous, the decision trace $T_{e1} = \{$<id1,1>$\}$ is added to the set of bad traces after backtracking. When we explore <A,2>-<id2,2>, we observe that its decision trace, $\{$<id2,2>,<id1,1>$\}$, contains T_{e1} as subset, and so we skip this path.

The search returns a set of candidate decision traces that may not be complete: for some hotspot the candidates may not indicate which changeset entry should be chosen. In this case, for each such hotspot we retain the original program expression. Each decision trace is thus extended into a complete trace. We then select one complete trace such that the number of hotspots at which the selected alternative differs from the original one is minimal. Before presenting the so obtained patch to the user, the patch is checked again for correctness, using some more sophisticated testing method.

Algorithm 5. PCPointExplored

---

input: Program choice point p, reference to a set of good traces g, reference
     to a set of bad traces b.

begin
   if *All choices of p are marked bad* **then**
      if $\exists$ *prevProgramChoicePoint(p)* **then**
         $p\_prev \longleftarrow$ prevProgramChoicePoint(p)
         $p\_prev.$markCurrentChoiceBad$()$
      else
         exit search - no solution found
   else
      forall $c \in$ *choices marked as bad in p* **do**
         $d_b \longleftarrow$ getDecisionTrace(c)
         if $\nexists\ t \in b$ *with* $t \subseteq d_b$ **then**
            $b.$add(d_b)
            $g.$removeContradictingDecisionTraces(b)

end

3.4   Efficient Data Structure for Decision Traces

We present an efficient data structure for storing sets of decision traces. A decision trace is a set of elements, so this data structure holds *sets of sets of elements*. In Set Theory, sets of sets are usually referred as families of sets. We will stick to this notation. Assume $\mathfrak{F}$ is a family of sets and S is a set of elements. Following operations are implemented efficiently:

- Add/remove S to/from $\mathfrak{F}$. ($\mathfrak{F}$ is a family of decision traces, S is added.)
- Extract all sets of elements from $\mathfrak{F}$ that contain S as subset. ($\mathfrak{F}$ is a family of good decision traces, S is a new bad decision trace. We remove all decision traces from $\mathfrak{F}$ containing S.)
- Check if $\mathfrak{F}$ contains S as subset. (S is a new good decision trace, if it does not contain any bad decision trace, i.e., a set in $\mathfrak{F}$ as subset.)

Figure 4 shows the representation of a family of three sets S_1-S_3. We store sets in their original representation together with their sizes (Figure 4/Left). Additionally, we store each element in a reverse lookup map, mapping set elements to set references, stating in which sets this element occurs (Figure 4/Right).

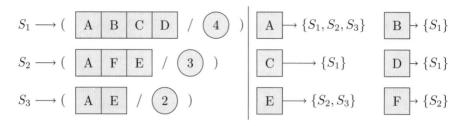

Fig. 4. Data structure for family of decision traces

Adding/removing a set of elements is not expensive. We have to iterate once over the new set for adding/removing the respective map entries.

To find all sets in $\mathfrak{F}$ that contain S as subset, we derive the cut set of the reverse lookup entries of the elements contained in S. The references in the cut set are the references to the searched sets. For the example, assume $S = \{A, F, E\}$. The cut set of the three reference sets contains only one element: S_2, so $S \subseteq S_2$.

For checking if S contains a set from $\mathfrak{F}$ as subset, we create an empty map M, mapping set references to a counter. For each element in S, we get the reference set of it using the reverse lookup map. For each reference r in this set, we look up if there exists an entry for it in map M. If there exists an entry, we increase the counter of r in M by one. If there exists no entry, we insert a new entry, with the counter set to one. After all elements from S are processed, we iterate through the entries in the map M. If for any map entry $\langle r', c \rangle$, the value of counter c is equal to the size of the set referenced by r', S contains at least one set from $\mathfrak{F}$ as subset, the set referenced by r'. For the example, assume $S = \{A, C, D, E\}$. We apply the procedure, and we get the map $M = \{S_1 \to 3, S_2 \to 2, S_3 \to 2\}$ as interim result. The counter of S_3 matches the size of S_3, so $S_3 \subseteq S$.

The depth-first search iteratively adds/removes (due backtracking and forward search) elements to/from a set of elements (decision trace) S, which has to be checked every time for the inclusion in some set from $\mathfrak{F}$ as subset. As discussed, this allows us to efficiently prune the search. Since this check is performed very often, it must be implemented efficiently, and so our implementation of the procedure discussed above is iterative: whenever one element of S is modified, the map M is adjusted by increasing/decreasing the respective counters.

4   Experiments

We demonstrate the feasibility of our approach by means of an experiment using Quicksort implementations. The implementations were obtained automatically from the web using *Google Code Search*[TM], a search engine for source code that supports searching for different programming languages and for regular expressions. We searched for Java implementations and typical Quicksort signatures. The relevant Quicksort methods, together with all dependencies, were fetched from the obtained implementations. An specification and an adapter were generated to supply an unique interface for executing the different sorting algorithms.

Duplicates were removed, and the compilable implementations were checked automatically for correctness, which partitioned them into two categories: *correct* and *defective*. We obtained a total number of 174 source files; 88 of them were parse- and compilable, and the Quicksort method extractable with all its dependencies. Of these 88 source files, 76 were *correct* and 12 were *defective*. A closer look at the defective implementatiosn showed that two contained an empty Quicksort method, leaving 10 *defective* implementations for our experiments.

For the search of hotspots, we focused on *off-by-one* errors, in which the bounds of a loop are wrong by one unit, or a `<=` instead of a `<` comparison is used. So our changeset C was created as follows:

- For each program location `EXPRESSION1 < EXPRESSION2`, we create the change-set entry $\widehat{X} \rightarrow \{$ `EXPRESSION1 < EXPRESSION, EXPRESSION1 <= EXPRESSION2, EXPRESSION1 > EXPRESSION2, EXPRESSION1 >= EXPRESSION2`$\}$, so that each comparison operator is tried as replacement. The same is applied for all other possible comparison operators.
- For each program location `EXPRESSION1 - EXPRESSION2`, we create the changeset entry $\widehat{X} \rightarrow \{$ `EXPRESSION1 - EXPRESSION2, EXPRESSION1` $\}$. The same is applied for the `+` operator.

We apply our search strategy to changeset C on 84 test inputs (all arrays of length three or less with entries between 0 and 3). We return a minimal patch when it exists.

Table 1 shows our results. For each implementation, *Domain* denotes the domain it was fetched from, *LOC* denotes the lines of code of the extracted algorithm, *GT* and *BT* denote the number of good and bad decision traces that have been stored when the search terminates; *PC-points* denotes the number of choice points that were introduced, *Patch Size* denotes the number of code changes in the patch, and *Time* denotes the runtime of the search algorithm in seconds. Quicksort algorithms #2 and #5 are very similar, but not identical. Four out of ten Quicksort algorithms were fixed fully automatically. All experiments were performed on an Intel Core 2 Duo 2.26GHz^{TM} system with 3GB physical memory.

Table 1. Experimental results on Quicksort algorithms

Domain	LOC	GT	BT	PC-points	Patch Size	Time
1 framwork.googlecode.com	29	-	-	7	no fix	2
2 www.cs.iastate.edu	32	24	261	10	1	524
3 geo.jm-art.cz	29	8	36	11	6	79
4 raider.muc.edu	24	-	-	7	no fix	5
5 archive.godatabase.org	27	24	261	10	1	442
6 www.jeckle.de	22	-	-	8	no fix	158
7 www.cs.indiana.edu	35	30	162	9	3	440
8 www.cse.buffalo.edu	50	-	-	16	no fix	4
9 gwt-greflect.googlecode.com	32	-	-	11	no fix	4
10 downloads.sourceforge.net	35	-	-	11	no fix	3

5 Conclusions

We have presented an approach for automatic bug fixing of Java programs that uses search techniques to explore the behaviour of program variants (candidates for a fix) on test inputs. The approach has been implemented on top of Java Pathfinder (JPF), which allows to encapsulate all program variants into one single meta-program, and use the JPF model checker to search all variants on all inputs. We have designed an efficient search strategy for early pruning unsuitable variants, and we have provided an efficient implementation with a suitable data structure.

We have tested the approach on implementations of Quicksort obtained through an automatic web search. Under the assumption that the bug was caused by "off-by-one" errors, four out of ten faulty implementations could be automatically repaired.

While the idea of exploring a set of program variants using some kind of systematic search is not new, we think that our particular design choices have two strong points. First, our search strategy makes the approach very suitable for finding fixes requiring multiple changes in different points of the code. Second, our approach fits very well the functionality offered by JPF, which greatly reduces the implementation effort and allows profiting from a very mature tool. On the other side, we require the programmer to specify the syntactic constructs where to look for bugs, and the alternative constructs that can be tried for a fix, which can be too restrictive in important cases.

Acknowledgments

We thank several anonymous referees for very helpful comments and suggestions.

References

1. Ball, T., Naik, M., Rajamani, S.K.: From symptom to cause: localizing errors in counterexample traces. In: POPL, pp. 97–105 (2003)
2. Ball, T., Rajamani, S.K.: The slam toolkit. In: Berry, G., Comon, H., Finkel, A. (eds.) CAV 2001. LNCS, vol. 2102, pp. 260–264. Springer, Heidelberg (2001)
3. Clarke, E.M., Kroening, D., Lerda, F.: A tool for checking ansi-c programs. In: Jensen, K., Podelski, A. (eds.) TACAS 2004. LNCS, vol. 2988, pp. 168–176. Springer, Heidelberg (2004)
4. Cleve, H., Zeller, A.: Locating causes of program failures. In: Roman, G.-C., Griswold, W.G., Nuseibeh, B. (eds.) ICSE, pp. 342–351. ACM, New York (2005)
5. Griesmayer, A., Staber, S., Bloem, R.: Automated fault localization for c programs. Electr. Notes Theor. Comput. Sci. 174(4), 95–111 (2007)
6. Groce, A., Chaki, S., Kroening, D., Strichman, O.: Error explanation with distance metrics. STTT 8(3), 229–247 (2006)
7. Groce, A., Visser, W.: What went wrong: Explaining counterexamples. In: Ball, T., Rajamani, S.K. (eds.) SPIN 2003. LNCS, vol. 2648, pp. 121–135. Springer, Heidelberg (2003)

8. Hailpern, B., Santhanam, P.: Software debugging, testing, and verification. IBM Systems Journal 41(1), 4–12 (2002)
9. Jobstmann, B., Griesmayer, A., Bloem, R.: Program repair as a game. In: Etessami, K., Rajamani, S.K. (eds.) CAV 2005. LNCS, vol. 3576, pp. 226–238. Springer, Heidelberg (2005)
10. Jones, J.A., Harrold, M.J.: Empirical evaluation of the tarantula automatic fault-localization technique. In: Redmiles, D.F., Ellman, T., Zisman, A. (eds.) ASE, pp. 273–282. ACM, New York (2005)
11. Staber, S., Jobstmann, B., Bloem, R.: Finding and fixing faults. In: Borrione, D., Paul, W. (eds.) CHARME 2005. LNCS, vol. 3725, pp. 35–49. Springer, Heidelberg (2005)
12. Visser, W., Havelund, K., Brat, G.P., Park, S., Lerda, F.: Model checking programs. Autom. Softw. Eng. 10(2), 203–232 (2003)
13. Wang, C., Yang, Z., Ivancic, F., Gupta, A.: Whodunit? causal analysis for counterexamples. In: Graf, S., Zhang, W. (eds.) ATVA 2006. LNCS, vol. 4218, pp. 82–95. Springer, Heidelberg (2006)
14. Weimer, W., Nguyen, T.V., Le Goues, C., Forrest, S.: Automatically finding patches using genetic programming. In: ICSE, pp. 364–374. IEEE, Los Alamitos (2009)
15. Zeller, A.: Isolating cause-effect chains from computer programs. In: SIGSOFT FSE, pp. 1–10 (2002)

Range Analysis of Microcontroller Code Using Bit-Level Congruences

Jörg Brauer[1], Andy King[2], and Stefan Kowalewski[1]

[1] Embedded Software Laboratory, RWTH Aachen University, Germany
[2] Portcullis Computer Security, Pinner, HA5 2EX, UK

Abstract. Bitwise instructions, loops and indirect data access pose difficult challenges to the verification of microcontroller programs. In particular, it is necessary to show that an indirect write does not mutate registers, which are indirectly addressable. To prove this property, among others, this paper presents a relational binary-code semantics and details how this can be used to compute program invariants in terms of bit-level congruences. Moreover, it demonstrates how congruences can be combined with intervals to derive accurate ranges, as well as information about strided indirect memory accesses.

1 Introduction

Microcontroller assembly code[1] presents different challenges to verification than those posed by programs written in high-level languages. Microcontroller code typically consists of a loop in which input ports are read. Data is then stored and processed – often using bitwise operations – before values are written to output ports. Bitwise operations and control logic formulated in terms of status flags necessitate reasoning at the granularity of bits. This presents one problem.

On hardware such as the ATMEL ATmega16 [1], any verification argument must also pay special attention to the targets of indirect writes[2]. An indirect write is a store operation in which the contents of one register are stored at a target address that is held in another register. On the ATmega family of microcontrollers, registers are reserved locations in the same address space as the SRAM. Thus, it is possible to mutate a register, such as the stack pointer, if the target coincides with the address of the register. One approach to microcontroller verification is to assume that indirect writes never mutate registers [20]. Though appealing in its simplicity, this assumption is dubious for handcrafted assembly code, and it is not unknown for compilation itself to introduce errors [12]. The problem of reasoning about targets is compounded by the fact that indirect writes often arise in loops that are, for example, responsible for data initialisation. Then the same store operation may write to a number of different targets. Another problem is therefore showing that all targets are within range [5].

---

[1] We often refer to assembly code, although our implementation operates on a disassembled binary, and thus, does not rely on correctness of assemblers and linkers.

[2] We illustrate our method for the ATmega16 platform, but the techniques are easily transferable to other platforms as well as high-level languages.

S. Kowalewski and M. Roveri (Eds.): FMICS 2010, LNCS 6371, pp. 82–98, 2010.
© Springer-Verlag Berlin Heidelberg 2010

```
0x50: LDI R17 0      0x56: LPMPI R0 Z
0x51: LDI R26 96     0x57: STPI X R0
0x52: LDI R27 0      0x58: CPI R26 99
0x53: LDI R30 66     0x59: CPC R27 R17
0x54: LDI R31 0      0x5A: BRNE -5
0x55: RJUMP 2        0x5B: RET
```

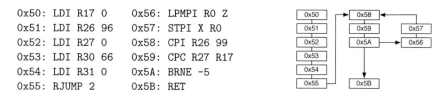

Fig. 1. An initialisation loop for the ATMEL ATmega16

1.1 Illustrative Example

This paper addresses the problem of statically analysing the targets of indirect writes, whilst simultaneously modelling data at the bit-level. Since the set of possible targets cannot be exactly determined statically, we employ abstract interpretation techniques [8] to compute a range of addresses that includes all possible targets. If the enclosing range is suitably tight, it is possible to verify that the registers are not overwritten. Figure 1 illustrates some ATmega16 assembly code. The instructions at locations 0x50 - 0x54 assign 8-bit registers to (decimal) constants. The relative jump passes control to location 0x58. The LPMPI R0 Z instruction first loads R0 with the contents of the byte at the address in program memory stored in the 16-bit Z register, then Z is incremented. Z is obtained by concatenating the 8-bit registers R30 and R31. Likewise, the 8-bit registers R26 and R27 constitute the 16-bit X register. STPI X R0 stores the contents of R0 into the byte at address X and then increments X.

The ATmega has a Harvard architecture, and hence, program memory is separate from SRAM. Location 98, for instance, in program memory is different from location 98 in SRAM. Thus, program memory is accessed with special instructions such as LPMPI. Therefore, detecting self-modifying code, which we do not consider, is trivial. The instructions CPI R26 99 and CPC R27 R17 compare X against 99, setting the zero flag if X equals 99. Control loops back to location 0x56 iff the zero flag is cleared, that is, if X is not equal to 99. The net effect of the code is to copy the contents of three locations in program memory starting at 66 into the SRAM locations $96 - 98$. This initialises three global variables to constant values.

A non-relational interval analysis as described in [5] can derive that $X \in [96, 99]$ in program location 0x5A. The interval analyser derives the bound on X based on the combination of CPI/CPC instructions followed by BRNE. However, it fails to discover that $Z \in [66, 69]$ and has to assume that the loop body could be entered with values $X \in [96, 98] \wedge Z \in [66, 69]$, $X \in [96, 98] \wedge Z \in [66, 70]$, and so forth, which eventually yields $Z \in [0, 65535]$. If the CPI/CPC instructions were to restrict Z instead of X, then the value of X were unbounded. This is in fact a well-known drawback of non-relational interval analysis. To resolve this type of imprecision, we combine the results of a relational analysis for equalities with a computationally cheap interval analysis, with the goal of deriving that X is incremented only in combination with Z, and consequently that $X \in [96, 98] \wedge Z \in [66, 68]$ when the indirect loads/stores are executed.

1.2   Approach

In microcontroller code for the ATmega16 platform, a memory region typically is statically reserved rather than dynamically allocated. Thus, the address of the start of a region that is used as an array is fully determined. Hence, when verifying such code, it is not necessary to use a symbolic name to refer to a memory region: an address will suffice. The force of this is that there is no need to adopt a memory model in which regions with different symbolic names are assumed to be non-interfering. Symbolic memory models are often employed when the position of a region is unknown, as with dynamically allocated memory in C, but this nevertheless compromises soundness [3]. Furthermore, when analysing statically reserved regions, it is even possible to infer a relationship between each address of a region, and the contents of that address.

To represent such relations, we turn to linear congruences [2, 18]. In this classical abstract domain [13], the relationships between variables are described as systems of linear equations of the form $\sum_{i=0}^{n-1} c_i x_i \bmod m = d$, denoted by $\sum_{i=0}^{n-1} c_i x_i \equiv_m d$, where $c_i \in \mathbb{Z}$ are integer coefficients, x_i are variables, $m \in \mathbb{N}$ is a modulus, and $d \in \mathbb{Z}$ is an integer constant. Such a system may have none, one or many solutions, where a solution is an assignment to the values of the n variables $x_0, \ldots, x_{n-1}$ that satisfies each of the equations. For example, the system $u + 2v \equiv_{256} 3$ and $v + w \equiv_{256} 1$ has solutions $\{\langle 1 + 256k_1 + 2k_3, 1 + 256k_2 - k_3, k_3 \rangle \in [0, 255]^3\}$ where $k_1, k_2, k_3 \in \mathbb{Z}$. Such relationships arise between program variables, or memory locations in the case of microcontroller code, because of the modular nature of computer arithmetic. It is therefore natural to consider moduli corresponding to the size of a machine word [18]. Such systems can only represent linear relationships, but not ranges, and therefore, we adopt a more expressive class of congruences based on decomposing variables into their consistent bits [15].

For instance, suppose u is represented by an unsigned byte whose bits are $\langle u_0, \ldots, u_7 \rangle$ where $u_i \in \{0, 1\}$ and the value of u is $\sum_{i=0}^{7} 2^i u_i$. Suppose too that v and w are likewise represented by $\langle v_0, \ldots, v_7 \rangle$ and $\langle w_0, \ldots, w_7 \rangle$. Then the above system can be expressed as $\sum_{i=0}^{7} 2^i (u_i + 2v_i) \equiv_{256} 3$, $\sum_{i=0}^{7} 2^i (v_i + w_i) \equiv_{256} 1$ without any loss of information. It has been shown how such systems can be applied to verify bit-twiddling algorithms [15, 16].

1.3   Contributions

In this paper, we make the following contributions. (1) We deploy congruence systems to derive program invariants for assembly code at the level of bits. (2) Further, we combine intervals [5] and congruence relations to derive accurate ranges. To do so, we present a new algorithm for refining the precision of abstract descriptions in both domains. (3) We show how a contiguous range, such as $[0, 6]$, can be refined to a set of non-contiguous values, such as $\{0, 2, 4, 6\}$, by applying congruences to ranges. (4) To summarise, this paper shows by that it is possible to infer accurate ranges using congruences and intervals, and thereby verify the correctness of microcontroller assembly code.

2   Abstract Domains

This section briefly reviews results on the abstract domains our work builds on, namely intervals and congruences. In the following, let $m = 2^w$ where $w = 8$ is the word-length of the microcontroller, $\mathbb{Z}_m = \{i \in \mathbb{N} \mid 0 \leq i \leq m - 1\}$, and let $\mathcal{V} = \{v_0, \ldots, v_{n-1}\}$ be a set of variables for some $n \in \mathbb{N}$. Further, let $\mathcal{P}$ denote the set of program locations (or instructions, equivalently).

2.1   Intervals

The interval abstract domain, probably the most widely used numerical domain, is used to over-approximate the value-sets of memory cells. In case of the 8-bit ATmega16, a memory location can hold a contiguous subset of values in $\mathbb{Z}_m$ defined through its bounds. Denote the domain Int. A partial order on intervals is induced by the subset relation over the concrete value-sets. Then, $(\mathsf{Int}, \subseteq)$ forms a complete lattice with $\bot = \emptyset$ and $\top = \mathbb{Z}_m$. Define auxiliary functions $\mathsf{fst} : \mathsf{Int} \to \mathbb{Z}_m$ and $\mathsf{snd} : \mathsf{Int} \to \mathbb{Z}_m$ that map intervals to their bounds. Abstraction $\alpha_{\mathsf{Int}} : 2^{\mathbb{Z}_m} \to \mathsf{Int}$ and concretisation $\gamma_{\mathsf{Int}} : \mathsf{Int} \to 2^{\mathbb{Z}_m}$ are defined as

$$\alpha_{\mathsf{Int}}(v) = \begin{cases} \emptyset & : \bot \\ [\min(v), \max(v)] & : \text{otherw.} \end{cases} \qquad \gamma_{\mathsf{Int}}(i) = \{z \in \mathbb{Z}_m \mid \mathsf{fst}(i) \leq z \leq \mathsf{snd}(i)\}$$

for $i \in \mathsf{Int}$ and $v \subseteq \mathbb{Z}_m$. An abstract interpretation framework for deriving non-relational interval abstractions of microcontroller code has been described in [5], however, space constraints prevent us from repeating these results here. We assume that for each program location $p \in \mathcal{P}$ and each memory location $v \in \mathcal{V}$, an interval abstraction has been computed, given through a map $I : \mathcal{V} \times \mathcal{P} \to \mathsf{Int}$.

2.2   Congruences

Additionally, our analysis is based on representing Boolean functions as congruence systems. To explain this idea, let $\mathsf{sol}(f)$ denote the set of solutions of a Boolean function f over n propositional variables. Our method relies on the computation of the so-called *congruent closure*, which yields a congruence system c over n bitwise variables such that $\mathsf{sol}(f) \subseteq \mathsf{sol}(c) \cap \mathbb{B}^n$ with $\mathbb{B} = \{0, 1\}$ holds. For example, given a function $f = x_1 \wedge (x_2 \vee x_3)$, we have $\mathsf{sol}(f) = \{\langle 1, 0, 1 \rangle, \langle 1, 1, 0 \rangle, \langle 1, 1, 1 \rangle\}$. Congruent closure, with a fixed modulo of 4, then computes $c = (x_1 \equiv_4 1)$. The solutions of this congruence equation are $\mathsf{sol}(c) \cap \mathbb{B}^3 = \{\langle 1, x_2, x_3 \rangle \mid x_2, x_3 \in \mathbb{B}\}$. Note that $\mathsf{sol}(c) \setminus \mathsf{sol}(f) = \{\langle 1, 0, 0 \rangle\}$.

Definition 1. The operator $\mathsf{cong} : 2^{\mathbb{B}^{nw}} \to 2^{\mathbb{B}^{nw}}$ is defined:

$$\mathsf{cong}(S) = \left\{ \boldsymbol{x} \in \mathbb{B}^{nw} \;\middle|\; \begin{array}{l} \{\boldsymbol{y}_0, \ldots, \boldsymbol{y}_{k-1}\} \subseteq S \wedge \{\lambda_0, \ldots, \lambda_{k-1}\} \subseteq \mathbb{Z} \wedge \\ \sum_{j=0}^{j<k} \lambda_j \equiv_{2^w} 1 \qquad \wedge \boldsymbol{x} \equiv_{2^w} \sum_{j=0}^{j<k} \lambda_j \boldsymbol{y}_j \end{array} \right\}$$

An algorithm for deriving optimal congruent abstractions of Boolean formulae was described by King and Søndergaard [16]. Given a formula φ, the key idea of their method is to derive a congruent abstraction $\alpha_{\mathsf{Cong}}(\varphi)$ through successive calls to a SAT solver. Therefore, their algorithm is similar in spirit to the symbolic implementation of a best transformer as described by Reps et al. [21]. In the following, let Cong denote the domain of bit-level congruences over $\mathcal{V}$.

3   Worked Examples

We illustrate the power of bit-level reasoning using the congruence domain for some illustrative sequences of ATmega16 assembly. The key idea of our approach is to derive a template transfer function for each instruction using SAT solving up-front, and then instantiate the transfer functions to infer program invariants. The invariants are then strengthened with intervals, yielding more precise representations of congruences as well as intervals.

3.1   Reasoning about Bit-Wise Operations

Consider the instruction EOR R0 R1, which computes the exclusive-or of registers R0 and R1 and stores the result in R0. First, a template abstraction of this instruction that does not depend on the concrete registers R0 and R1 is synthesised from a Boolean encoding. To express the semantics of EOR r s, introduce bit-vectors $r[i]$ and $s[i]$ for the inputs as well as $r'[i]$ and $s'[i]$ for the outputs (with $0 \leq i \leq 7$). Then, EOR r s is encoded symbolically as

$$[\![\text{EOR } r \text{ } s]\!] = \bigwedge_{i=0}^{7} \left(r'[i] \leftrightarrow r[i] \oplus s[i] \wedge s'[i] \leftrightarrow s[i] \right)$$

where $\oplus$ denotes the Boolean exclusive-or. By computing the congruent closure of $[\![\text{EOR } r \text{ } s]\!]$ with a modulus of 256, denoted α_{Cong}, we obtain:

$$\alpha_{\mathsf{Cong}}([\![\text{EOR } r \text{ } s]\!]) = \begin{cases} \bigwedge_{i=0}^{7} (128 \cdot r'[i] \equiv_{256} 128 \cdot r[i] + 128 \cdot s[i]) \wedge \\ \bigwedge_{i=0}^{7} s'[i] \equiv_{256} s[i] \end{cases}$$

Note that $\mathsf{sol}(\alpha_{\mathsf{Cong}}([\![\text{EOR } r \text{ } s]\!])) = \mathsf{sol}([\![\text{EOR } r \text{ } s]\!])$, and thus, this congruent transfer function is just as accurate as its Boolean counterpart.

3.2   Relational Composition without Ranges

In the previous example, we have seen how a template abstraction of a single instruction is derived. Here, we consider the program fragment EOR R0 R1; EOR R1 R0; EOR R0 R1 and the instantiation of templates. In [15], it was shown that best transformers for blocks (sequences of instructions) can be obtained by encoding the sequence propositionally as a whole. Since our goal is to derive range information for different program locations that may be located in the middle of a block, we deviate from following this approach, and combine the obtained transfer functions using relational composition $\circ : \mathsf{Cong} \times \mathsf{Cong} \to \mathsf{Cong}$.

A template transfer function c, derived analogously to the first example, is instantiated with the corresponding variables $\boldsymbol{r0}$, $\boldsymbol{r1}$, $\boldsymbol{r0'}$, and $\boldsymbol{r1'}$, which amounts to renaming variables in the template. This gives $c_1 = c(\boldsymbol{r0}, \boldsymbol{r1}, \boldsymbol{r0'}, \boldsymbol{r1'})$, $c_2 = c(\boldsymbol{r1}, \boldsymbol{r0}, \boldsymbol{r1'}, \boldsymbol{r0'})$, and $c_3 = c(\boldsymbol{r0}, \boldsymbol{r1}, \boldsymbol{r0'}, \boldsymbol{r1'})$, for instance:

$$c_1 = \bigwedge\nolimits_{i=0}^{7} \left(128 \cdot \boldsymbol{r0'}[i] \equiv_{256} 128 \cdot \boldsymbol{r0}[i] + 128 \cdot \boldsymbol{r1}[i]\right) \wedge \bigwedge\nolimits_{i=0}^{7} \left(\boldsymbol{r1'}[i] \equiv_{256} \boldsymbol{r1}[i]\right)$$

To combine the effects of c_1 and c_2, introduce additional disjoint bit-vectors $\boldsymbol{r0''}$ and $\boldsymbol{r1''}$, and put $c_1' = c_1 \wedge \left(\wedge_{i=0}^{7}\boldsymbol{r0''}[i] \equiv_{256} \boldsymbol{r0}[i]'\right) \wedge \left(\wedge_{i=0}^{7}\boldsymbol{r1''}[i] \equiv_{256} \boldsymbol{r1}[i]'\right)$ and $c_2' = c_2 \wedge \left(\wedge_{i=0}^{7}\boldsymbol{r0''}[i] \equiv_{256} \boldsymbol{r0}[i]\right) \wedge \left(\wedge_{i=0}^{7}\boldsymbol{r1''}[i] \equiv_{256} \boldsymbol{r1}[i]\right)$. The net effect of this construction is to relate the outputs of c_1 to the inputs of c_2. Then, define $c_1 \circ c_2 = \exists_{\boldsymbol{r0''}, \boldsymbol{r1''}}(\exists_{\boldsymbol{r0'}, \boldsymbol{r1'}}(c_1') \wedge \exists_{\boldsymbol{r0}, \boldsymbol{r1}}(c_2'))$ where the operation $\exists_{\boldsymbol{X}}(f)$ eliminates the variables $\boldsymbol{X}$ from f using projection. Observe that projection can be implemented by computing upper triangular form after reordering the variables in the system [18, 15]. As a result, we obtain:

$$c_1 \circ c_2 = \bigwedge\nolimits_{i=0}^{7} \left(\boldsymbol{r1'}[i] \equiv_{256} \boldsymbol{r0}[i]\right) \wedge \bigwedge\nolimits_{i=0}^{7} \left(128 \cdot \boldsymbol{r0'}[i] \equiv_{256} 128 \cdot (\boldsymbol{r0}[i] + \boldsymbol{r1}[i])\right)$$

That is, after the second instruction, register R1 holds the original value of R0. Further, by computing $c_1 \circ c_2 \circ c_3$ analogously, we derive:

$$c_1 \circ c_2 \circ c_3 = \bigwedge\nolimits_{i=0}^{7} \left(\boldsymbol{r0'}[i] \equiv_{256} \boldsymbol{r1}[i]\right) \wedge \bigwedge\nolimits_{i=0}^{7} \left(\boldsymbol{r1'}[i] \equiv_{256} \boldsymbol{r0}[i]\right)$$

This congruent representation reveals that the sequence of instructions performs an in-place swapping of R0 and R1 using consecutive exclusive-or operations.

3.3   Reasoning about Ranges Using Invariants

Recall again the example program from Fig. 1, which copies three values from program memory into SRAM. The interval analysis infers a map $I : \mathcal{V} \times \mathcal{P} \rightarrow \mathsf{Int}$, which states that before instruction 0x5A is executed, the registers X and Z hold the values $I(\mathtt{X}, \mathtt{0x5A}) = [96, 99]$ and $I(\mathtt{Z}, \mathtt{0x5A}) = [0, 65535]$.

To derive program invariants, we express the behaviour of the program fragment in terms of a flowchart program $\langle \mathcal{P}, \mathcal{V}, p_0, T \rangle$, where $\mathcal{P}$ is the set of program locations, $\mathcal{V}$ is the set of program variables, $p_0 \in \mathcal{P}$ is the initial program location and $T \subseteq \mathcal{P} \times \mathcal{P}$ defines the possible transitions between the instructions as given by the control flow graph. Consequently, we have $\mathcal{P} = \{\mathtt{0x50}, \ldots, \mathtt{0x5A}\}$, $\mathcal{V} = \{\mathtt{R17}, \mathtt{R26}, \mathtt{R27}, \mathtt{R30}, \mathtt{R31}\}$ and $p_0 = \mathtt{0x50}$. The semantics of the program can be stated as the least fixed point of a system of equations, given through:

- $\mathsf{inv}(p_0) = \bigwedge_{v \in \mathcal{V}} \left(\bigwedge_{i=0}^{7} v'[i] \equiv_{256} v[i]\right)$ for the initial program location p_0.
- $\mathsf{inv}(p_j) = \bigsqcup_{(p_i, p_j) \in T}(\mathsf{inv}(p_i) \circ c_{i,j})$, where $c_{i,j}$ denotes the instantiated congruent transfer function connecting $p_i \in \mathcal{P}$ and $p_j \in \mathcal{P}$.

Here, $\bigsqcup$ denotes the least upper bound operator over congruences as defined in [15]. Applying the first equation $\mathsf{inv}(p_{\mathtt{0x51}}) = \mathsf{inv}(p_0) \circ c_{\mathtt{0x50}}$ then gives

$$\mathsf{inv}(p_{\mathtt{0x51}}) = \begin{cases} \bigwedge_{i=0}^{7} \left(\boldsymbol{r17'}[i] \equiv_{256} 0\right) \quad \wedge \\ \bigwedge_{i=0}^{7} \left(\boldsymbol{r26'}[i] \equiv_{256} \boldsymbol{r26}[i]\right) \wedge \bigwedge_{i=0}^{7} \left(\boldsymbol{r27'}[i] \equiv_{256} \boldsymbol{r27}[i]\right) \wedge \\ \bigwedge_{i=0}^{7} \left(\boldsymbol{r30'}[i] \equiv_{256} \boldsymbol{r30}[i]\right) \wedge \bigwedge_{i=0}^{7} \left(\boldsymbol{r31'}[i] \equiv_{256} \boldsymbol{r31}[i]\right) \end{cases}$$

and thereafter, the invariant is stable. To express the program invariant $\mathsf{inv}(p_{\mathtt{0x5A}})$, let $\langle\!\langle \boldsymbol{x} \rangle\!\rangle = \sum_{i=0}^{7} 2^i \boldsymbol{x}[i]$. Proceeding with the computations eventually yields:

$$\mathsf{inv}(p_{\mathtt{0x5A}}) = \begin{cases} (\langle\!\langle \boldsymbol{r26'} \rangle\!\rangle - \langle\!\langle \boldsymbol{r30'} \rangle\!\rangle \equiv_{256} 30) \wedge \\ \bigwedge_{i=0}^{7} (\boldsymbol{r17'}[i] \equiv_{256} 0 \wedge \boldsymbol{r27'}[i] \equiv_{256} 0 \wedge \boldsymbol{r31'}[i] \equiv_{256} 0) \end{cases}$$

From $\mathsf{inv}(p_{\mathtt{0x5A}})$ and $I(\mathtt{X}, \mathtt{0x5A}) = [96, 99]$, we can now derive $I(\mathtt{Z}, \mathtt{0x5A}) = [66, 69]$. In the following, we will first see how program invariants of this kind are derived for arbitrary assembly programs, and then describe a systematic way of refining congruences and intervals in parallel. This operation amounts to triangularisation and checking satisfiability in order to strengthen the descriptions in both domains. Formally speaking, we will derive an operator $\mathsf{reduce} : \mathsf{Int} \times \mathsf{Cong} \rightarrow \mathsf{Int} \times \mathsf{Cong}$ such that $\mathsf{reduce}(i, c) \sqsubseteq (i, c)$ for $(i, c) \in \mathsf{Int} \times \mathsf{Cong}$ (cf. Sect. 6).

4   Relational Semantics for Assembly Code

In his seminal paper on congruence analysis, Granger [13] lamented the difficulty of handcrafting transformers for the congruence domain. However, since each of the 131 instructions on the ATmega16 has a well-defined semantics on the level of bits, we synthesise templates of transfer functions, based on a propositional encoding of the instructions and the computation of congruent closure to remedy this difficulty. When modelling the effects of instructions, no abstraction is applied, such that the formulae define the concrete semantics of the instructions.

Instructions for the ATmega platform have either zero, one, or two operands. Here, we present a relational encoding $[\![\cdot]\!]$ for a representative subset of the instruction-set. The semantics for other instructions can be derived analogously from the instruction set manual [1]. Given a set of memory locations accessed by an instruction, its encoding is given over disjoint bit-vectors for representing each accessed memory location, where the outputs are primed. Formally speaking, given a set of program variables $\mathcal{V}$, the Boolean formulae $[\![\cdot]\!]$ are defined over $\mathbb{B}_{\mathbf{V} \cup \mathbf{V'}}$, where $\mathbf{V} = \{\boldsymbol{v}[i] \mid v \in \mathcal{V}, 0 \le i \le 7\}$, $\mathbf{V'} = \{\boldsymbol{v'}[i] \mid v \in \mathcal{V}, 0 \le i \le 7\}$, and $\mathbb{B}_Y$ defines the class of Boolean formulae over propositional variables Y. Additionally, we require $\mathbf{V} \cap \mathbf{V'} = \emptyset$.

4.1   Copy and Load Instructions

The instruction MOV r s copies a register s into r. Similarly, given $c \in \mathbb{Z}_m$, the instruction LDI r c loads the constant value c into r. To express, introduce a bit-vector $\boldsymbol{c} \in \mathbb{B}^8$ with $\langle\!\langle \boldsymbol{c} \rangle\!\rangle = $ c. The semantics of these instructions can be encoded relationally over bit-vectors $\boldsymbol{r}$, $\boldsymbol{s}$, $\boldsymbol{r'}$ and $\boldsymbol{s'}$ as:

$$[\![\text{MOV r s}]\!] = \bigwedge_{i=0}^{7} (\boldsymbol{r'}[i] \leftrightarrow \boldsymbol{s}[i]) \wedge \bigwedge_{i=0}^{7} (\boldsymbol{s'}[i] \leftrightarrow \boldsymbol{s}[i])$$
$$[\![\text{LDI r c}]\!] = \bigwedge_{i=0}^{7} (\boldsymbol{r'}[i] \leftrightarrow \boldsymbol{c}[i])$$

Computing the congruent closure of $[\![\text{MOV r s}]\!]$, e.g., yields:

$$\alpha_{\mathsf{Cong}}([\![\text{MOV r s}]\!]) = \bigwedge_{i=0}^{7} (\boldsymbol{r'}[i] \equiv_{256} \boldsymbol{s}[i]) \wedge \bigwedge_{i=0}^{7} (\boldsymbol{s'}[i] \equiv_{256} \boldsymbol{s}[i])$$

Observe that for these instructions, a modulus of 2 would suffice, but this is not always so. However, choosing the modulus to match the register-length is safe. Moreover, note that the status register (called SREG in case of the ATmega16) is not affected by these instructions, which is different for logical or arithmetic instructions. Overall, the status register contains 8 different flags that can be affected by instructions: carry flag C, zero flag Z, negative flag N, overflow flag O, sign flag S, half-carry flag H, transfer flag T, and interrupt flag I. The exact way these bits are set or cleared, however, depends on the concrete instruction.

4.2 Bitwise Instructions

As bitwise operations, the ATmega16 supports bitwise-and (AND), bitwise-and with a constant value (ANDI), bitwise negation (COM), exclusive-or (EOR), bitwise-or (OR), and bitwise-or with a constant (ORI). The effects of these operations on the destination register, denoted $\theta(\text{op})$, are bit-blasted as follows:

$$
\begin{aligned}
\theta(\text{AND } r\ s) &= \bigwedge_{i=0}^{7} \left(r'[i] \leftrightarrow r[i] \wedge s[i] \right) \wedge \bigwedge_{i=0}^{7} \left(s'[i] \leftrightarrow s[i] \right) \\
\theta(\text{COM } r) &= \bigwedge_{i=0}^{7} \left(r'[i] \leftrightarrow \neg r[i] \right) \\
\theta(\text{EOR } r\ s) &= \bigwedge_{i=0}^{7} \left(r'[i] \leftrightarrow r[i] \oplus s[i] \right) \wedge \bigwedge_{i=0}^{7} \left(s'[i] \leftrightarrow s[i] \right) \\
\theta(\text{OR } r\ s) &= \bigwedge_{i=0}^{7} \left(r'[i] \leftrightarrow r[i] \vee s[i] \right) \wedge \bigwedge_{i=0}^{7} \left(s'[i] \leftrightarrow s[i] \right)
\end{aligned}
$$

The encodings for ANDI r c and ORI r c are derived by replacing $s[i]$ in the respective formulae with $c[i]$ defined as above. As an example, consider the abstraction of COM r, which flips all bits in r:

$$
\alpha_{\text{Cong}}(\theta(\text{COM } r)) = \bigwedge_{i=0}^{7} \left(128 \cdot r'[i] \equiv_{256} 128 \cdot r[i] + 128 \right)
$$

Bitwise instructions also alter status flags. These effects are encoded in formulae $\psi(\text{op})$, leading to an encoding $[\![\text{op}]\!] = \theta(\text{op}) \wedge \psi(\text{op})$. AND r s, for instance, behaves as follows with respect to the status flags: It clears the overflow flag, sets the negative flag iff $r'[7]$ is set, sets the sign flag to $N' \oplus O'$, and sets the zero flag iff all bits in r' are cleared. The other flags remained unchanged. To express, let $\text{id}(x) = x' \leftrightarrow x$. Then:

$$
\psi(\text{AND } r\ s) = \begin{cases} \neg O' \ \wedge \ \ \ Z' \leftrightarrow (\bigwedge_{i=0}^{7} \neg r'[i]) \wedge \text{id}(T) \ \wedge N' \leftrightarrow r'[7] \ \wedge \\ \text{id}(C) \wedge \ \ \ S' \leftrightarrow N' \oplus O' \ \ \ \ \ \ \wedge \text{id}(H) \wedge \text{id}(I) \end{cases}
$$

Encodings $\psi(\text{op})$ for ANDI, EOR, OR, and ORI are equal to this case. COM differs in that it always sets the carry flag. Observe that the congruence domain is too weak to express the relationship on Z', but it can represent the other ones.

4.3 Shifts

In terms of shifts, the ATmega16 supports arithmetic shift right (ASR), logical shift left (LSL), logical shift right (LSR), rotate left through carry (ROL), and rotate right through carry (ROR). All these operations shift the value of the source register by a single position, shifts by a higher or variable number of positions are not supported. ASR r shifts all bits in r to the right, the most significant (MSB) bit is held constant, and the least significant bit (LSB) is shifted into the carry. Thus, the instruction divides a signed r by two without changing its sign. LSR r behaves analogously for an unsigned value. LSL r multiplies r by two, shifting the MSB into the carry and clearing the LSB. ROL r and ROR r are used to multiply and divide multi-byte signed and unsigned values by two, by shifting the carry flag into the LSB/MSB of r and shifting the value of the MSB/LSB bit into the carry. Expressed in propositional logic, this gives:

$$\theta(\texttt{ASR r}) = \bigwedge_{i=0}^{6} \left(r'[i] \leftrightarrow r[i+1]\right) \wedge r'[7] \leftrightarrow r[7] \wedge C' \leftrightarrow r[0]$$
$$\theta(\texttt{LSL r}) = \bigwedge_{i=0}^{6} \left(r'[i+1] \leftrightarrow r[i]\right) \wedge \neg r'[0] \wedge C' \leftrightarrow r[7]$$
$$\theta(\texttt{ROR r}) = \bigwedge_{i=0}^{6} \left(r'[i] \leftrightarrow r[i+1]\right) \wedge r'[7] \leftrightarrow C \wedge C' \leftrightarrow r[0]$$

Encodings for LSR and ROL are specified similarly. The updates of the status flags are then expressed analogously to before with $[\![\mathsf{op}]\!] = \theta(\mathsf{op}) \wedge \psi(\mathsf{op})$ and $\psi(\mathsf{op}) = \varphi(\mathsf{op}) \wedge \xi(\mathsf{op})$, where

$$\varphi(\mathsf{op}) = \begin{cases} N' \leftrightarrow r'[7] & \wedge\ Z' \leftrightarrow \bigwedge_{i=0}^{7} \neg r'[i] \ \wedge\ \mathsf{id}(T)\ \wedge\ \mathsf{id}(I)\ \wedge \\ O' \leftrightarrow N' \oplus C' \wedge S' \leftrightarrow N' \oplus O' & \wedge\ \mathsf{id}(H) \end{cases}$$

is the same among all shift instructions, whereas $\xi(\mathsf{op}) = C' \leftrightarrow r[0]$ for $\mathsf{op} \in \{\texttt{ASR}, \texttt{LSR}, \texttt{ROR}\}$ and $\xi(\mathsf{op}) = C' \leftrightarrow r[7]$ otherwise.

4.4   Arithmetic Instructions

Let us consider encodings for two arithmetic instructions, in this case for summing up two registers (ADD) and incrementing a register by 1 (INC). Here, ADD r s is expressed using a cascade of full-adders using additional carry bits c:

$$\theta(\texttt{ADD r s}) = \left(\bigwedge_{i=0}^{7} r'[i] \leftrightarrow r[i] \oplus s[i] \oplus c[i]\right) \wedge \neg c[0] \wedge$$
$$\left(\bigwedge_{i=0}^{6} c[i+1] \leftrightarrow (r[i] \wedge s[i]) \vee (r[i] \wedge c[i]) \vee (s[i] \wedge c[i])\right)$$
$$\theta(\texttt{INC r}) = \bigwedge_{i=0}^{7}(r'[i] \leftrightarrow r[i] \oplus \bigwedge_{j=0}^{i-1} r[j])$$

Bit-wise encodings for other arithmetic instructions such as computation of the two's complement (NEG) or subtraction (SUB) are derived accordingly. The effects $\psi(\mathsf{op})$ on the status register can be derived analogously to the previous examples to obtain $[\![\mathsf{op}]\!] = \psi(\mathsf{op}) \wedge \theta(\mathsf{op})$. Abstracting the increment using congruences then gives:

$$\alpha_{\mathsf{Cong}}(\theta(\texttt{INC r})) = (\langle\!\langle r \rangle\!\rangle' \equiv_{256} \langle\!\langle r \rangle\!\rangle + 1)$$

Using the same approach, Boolean encodings for the complete instruction set of the ATmega16 and the corresponding congruent abstractions are computed. For instance, branching instructions such as BRNE do not alter the status of the addressable memory, but only the program counter, which is implicitly encoded in the control flow graph. Compare instructions such as CP, CPC, or CPI subtract two values, but they only alter the status flags accordingly and do not store the result at a memory location.

5 A Discussion of Soundness

As stated in Sect. 3.3 already, defining a program analysis over congruences amounts to the application of four operations: instantiating template functions, relational composition $\circ$, join $\sqcup$, and checking entailment $\models$. Since congruences satisfy the finite ascending chain condition, no widening is needed [18]. We make no contributions in this regard. However, two open issues warrant discussion: the effect of indirect stores on the validity of invariants and relationships between addresses of a region and the contents of that address.

In Sect. 3.3, we have not modelled the effects of indirect stores on memory locations 96–98 in SRAM. Thus, no relational constraints are put onto these memory locations. However, suppose that a value is copied from s into a target register r using a direct access, which generates an equality constraint $\bigwedge_{i=0}^{7} r[i] \equiv_{256} s[i]$, and later r is overwritten using an indirect store. Following the approach described so far, the equality constraint remains in the program invariant, which is unsound. The strength of using a concrete memory model, where each cell is represented by an integer address, is that the intervals provide an upper-approximation of the targets of indirect stores. Hence, we can simply modify the $\circ$ operator such that all constraints on targets of indirect writes are eliminated when $\circ$ is applied. This is achieved by removing all equalities that involve the target register from the invariant. This strategy recovers soundness. As a matter of fact, this method typically yields the same results as if the constraints on the targets were joined (since indirect stores are modelled as weak updates).

Even though it is not possible to derive relationships on the targets of indirect stores using weak updates, it is possible to derive a relationship between indirectly written locations and their contents. To illustrate, suppose we have an indirect store operation ST X R0, and a program invariant is generated. Then, if the invariant exhibits a relationship between X and R0, it follows that if a target memory location is written (which cannot be guaranteed), the target address is congruently related to the source register R0 as described by the invariant.

6 Reducing Abstract Descriptions

Thus far we have derived bit-level invariants, which are systems of linear congruences. In this section, we show how congruences and intervals are combined to derive more precise abstractions in both domains. Finally, strides – that is, sets of values that are separated by a constant $k \in \mathbb{N}$ – are extracted from the refined ranges.

6.1 A Reduce Operator

Given $S_1, S_2 \subseteq \mathbb{B}^{nw}$, where S_1 represents the models of the interval abstraction and S_2 represents the models of the congruent invariant, we construct $S_1 \cap S_2$ formally. To represent the models of intervals, let $\ell_i, u_i \in \mathbb{B}^w$ denote bitwise encodings of the extremal values of $v_i \in \mathcal{V}$ for a fixed $p \in \mathcal{P}$ as defined through the map $I : \mathcal{V} \times \mathcal{P} \to \mathsf{Int}$. Then:

Definition 2. The operator $\text{cube} : 2^{\mathbb{B}^{nw}} \to 2^{\mathbb{B}^{nw}}$ is defined:

$$\text{cube}(S) = \left\{ \boldsymbol{x} \in \mathbb{B}^{nw} \; \middle| \; \begin{array}{ll} \forall i \in [0, n-1] : \boldsymbol{\ell}_i, \boldsymbol{u}_i \in S & \wedge \\ \ell_i' = \langle\!\langle\langle \boldsymbol{\ell}_i[0], \ldots, \boldsymbol{\ell}_i[w-1]\rangle\rangle\!\rangle & \wedge \\ u_i' = \langle\!\langle\langle \boldsymbol{u}_i[0], \ldots, \boldsymbol{u}_i[w-1]\rangle\rangle\!\rangle & \wedge \\ \ell_i' \leq \langle\!\langle\langle \boldsymbol{x}[iw], \ldots, \boldsymbol{x}[iw+w-1]\rangle\rangle\!\rangle \leq u_i' \end{array} \right\}$$

It is straightforward to show that $\text{cube} : 2^{\mathbb{B}^{nw}} \to 2^{\mathbb{B}^{nw}}$ and $\text{cong} : 2^{\mathbb{B}^{nw}} \to 2^{\mathbb{B}^{nw}}$ are closure operators, that is, extensive, increasing and idempotent. Further, suppose $S_1, S_2, \ldots \subseteq \mathbb{B}^{nw}$. If $\text{cube}(S_i) = S_i$ for all $i \in \mathbb{N}$ then $\text{cube}(\cap_{i \in \mathbb{N}} S_i) = \cap_{i \in \mathbb{N}} S_i \text{m}$, and if $\text{cong}(S_i) = S_i$ for all $i \in \mathbb{N}$ then $\text{cong}(\cap_{i \in \mathbb{N}} S_i) = \cap_{i \in \mathbb{N}} S_i$. To derive Galois connections, and accordingly safety of our computations, we define abstraction and concretisation as follows:

Definition 3. The abstraction and concretisation maps are defined as:

$$\alpha_{\text{cube}}(S) = \cap\{S' \subseteq \mathbb{B}^{nw} \mid S \subseteq S' \wedge S' = \text{cube}(S')\} \qquad \gamma_{\text{cube}}(S) = S$$
$$\alpha_{\text{cong}}(S) = \cap\{S' \subseteq \mathbb{B}^{nw} \mid S \subseteq S' \wedge S' = \text{cong}(S')\} \qquad \gamma_{\text{cong}}(S) = S$$

Then, any subset of $\mathbb{B}^{nw}$ (or equivalently $\mathbb{Z}_m$) closed under affine combination can be represented congruently. A similar observation holds for the cube of S. Further, we have $\text{cube}(S) = S$ iff there exists $\ell_0', \ldots, \ell_{n-1}' \in [-2^{w-1}, 2^{w-1} - 1]$ and $u_0', \ldots, u_{n-1}' \in [-2^{w-1}, 2^{w-1} - 1]$ such that:

$$S = \left\{ \boldsymbol{x} \in \mathbb{B}^{nw} \; \middle| \; \forall i \in [0, n-1] : \ell_i' \leq \langle\!\langle\langle \boldsymbol{x}[iw], \ldots, \boldsymbol{x}[iw+w-1]\rangle\rangle\!\rangle \leq u_i' \right\}$$

For congruences, it is $\text{cong}(S) = S$ iff there exists a matrix $[A \mid \boldsymbol{b}] \in \mathbb{Z}^{k,nw+1}$ such that $S = \{\boldsymbol{x} \in \mathbb{B}^{nw} \mid A\boldsymbol{x} \equiv_{2^w} \boldsymbol{b}\}$.

Finally, we present a constructive approach to computing the affine intersection between S_1 and S_2. This construction is based on strengthening S_2 using constraints from S_1 (or I, respectively). The key idea in this construction is introduce fresh equalities to express the non-negativity of $\langle\!\langle \boldsymbol{v}_i \rangle\!\rangle - \langle\!\langle \boldsymbol{\ell}_i \rangle\!\rangle$ and $\langle\!\langle \boldsymbol{u}_i \rangle\!\rangle - \langle\!\langle \boldsymbol{v}_i \rangle\!\rangle$ in order to enforce $\langle\!\langle \boldsymbol{\ell}_i \rangle\!\rangle \leq \langle\!\langle \boldsymbol{v}_i \rangle\!\rangle \leq \langle\!\langle \boldsymbol{u}_i \rangle\!\rangle$. This is achieved by imposing a zero-constraint on the MSB of the difference, which corresponds to the sign bit. This construction is followed by putting the resulting system into upper triangular form.

Proposition 1. Suppose $\ell_0', \ldots, \ell_{n-1}', u_0', \ldots, u_{n-1}' \in [0, 2^w - 1]$ and let $[A \mid \boldsymbol{b}] \in \mathbb{Z}^{k,nw+1}$. Define

$$S_1 = \left\{ \boldsymbol{x} \in \mathbb{B}^{nw} \mid \forall i \in [0, n-1] : \ell_i' \leq \langle\!\langle\langle \boldsymbol{x}[iw], \ldots, \boldsymbol{x}[iw+w-1]\rangle\rangle\!\rangle \leq u_i' \right\}$$
$$S_2 = \{\boldsymbol{x} \in \mathbb{B}^{nw} \mid A\boldsymbol{x} \equiv_{2^w} \boldsymbol{b}\}$$

Let $\boldsymbol{e}, \boldsymbol{f} \in \mathbb{B}^w$ such that $\boldsymbol{e} = \langle 0, 0, \cdots, 0, 1 \rangle$ and $\boldsymbol{f} = \langle 1, 2, \cdots, 2^{w-2}, 2^{w-1} \rangle$. Moreover, let $A' \in \mathbb{Z}^{k+4n,3nw}$, $E \in \mathbb{Z}^{n,nw}$ and $F \in \mathbb{Z}^{n,nw}$ defined by:

$$A' = \begin{bmatrix} E & 0 & 0 \\ 0 & E & 0 \\ 0 & -F & F \\ F & 0 & -F \\ 0 & 0 & A \end{bmatrix} \qquad E = \begin{bmatrix} \boldsymbol{e} & 0 & \cdots & 0 \\ 0 & \boldsymbol{e} & \cdots & 0 \\ \vdots & \vdots & \vdots & \vdots \\ 0 & 0 & \cdots & \boldsymbol{e} \end{bmatrix} \qquad F = \begin{bmatrix} \boldsymbol{f} & 0 & \cdots & 0 \\ 0 & \boldsymbol{f} & \cdots & 0 \\ \vdots & \vdots & \vdots & \vdots \\ 0 & 0 & \cdots & \boldsymbol{f} \end{bmatrix}$$

Additionally, let $l \in \mathbb{Z}^n$, $u \in \mathbb{Z}^n$, $b' \in \mathbb{Z}^{k+4n}$ where

$$l = \begin{bmatrix} \ell'_0 \\ \ell'_1 \\ \vdots \\ \ell'_{n-1} \end{bmatrix} \qquad u = \begin{bmatrix} u'_0 \\ u'_1 \\ \vdots \\ u'_{n-1} \end{bmatrix} \qquad b' = \begin{bmatrix} 0 \\ 0 \\ l \\ u \\ b \end{bmatrix} \qquad x' = \begin{bmatrix} z \\ y \\ x \end{bmatrix}$$

Then $S_1 \cap S_2 = \{x \in \mathbb{B}^{nw} \mid A'x' \equiv_{2^w} b'\}$.

Refining intervals follows a method for maximising values in Boolean formulae described by Codish et al. [6] using successive calls to a decision procedure. The key idea is to maximise single bits – starting from the MSB – and checking satisfiability of a system of linear 0/1 constraints using SAT [15]. We use SAT solving because triangularisation only provides an incomplete decision procedure for 0/1 variables. In the following definition, the symbol : denotes the concatenation of bit-vectors.

Definition 4. Define $\max(A, b, i) = \mathsf{extr}(A, b, i, w, 0, 1)$ where $\mathsf{extr}(A, b, i, j, v_1, v_2)$:

- ϵ if $j = 0$.
- $\langle v_1 \rangle : \mathsf{extr}(\begin{bmatrix} e_i \\ A \end{bmatrix}, \begin{bmatrix} v_1 \\ b \end{bmatrix}, i-1, j-1, v_2, v_2)$ if $\begin{bmatrix} e_i \\ A \end{bmatrix} x \equiv_{2^w} \begin{bmatrix} v_1 \\ b \end{bmatrix}$ is satisfiable.
- $\langle \neg v_1 \rangle : \mathsf{extr}(\begin{bmatrix} e_i \\ A \end{bmatrix}, \begin{bmatrix} \neg v_1 \\ b \end{bmatrix}, i-1, j-1, v_2, v_2)$ otherwise.

Conversely define $\min(A, b, i) = \mathsf{extr}(A, b, i, w, 1, 0)$. Finally, reduce follows from the combination of min, max, and $\cap$:

Corollary 1. Let $S_1 \cap S_2 = Ax \equiv_{2^w} b$. Then $\mathsf{reduce}(S_1, S_2) = (I', Ax \equiv_{2^w} b)$ where $I' = \langle [\min(A, b, 0), \max(A, b, 0)], \ldots, [\min(A, b, n-1), \max(A, b, n-1)] \rangle$.

Example 1. Suppose $w = 4$, $n = 2$ and $S_2 = \{x \in \mathbb{B}^8 \mid Ax \equiv_{2^4} b\}$ where

$$A = \begin{bmatrix} 1 & 0 & 0 & 0 & -1 & 0 & 0 & 0 \\ 0 & 1 & 0 & 0 & 0 & -1 & 0 & 0 \\ 0 & 0 & 1 & 0 & 0 & 0 & -1 & 0 \\ 0 & 0 & 0 & 1 & 0 & 0 & 0 & -1 \\ 0 & 0 & 0 & 0 & 1 & 0 & 0 & 0 \end{bmatrix} \qquad b = \begin{bmatrix} 0 \\ 0 \\ 0 \\ 0 \\ 0 \end{bmatrix}$$

To interpret $[A \mid b]$, let $u = \langle x[0], x[1], x[2], x[3] \rangle$ and $v = \langle x[4], x[5], x[6], x[7] \rangle$. Then the system $Ax \equiv_{2^4} b$ implies that $\langle\langle u \rangle\rangle \equiv_{2^w} \langle\langle v \rangle\rangle$ and $\langle\langle v \rangle\rangle \equiv_2 0$. Now let

$$S_1 = \{x \in \mathbb{B}^8 \mid 4 \le \langle\langle u \rangle\rangle \le 15 \wedge 0 \le \langle\langle v \rangle\rangle \le 7\}$$

and consider $S_1 \cap S_2$ as characterised by $[A' \mid b']$ which is:

$$\left[\begin{array}{cccc|cccc|cccc|cccc|cccc|c}
0&0&0&1&0&0&0&0&0&0&0&0&0&0&0&0&0&0&0&0&0\\
0&0&0&0&0&0&0&1&0&0&0&0&0&0&0&0&0&0&0&0&0\\
0&0&0&0&0&0&0&0&0&0&0&1&0&0&0&0&0&0&0&0&0\\
0&0&0&0&0&0&0&0&0&0&0&0&0&0&0&1&0&0&0&0&0\\
0&0&0&0&0&0&0&0&-1&-2&-4&-8&0&0&0&0&1&2&4&8&4\\
0&0&0&0&0&0&0&0&0&0&0&0&-1&-2&-4&-8&0&0&0&0&0\\
1&2&4&8&0&0&0&0&0&0&0&0&0&0&0&0&-1&-2&-4&-8&15\\
0&0&0&0&1&2&4&8&0&0&0&0&0&0&0&0&0&0&0&0&7\\
0&0&0&0&0&0&0&0&0&0&0&0&1&0&0&0&-1&0&0&0&0\\
0&0&0&0&0&0&0&0&0&0&0&0&0&1&0&0&0&-1&0&0&0\\
0&0&0&0&0&0&0&0&0&0&0&0&0&0&1&0&0&0&-1&0&0\\
0&0&0&0&0&0&0&0&0&0&0&0&0&0&0&1&0&0&0&-1&0\\
0&0&0&0&0&0&0&0&0&0&0&0&0&0&0&0&1&0&0&0&0
\end{array}\right]$$

Putting this into a triangular form, we achieve:

$$\left[\begin{array}{cccc|cccc|cccc|cccc|cccc|c}
1&2&4&8&0&0&0&0&0&0&0&0&-1&-2&-4&-8&0&0&0&0&15\\
0&0&0&1&0&0&0&0&0&0&0&0&0&0&0&0&0&0&0&0&0\\
0&0&0&0&1&2&4&8&0&0&0&0&0&0&0&0&-1&-2&-4&-8&7\\
0&0&0&0&0&0&0&1&0&0&0&0&0&0&0&0&0&0&0&0&0\\
0&0&0&0&0&0&0&0&-1&-2&-4&-8&0&0&0&0&1&2&4&8&4\\
0&0&0&0&0&0&0&0&0&0&0&1&0&0&0&0&0&0&0&0&0\\
0&0&0&0&0&0&0&0&0&0&0&0&-1&-2&-4&-8&0&0&0&0&0\\
0&0&0&0&0&0&0&0&0&0&0&0&0&0&0&1&0&0&0&0&0\\
0&0&0&0&0&0&0&0&0&0&0&0&1&0&0&0&-1&0&0&0&0\\
0&0&0&0&0&0&0&0&0&0&0&0&0&1&0&0&0&-1&0&0&0\\
0&0&0&0&0&0&0&0&0&0&0&0&0&0&1&0&0&0&-1&0&0\\
0&0&0&0&0&0&0&0&0&0&0&0&0&0&0&1&0&0&0&-1&0\\
0&0&0&0&0&0&0&0&0&0&0&0&0&0&0&0&1&0&0&0&0
\end{array}\right]$$

Here, rows 3 and 4 impose the constraint $\langle\!\langle v \rangle\!\rangle \leq 7$ by requiring $7 - \langle\!\langle v \rangle\!\rangle \geq 0$. The constraints can be projected from $S_1 \cap S_2$, which yields $u[3] \equiv_{2^w} 0$, and thus, $\langle\!\langle u \rangle\!\rangle \leq 7$. With $u[0] \equiv_{2^w} 0$, applying SAT yields $4 \leq \langle\!\langle u \rangle\!\rangle \leq 6$. Note, however, that more precise congruences could be extracted by encoding the equation system in propositional logic and recomputing congruent closure.

6.2   Refinement for Strides

For $p \in \mathcal{P}$, the respective invariant $inv(p)$, and a variable $v \in \mathcal{V}$, let $i \in \mathbb{N}$ be the maximum index of bit-vector v such that $inv(p)$ contains relations $v[j] \equiv_{256} k_j$ for all $0 \leq j \leq i$ and $k_j \in \{0, 1\}$. The size of the stride is then defined by 2^{i+1}, and the set of possible values constrained by the invariant is given through $Z = \{(\sum_{j=0}^{i} 2^j v[j]) + k \cdot 2^{i+1} \mid k \in \mathbb{N}\}$. Thus, the resulting value-set is $I(v, p) \cap Z$.

Table 1. Optimality of synthesised transfer functions

Class	Instructions	$\mathsf{sol}(\alpha([\![c]\!])) = \mathsf{sol}([\![c]\!])$?
load & copy	LDI, MOV	yes
shift	ASR, LSL, LSR, ROL, ROR	yes
logical	COM, EOR, SWAP	yes
logical	AND, ANDI, OR, ORI	no
arithmetic	ADC, ADD, DEC, INC, NEG, SBC, SUB, SUBI	yes
arithmetic	MUL, MULS, MULSU	no
compare	CP, CPC, CPI	no
branching	BRBC, BRBS, ...	no

7 Experiments

We have integrated the ideas and algorithms described in this paper into the [MC]SQUARE verification platform for microcontroller binary code. In this section, we discuss our experiences with respect to optimality and the runtime requirements. All experiments were performed on a MacBook Pro, equipped with a 2.4 Ghz dual-core processor and 4 GB of RAM.

7.1 Optimality

Let $\alpha_{\mathsf{Cong}}([\![f]\!])$ denote a transfer function synthesised from a Boolean encoding $[\![f]\!]$. The congruence domain is optimal for abstracting f iff $\mathsf{sol}(\alpha_{\mathsf{Cong}}([\![f]\!])) = \mathsf{sol}([\![f]\!])$. Considering the classes of instructions that were described Sect. 4, optimality results given in Tab. 1 are obtained (ignoring the effects of arithmetic and logical instructions on the status register). Observe that compare and branching instructions, which are required to handle conditional branches and loop conditions, sometimes cannot be modelled precisely (recall the congruent abstraction of $\mathbf{Z}' \leftrightarrow \bigwedge_{i=0}^{7}(\neg \mathbf{r}'[i])$). This drawback, however, is remedied through the interval analysis, which constrains the ranges through branching conditions.

7.2 Runtime

Synthesing transfer functions up-front requires less than 1s for each instruction. Abstracting INC r, e.g., requires 17 SAT instances over 32 propositional variables to be solved with an overall runtime of 0.18s using SAT4J. Composing congruences is implemented using triangularisation, as is $\sqcup$. For the initialisation loop in Sect. 3.3, the loop invariant stabilised after 2 iterations, which led to 18 applications of $\circ$ and 2 applications of $\sqcup$, which required $0.3s$ overall. The runtime for operations on matrices is very susceptible to the number of variables in the system, and hence, $\mathbf{r17}$, $\mathbf{r26}$, $\mathbf{r27}$, $\mathbf{r30}$, and $\mathbf{r31}$ were eliminated prior to range-refinement as they are unrelated to the invariant. Since the runtime grows polynomially with the number of bits, computing invariants for complete programs is not tractable. Instead, an invariant generator should detect program fragments where the interval analyser loses precision.

Computing reduce to derive refined ranges requires 16 SAT instances to be solved which amounts to 0.25s. That is, two instances for each bit are required, whereas deriving strides is linear in the number of congruence relations.

8   Related Work

Defining and computing transformers for relational domains has been an active topic in abstract interpretation for decades, and numerous techniques for expressing relational constraints have been described [11, 17]. Most existing approaches, however, operate on unbounded integers, with the additional duty to verify that no overflow can occur [10]. The technique from [22] suggests to revise the truncation map to reflect overflows for polyhedral analysis.

In assembly code for 8-bit architectures, overflows can be observed commonly due to the limited bit-width. Therefore, it is natural to deploy congruence relations [18, 13] where the modulus is 256. Instead of expressing ranges in a domain that handles wraps, our approach combines relational invariants with computationally inexpensive intervals [5]. The idea of reducing two abstract descriptions in parallel was already formalised by Cousot and Cousot [9]. Later, Codish et al. [7] have applied a similar technique to pair and set-sharing analysis.

The difficulty of designing optimal transfer functions was already discussed in [11]. However, it took several decades until it was observed that optimal transformers can be derived for any abstract domain that satisfies the ascending chain condition [21]. Our work builds on this to remedy both the difficulty and the workload of handcrafting transfer functions for the complete instruction set of the microcontroller as in [4]. Contemporaneously to [21], Regehr et al. [20] observed that optimal transfer functions for interval analysis of ATmega16 assembly can be derived using BDDs. However, the time needed for computing best transformers is considerably longer due to the use of BDD-based encodings without abstraction.

9   Conclusion and Future Work

We have shown that bit-level congruences provide a suitable means for deriving invariants for assembly code. We have detailed techniques for verifying, inferring, and refining ranges in presence of indirect reads and writes. The work calls for further research into the handling of indirect stores in order to derive strong updates instead of weak updates. Existing work on lifting abstract interpreters to quantified domains [14] could serve as a basis for this. Another interesting application is model checking, where congruences could be used to reduce the over-approximation introduced through abstractions [19] similar to the refinement described in Sect. 6, leading to smaller state spaces and fewer false alarms.

Acknowledgements

This work was supported, in part, by a Royal Society industrial secondment and the UMIC Research Centre at the RWTH Aachen University.

References

1. Atmel Corporation. 8-bit AVR Instruction Set (July 2008)
2. Bagnara, R., Dobson, K., Hill, P., Mundell, M., Zaffanella, E.: Grids: A domain for analyzing the distribution of numerical values. In: Puebla, G. (ed.) LOPSTR 2006. LNCS, vol. 4407, pp. 219–235. Springer, Heidelberg (2007)
3. Balakrishnan, G., Reps, T.W.: WYSINWYX: What You See Is Not What You eXecute. ACM Trans. Program. Lang. Syst. (to appear, 2010)
4. Brauer, J., King, A.: Automatic abstraction for intervals using boolean formulae. In: SAS 2010. LNCS. Springer, Heidelberg (2010)
5. Brauer, J., Noll, T., Schlich, B.: Interval analysis of microcontroller code using abstract interpretation of hardware and software. In: SCOPES. ACM, New York (to appear, 2010)
6. Codish, M., Lagoon, V., Stuckey, P.J.: Logic programming with Satisfiability. Theory and Practice of Logic Programming 8(1), 121–128 (2008)
7. Codish, M., Mulkers, A., Bruynooghe, M., García de la Banda, M.J., Hermenegildo, M.V.: Improving abstract interpretations by combining domains. ACM Trans. Program. Lang. Syst. 17(1), 28–44 (1995)
8. Cousot, P., Cousot, R.: Abstract interpretation: A unified lattice model for static analysis of programs by construction or approximation of fixpoints. In: POPL, pp. 238–252. ACM, New York (1977)
9. Cousot, P., Cousot, R.: Systematic design of program analysis frameworks. In: POPL, pp. 269–282 (1979)
10. Cousot, P., Cousot, R., Feret, J., Mauborgne, L., Mine, A., Monniaux, D., Rival, X.: The Astrée analyser. In: Sagiv, M. (ed.) ESOP 2005. LNCS, vol. 3444, pp. 21–30. Springer, Heidelberg (2005)
11. Cousot, P., Halbwachs, N.: Automatic Discovery of Linear Restraints Among Variables of a Program. In: POPL, pp. 84–97. ACM Press, New York (1978)
12. Eide, E., Regehr, J.: Volatiles are miscompiled, and what to do about it. In: EMSOFT, pp. 255–264. ACM, New York (2008)
13. Granger, P.: Static analysis of linear congruence equalities among variables of a program. In: Abramsky, S. (ed.) CAAP 1991 and TAPSOFT 1991. LNCS, vol. 493, pp. 169–192. Springer, Heidelberg (1991)
14. Gulwani, S., McCloskey, B., Tiwari, A.: Lifting abstract interpreters to quantified logical domains. In: POPL, pp. 235–246. ACM, New York (2008)
15. King, A., Søndergaard, H.: Inferring congruence equations using SAT. In: Gupta, A., Malik, S. (eds.) CAV 2008. LNCS, vol. 5123, pp. 281–293. Springer, Heidelberg (2008)
16. King, A., Søndergaard, H.: Automatic abstraction for congruences. In: Barthe, G., Hermenegildo, M. (eds.) VMCAI 2010. LNCS, vol. 5944, pp. 281–293. Springer, Heidelberg (2010)
17. Miné, A.: The Octagon Abstract Domain. Higher-Order and Symbolic Computation 19(1), 31–100 (2006)

18. Müller-Olm, M., Seidl, H.: Analysis of Modular Arithmetic. ACM Trans. Program. Lang. Syst. 29(5) (August 2007)
19. Noll, T., Schlich, B.: Delayed nondeterminism in model checking embedded systems assembly code. In: Yorav, K. (ed.) HVC 2007. LNCS, vol. 4899, pp. 185–201. Springer, Heidelberg (2008)
20. Regehr, J., Reid, A.: HOIST: A system for automatically deriving static analyzers for embedded systems. Operating Systems Review 38(5), 133–143 (2004)
21. Reps, T., Sagiv, M., Yorsh, G.: Symbolic Implementation of the Best Transformer. In: Steffen, B., Levi, G. (eds.) VMCAI 2004. LNCS, vol. 2937, pp. 252–266. Springer, Heidelberg (2004)
22. Simon, A., King, A.: Taming the wrapping of integer arithmetic. In: Riis Nielson, H., Filé, G. (eds.) SAS 2007. LNCS, vol. 4634, pp. 121–136. Springer, Heidelberg (2007)

An Automated Translator for Model Checking Time Constrained Workflow Systems

Ahmed Shah Mashiyat, Fazle Rabbi, Hao Wang, and Wendy MacCaull

Centre for Logic and Information
St. Francis Xavier University
Antigonish, Canada
{x2008ooc,x2010mcf,hwang,wmaccaul}@stfx.ca

Abstract. Workflows have proven to be a useful conceptualization for the automation of business processes. While formal verification methods (e.g., model checking) can help ensure the reliability of workflow systems, the industrial uptake of such methods has been slow largely due to the effort involved in modeling and the memory required to verify complex systems. Incorporation of time constraints in such systems exacerbates the latter problem. We present an automated translator, *YAWL2DVE-t*, which takes as input a time constrained workflow model built with the graphical modeling tool YAWL, and outputs the model in DVE, the system specification language for the distributed LTL model checker DiVinE. The automated translator, together with the graphical editor and the distributed model checker, provides a method for rapid design, verification and refactoring of time constrained workflow systems. We present a realistic case study developed through collaboration with the local health authority.

Keywords: Workflow Systems, Modeling, Time, Automated Translation, Distributed Model Checking.

1 Introduction

Workflow Management Systems (WfMSs) improve business processes by identifying needs, reducing waste and duplication of work, ensuring completion of projects on time and in accordance with plans, improving efficiency, facilitating documentation, and creating solutions based on the analyzed process requirements. WfMSs such as Staffware, WebSphere MQ Workflow, FLOWer, SAP Workflow, YAWL are adopted widely in the industry because they facilitate the visualization and analysis of a business process. Many of today's workflows are complex requiring a high degree of flexibility, massive data and knowledge management, and complex timing [1]. However, the resulting implementations of unverified large and complex workflow models are at risk of undesirable runtime executions. Current WfMSs facilitate the enactment of workflows with some degree of fault-tolerance, e.g., exception handling, but formal verification capacity is limited.

S. Kowalewski and M. Roveri (Eds.): FMICS 2010, LNCS 6371, pp. 99–114, 2010.

Model checking is an automatic analysis method, which explores all possible states of a modeled system to verify whether the system satisfies a formally specified property. It is widely used in industrial applications, e.g., computer hardware and software, and has great potential for verifying models of complex and distributed business processes. Un-timed model checkers like SPIN and SMV can generally only represent and verify the *qualitative* temporal relations between events, which constrains their use for verifying real-time systems. *Timed* model checking, the method to formally verify real-time systems, is attracting increasing attention from both the model checking community and the real-time community. An extensive survey of formal methods for the specification and verification of timed systems in [2] contains references of over 200 publications. Despite the intensity of research dedicated to the specification and validation of real-time requirements, relatively little work has been done on formally modeling time-constrained workflows and their verification. When time becomes a factor in the activities running concurrently, the notion of time is required to precisely model in the workflow. *Quantified* time notions, including time instance and duration must be taken into account for timed model checking. For example in a safety critical application such as in an emergency department, after an emergency case arrives at the hospital, standard model checking can only verify whether *"The patient receives a certain treatment"*, but to save the patient's life, it should be verified whether *"The patient receives a certain treatment within half an hour"*.

There are different approaches for modeling and verifying time constraints for workflow systems. Marjanovic et al. [3] provides a conceptual model to specify and verify timing aspects of production workflow; however, a production workflow lacks the notion of delay time between two consecutive tasks. Moreover, the verification is with respect to a chosen execution sequence. Many formalisms with time extensions have been presented as the basis for timed model checkers. Two popular ones, due to their simple graphical representations and solid mathematical formalisms, are: (1) *timed automata* [4], which is an extension of finite-state automata with a set of clock variables to keep track of time (which is under certain circumstances decidable); (2) *time Petri Nets* [5], which is an extension of Petri Nets with timing constraints on the firing of transitions. The later should be distinguished from *timed Petri Nets* which can store information on both arcs and tokens and are undecidable. A validation method for workflow specifications using UPPAAL (a timed automata based model checker) is presented in [6]. Models in a timed automata based model checker can not represent at which time instant a transition is executed within a time region; such model checkers can only deal with a specification involving a time region or a pre-specified time instant and cannot store the exact time instant at which a transition is executed. However, the *stop-watch* automata [7], an extension of timed automata, is proposed to tackle this; unfortunately, as Krcál and Yi discussed in [8], since the reachability problem for this class of automata is undecidable, there is no guarantee for termination in the general case. An approach for time constrained workflow verification using time Petri Nets can also be found in [9].

Time Petri Net tools such as Romeo [10] (which can verify a subset of Timed CTL), TINA [11] (which can verify LTL) can also be used for time constrained workflow verification.

The *state explosion* problem often limits the applicability of the above tools for real world workflow models. Distributed model checkers exploit the power of distributed computing facilities so that much larger memory is available to accommodate the state space of the system model; parallel processing of the states can, moreover, reduce the verification time [12]. For these reasons, we are particularly interested in the distributed LTL model checker DiVinE [13].

Previously, we manually translated a number of workflow patterns [14] into DVE, the modeling language of DiVinE. These patterns, defined in [15], are well accepted as the basic building blocks for the design and development of workflow models. Building a model, using these patterns, is tedious and error-prone; so this approach is not feasible for large and complex models. The tool *YAWL2DVE* which can automatically convert a YAWL model into DVE was presented in [16] but it was unable to handle time constraints.

Here, we present *YAWL2DVE-t*, which can automatically translate a graphical time constrained YAWL workflow model into DVE, thus reducing the difficulty of representing a time constrained workflow system in the input language of a model checking tool. Use of DiVinE enables us to handle the huge memory requirement for real world complex models. This approach enhances the *"push button technology"* of verification to a further step, allowing the users to model the system in a graphical language, such as YAWL, input a temporal property (with or without time constraints) and immediately do the model checking. Users with little expertise modeling with the model checking language can easily use it.

The remainder of this paper is as follows: Section 2 presents some background topics; Section 3 describes the modeling and verification method of time constrained workflow; Section 4 presentes a case study and Section 5 concludes the paper and offers some directions for future work.

2   Preliminaries

This section provides background information about the tools used in this work. We begin by describing workflows and the workflow management system YAWL. Then we describe the DiVinE model checking tool and its modeling language.

2.1   Workflow and YAWL

For control purposes, workflow may be viewed as an abstraction of the real work under a chosen aspect that serves as virtual representation of the actual work. Therefore, a workflow is a collection of activities and the dependencies among those activities. The activities correspond to individual tasks in a business process. Dependencies determine the execution sequence of the activities and the data flow among these activities.

YAWL is a workflow management system, based on a concise and powerful modeling language. YAWL handles complex data, transformations, integration with organizational resources, and Web Service integration. YAWL uses a Petri net-based formalism extended with additional features to facilitate the modeling of complex workflows. A *workflow specification* in YAWL is a set of extended workflow nets (EWF-nets) which are made up of tasks, conditions and flow relations between them. A task (activity) is a description of a unit of work that may need to be performed as part of a workflow. The transfer of work between two tasks is done through a flow relation, which is depicted as unidirectional arrows in a YAWL model. In a YAWL model, every task must lie on a path from the start condition to the end condition. By default, a YAWL task can only have one outgoing flow and one incoming flow. When we need more outgoing flows from a task or incoming flows to a task, we have to use one of three kinds of split (for outgoing flows) and three corresponding kinds of join (for incoming flows); OR, XOR, and AND. The OR-Split is used to trigger some, but not necessarily all outgoing flows to other tasks. The XOR-Split is used to trigger only one outgoing flow. The AND-Split is used to start a number of task instances simultaneously. Corresponding XOR-Joins, OR-Joins, and AND-Joins are used to combine the incoming flows of a task. Tasks are either atomic or composite. Graphically in YAWL, an atomic task is represented by a rectangular box and a composite task is represented by a double rectangular box. Each task (either composite or atomic) can have multiple instances. Each atomic task can be assigned a timer called *Task Timeout*. It is also possible to set an activation type and an expiry value (Time units are Second, Minute, and Hour) for the timer. The timer can be activated either when a task is enabled or when it starts. A more detailed description of YAWL can be found in [17].

2.2   The DiVinE Model Checker and Its Modeling Language

DiVinE [18] is a distributed-memory explicit-state model checker, which employs the aggregate power of network-interconnected clusters to verify systems using distributed algorithms. DVE, the modeling language of DiVinE, is rich enough to describe systems made of synchronous and asynchronous processes communicating via shared memory and buffered or unbuffered channels. Like in Promela (the modeling language of SPIN), a model described in DVE consists of processes, message channels and variables. Each process, identified by a unique name, consists of a list of local variable declarations, process state declarations, initial state declaration and a list of transitions which start using the keyword *trans*. Variables can be global (declared at the beginning of DVE source code) or local (declared at the beginning of a process), they can be of `byte` or `int` type. A transition transfers a process from $stateid_1$ to $stateid_2$, the transition may contain a guard (which decides whether the transition can be executed), a synchronization (for communications between processes) and effects (which assign new values to local or global variables). Therefore, we have:

Transition ::= *stateid*₁ -> *stateid*₂ {Guard Sync Effect};

The Guard contains the keyword *guard* followed by a Boolean expression and the Effect contains the keyword *effect* followed by a list of assignments. The Sync follows the denotation for communication in the Communicating Sequential Processes (CSP) language, '!' for sending and '?' for receiving. The synchronization can be either asynchronous or rendezvous. Value(s) can be transferred in a channel identified by *chanid*. Declarations of channels follow declarations of global variables. Therefore, we have:

Sync ::= sync *chanid* ! SyncValue | *chanid* ? SyncVariable ;

Linear Temporal Logic (LTL) is a temporal logic which allows the specification of qualitative relationships between events. LTL has the following syntax given in Backus Naur form:

$$\phi ::= p|(\neg\phi)|(\phi \wedge \phi)|(\phi \vee \phi)|(X\ \phi)|(F\ \phi)|(G\ \phi)|(\psi\ U\ \phi)$$

where ϕ, ψ are formulas, and p is an atomic formula; $X\ \phi$ says that ϕ holds next time, $F\ \phi$ says that ϕ holds eventually, $G\ \phi$ says that ϕ holds globally, and $\psi\ U\ \phi$ says that ψ holds until ϕ holds.

In DiVinE, both the system model and the LTL formula are represented by automata. Then the model checking problem is reduced to detecting in the combined automaton graph whether or not there is an accepting cycle. If there is an accepting cycle, a counter example is produced. The model specification in DVE code is stored in a *.dve* file and the LTL properties are written in an *.ltl* file. DiVinE automatically generates a corresponding *property process* from the LTL formula, combines that process with the DVE code of the model, and produces a *.mdve* file. DiVinE uses identifiers to designate atomic formulas. For the simple clinical workflow in Fig. 1, let us assume we want to verify "In all cases a patient is released within 10 hours". Recalling that LTL formulas are built from propositional formulas using X, F, G, and U, we write, G (start_reception − > F (finish_patientRelease ∧ timeRequiredToReleasePatient)). We define *timeRequired-ToReleasePatient* as *timeDifference* <= *10*, where 10 means ten hours, *timeDifference* is a variable in the DVE code which stores the time difference between the start time of *Reception* and the finish time of *Patient Release*. In section 3.3, we show how to store the start time and the finish time of a task.

3   Modeling and Verification of Time Constrained Workflow

In our approach, first a workflow is modeled with YAWL, and then the model is translated into the DVE model specification by *YAWL2DVE-t*. Combining an LTL property with the DVE model specification, the DiVinE model checker determines whether the LTL property holds or not. If the property does not hold, DiVinE gives a counter example.

3.1   Timing Constraints and Their Representation in YAWL

When we talk about activities (or tasks) and the dependencies among them, time plays an important role. Several explicit time constraints have been identified for time management of an activity [19]. *Duration* is the time span required to finish a task. *Forced start time* prohibits executing some tasks before that certain time. *Deadline* is a time based scheduling constraint which requires that a certain activity be completed by a certain time [20]. A constraint, which forces an activity to be executed only on a certain fixed date, is referred to as a *fixed date constraint*. *Delay* is the time duration between two subsequent activities. Besides these explicit time constraints, some time constraints follow implicitly from the control dependencies and activity durations of a workflow model. They arise from the fact that an activity can start only when its predecessor activities have finished. Such constraints are called the *structural time constraints* since they abide by the control structure of the workflow [19]. The concept of *relative constraint* which limits the time distance (duration) between the starting/ending instants of two non-consecutive workflow activities can also be found in [21]. Yet another kind of constraint is a *periodic constraint*, which represents a periodic time interval, during which an activity can be started, for example, a task can be executed between Monday and Saturday of every week [22].

The YAWL execution engine supports only the *duration* and *deadline* constraints. However, we are using YAWL's graphical tool to model workflow for verifying properties. In modeling, we can assign a *delay* constraint in the control flow arc label between two consecutive tasks. Consequently we can model both *duration* and *delay* constraints which together are capable of modeling the timing aspects of almost any workflow [23]. *Duration* and *delay* are expressed in some basic time units and by integer value following the Gregorian calendar i.e., year, month, week, day, hour, and minute.

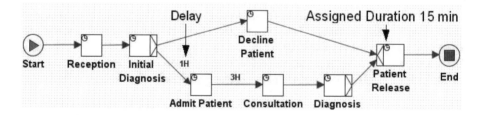

Fig. 1. Simple Clinical Workflow

In Fig. 1, *durations* and *delays* are shown in a simple clinical model designed by YAWL. Each task has a *duration* assigned to it. For example, *Patient Release* should be completed within fifteen minutes. Note that the *duration* assigned to each task is an integer value, thus constant. In real world, identifying a fixed *duration* for a particular task is unfeasible. Though we are assigning a constant value as *duration* of a task, the task can finish non-deterministically between any time from zero to *duration*. So it suffices to identify the maximum possible *duration* for any task.

Delay time in the labels of the connector of two tasks means that the later task should wait until the *delay* time is elapsed after completing the earlier task. For example, after admission, patients have to wait three hours to get a *Consultation*. No *delay* time in the label indicates that a task initiates immediately after completing its preceding task(s). *Initial Diagnosis* should be performed without any delay after *Reception*. Neither *duration* nor *delay* is a mandatory attribute of a task.

3.2   Modeling Time in DVE

DiVinE is an un-timed model checker which generally can not verify timed systems. Lamport [24] advocated *explicit-time description methods* using a general model construct, e.g., global integer variables or synchronization between processes commonly found in standard un-timed model checkers, to realize timed model checking. He presented an explicit-time description method, which we refer to as LEDM, using a clock-ticking process (*Tick*) to simulate the passage of time, and a pair of global variables to store the lower and upper bounds of the time for each modeled system process. The method has been implemented with popular model checkers SPIN and SMV. Explicit-time description methods have three advantages: (1) they do *not* need specialized languages or tools for time description. Therefore, they can be applied in standard un-timed model checkers; (2) they enable the accessing and storing of the current time [25], a useful feature for the preemptive scheduling problems; and (3) they enable the use of large-scale distributed model checkers (e.g., DiVinE) for the timed model checking. Recently, Van den Berg et al. [26] successfully applied LEDM to verify the safety of the railway inter-locking for one of Australia's largest railway companies.

```
process Tick {
   state tick;
   init tick;
   trans
        tick -> tick { guard (all durationᵢ && all delayᵢ) > 0 &&
               (atleast one durationᵢ || atleast one delayᵢ) != INFINITY;
               effect now = now + 1,
                      decrements all active durationᵢ,
                      decrements all active delayᵢ; } ;
}
```

Fig. 2. *Tick* process in DVE

In LEDM [24], the current time is represented by a global variable *now* that is incremented by an added *Tick* process (See Fig. 2). As mentioned earlier, standard model checkers can deal with only integer variables, and a real-time system can be modeled in discrete-time using an explicit-time description. So the *Tick* process increments *now* by 1. Note that in explicit-time description methods for standard model checkers, the real-valued time variables must be replaced by integer-valued ones. Therefore, these methods in general do not preserve continuous-time semantics; otherwise, an inherently infinite-state specification is produced and the verification is undecidable. However, these methods are sound for a commonly used class of real-time systems and their properties [27]. We believe workflow systems are ideally suited to this kind of analysis.

By assigning duration to a task and delay between two consecutive tasks as timing constraints, we can model time in a workflow system. A duration timing constraint forces the process, once initiated, to be finished within that time span. A delay constraint prohibits a task from being started, until the delay time has elapsed, counting the time from which the previous task has finished. Each system process P_i has two count-down timers, denoted as the global variable $duration_i$ and $delay_i$. A large enough integer constant, denoted as INFINITY, is initially assigned to the all $duration_i$ and $delay_i$ variables. Duration and delay timers with the value of INFINITY are not active and the *Tick* process will not decrement them. As *now* is incremented by 1, each non-INFINITY $duration_i$ and $delay_i$ is decremented by 1. Every model specification has a *Tick* process to simulates the time.

We observe that the value of *now* is limited by the size of type integer and careless incrementation can cause overflow error. This can be avoided by incrementing *now* using modular arithmetic, i.e., setting $now = (now + 1)$ mod MAXIMAL (MAXIMAL is the maximal integer value supported by the model checker). The limit of the maximum can be increased by linking several integers, i.e., when (int_1+1) mod MAXIMAL becomes zero, int_2 increments by 1, and so on.

3.3   Workflow Tasks in DVE

In this paper, we map a task (either composite or atomic) in YAWL to a DVE process; multiple instances of a task are mapped to multiple instances of the same process. Control flow paths are mapped to DVE channels and messages between processes are represented, without loss of granularity, by integers, in DVE. A task is enabled after the completion of its preceding task(s). The split and join structures of YAWL, introduced in section 2.1, are identified in the translation process and handled using different algorithms. Details of these algorithms can be found in our previous work [16]. In Fig. 3, we present a DVE process for a YAWL task.

Initially, all processes are in the *idle* state which indicates that tasks are not ready to start (In Fig. 3 process P_i is in *idle* state). An incoming message, through channel *ChanPrevProcess*, from a previous task activates the process P_i. A transition from the *idle* state to the *waiting* state represents that the task is initialized and a *delay* is assigned for the task as an effect. If the *delay* time for the task is zero then it can commit another transition where the *duration* of a task is assigned as effect. If the *delay* time for the task is not zero then the task has to wait until the *delay* time becomes zero. The passing of time is simulated

```
process Pi {
   state ..., idle,waiting, working;
   init idle;
   trans
      idle -> waiting { sync ChanPrevProcess?;
                           effect set delayi, set start_Pi to now;},
      waiting -> working { guard delayi==0; effect set durationi;},
         ... -> ... ,
      working -> idle { sync ChanNextProcess! ;
                           effect set durationi to INFINITY,
                               set delayi to INFINITY ,
                               set finish_Pi to now; };
}
```

Fig. 3. System process P_i in DVE

by the *tick* process (See Fig. 2). The task can be finished anytime within the *duration*. The transition from the *working* state to the *idle* state indicates that the task is finished. A message is sent through channel *ChanNextProcess* to activate the next process. As an *effect* of the transition the *duration* and *delay* time is set to INFINITY for that process. If any of the *duration* and *delay* timers is equal to zero, the transition in the *Tick* process is disabled. This forces the transition from the *working* state to the *idle* state for that process, if it is the only transition possible at this time. In this way, the *duration* and *delay* constraints are realized. To verify timed properties, we have to store the start time and finish time of all the processes. In this regard, for each process there are two global variables that store the start and end time. In Fig. 3, $start\_P_i$ stores the start time and $finish\_P_i$ stores the end time of process P_i.

3.4 YAWL2DVE-t: An Automated Translator

YAWL2DVE-t is an automated translator developed using Java, which can translate any workflow modeled using YAWL. It takes a YAWL (in XML) file as input and generates a *mdve* file as output; the mdve file can be combined with an *ltl* property file (may contain more than one property) and produce *dve* output file(s) (one for each property) which can be used for verification. The following steps are used in the translation by *YAWL2DVE-t*:

1. Parse XML and construct workflow components with timing information
2. Create links and channel numbers
3. Process multiple tasks
4. Generate DVE code from root net decomposition

For each task in the workflow model, *YAWL2DVE-t* will produce DVE code as described in section 3.3 . A part of the XML file for the simple clinical workflow in Fig. 1 is given in Fig. 4. The task ID's in the XML file are unique. An index and these ID's are used to generate unique channels for communication. In the

```
....
<task id="Consultation_7">
 <name>Consultation</name>
   <flowsInto>
      <nextElementRef id="Diagnosis_242" />
   </flowsInto>
   <join code="xor" />
   <split code="and" />
   <timer>
     <trigger>OnEnabled</trigger>
     <duration>PT5H</duration>
   </timer>
....
```

Fig. 4. Segment of XML File for Simple Clinical Workflow

DVE translation of the simple clinical workflow of Fig. 1, *YAWL2DVE-t* will create nine processes, one each for the *start* and *end* conditions, and seven for the tasks in between. The processes for the *start* and *end* conditions do not have any *delay* and *duration*, thus those processes are instantaneous. The *InputCondition_1* process (for *start* condition) will send a synchronization signal through the channel *'chan_InputCondition_1_0'*. The *Reception* process will be activated after receiving that signal and after completing its work (after the assigned *duration*) it will send a synchronization signal to the *Initial_Diagnosis* process through the channel *'chan_Reception_1'*. The *Initial_Diagnosis* process has an XOR-Split structure and can choose any of the channels non-deterministically to send a synchronization signal to the *Admit Patient* process or the *Decline Patient* process and the flow continues. The duration is stored in a *duration* tag in the XML file (*Consultation* task is assigned 5 hours as duration, see Fig. 4). The processes will be executed according to the workflow order, the next task reference is stored in a *nextElementRef* tag in the XML file. For each Net Decomposition (Composite task) of the workflow, a *NetDecomposition* instance will be created which contains one *InputCondition*, one *EndCondition*, and one or more task and condition instances.

A more detailed description (with algorithms) of step 1-4 can be found in our previous work [16].

4   Case Study and Property Verification

In this section we will examine how the above method can be useful for the verification of a workflow model with timing information. We study a Hospice Palliative Care workflow, which we are developing for the local health authority, the Guysborough Antigonish Strait Health Authority (GASHA), following the national Hospice Palliative Care model [28]. A number of sample specification properties are verified on the workflow model and a top level graphical view of the model, built with the YAWL modeling tool, is given in Fig. 5. Tabs across the top refer to composite tasks each of which give rise to a subnet. Subnets may also contains composite tasks. See the appendix for a more detailed view of the model.

4.1 A Hospice Palliative Care Workflow

Palliative Care refers to the medical or comfort care that reduces the severity of a disease or slows its progress rather than providing a cure. For incurable diseases, in cases where the cure is not recommended due to other health concerns, and when the patient does not wish to pursue a cure, palliative care becomes the focus of treatment. For example, if surgery cannot be performed to remove a tumor, radiation treatment might be tried to reduce its rate of growth, and pain management could help the patient manage physical symptoms. The term "Hospice Palliative Care" was coined to recognize the convergence of hospice and palliative care into one movement that has the same principles and norms of practice [28].

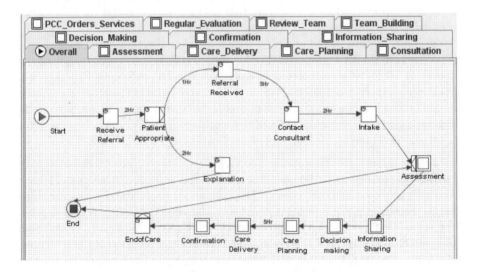

Fig. 5. Hospice Palliative Care Workflow Model for GASHA

The national model was developed to guide both the process of providing care to the patients and their families, and the development and function of hospice palliative care organizations. The model provides guidelines which they refer to as "norms of care" for quality of service, such as, "Requests for initial evaluation and ongoing follow-up are responded to within acceptable time frames". Based on this norm, an organization will develop a more specific standard of practice that will establish the minimum requirements to be met at all times [28], such as:

- "Requests for initial evaluation are responded to within 48 hours."
- "Requests for ongoing follow-up are responded to within 12 hours."

The timing information in this model is for illustration purpose, so it does not reflect the actual time in the real world. We are working with GASHA to greatly refine the details of the process of care and include information on time, access control and other process specific information. A pilot study is underway to transform the documentation from a paper based format to an electronic version; details gleaned from this pilot will substantially enhance the model.

The Hospice Palliative Care process involves six essential and several basic steps that guide the interaction between care givers, and the patient and family. After the patient referral is received, it is determined whether the patient is eligible for Hospice Palliative Care. If the patient is not eligible, the workflow will end with proper explanation. Otherwise the patient is sent for the next set of care tasks. A consultant will collect the medical information from the patient, identify his priorities, and determine whether the patient requires a consultation with physician(s). This completes the registration process and a profile is created and the patient enters into a iterative process called a therapeutic encounter. The next six tasks are essential and must be completed during each encounter. Each of them is represented as a composite task and has tasks (atomic or composite) in its 'Net-Decomposition'.

This model produces 144 processes with more than two thousands lines of code in DVE. Once the LTL properties are identified, they can be verified against the model (in DVE). If a property does not hold, the DiVinE model checker will produce a counter example. This approach greatly reduces the effort for modeling and rapid refactoring of a system model for verification. All we have to do is make a graphical representation of the workflow in YAWL, use the translator to get the DVE model for distributed verification and run DiVinE.

Property verification: Some properties of the Palliative Care model have been checked by the DVE model. The properties are Categorized into three groups: *safety properties, liveness properties,* and *time properties.* A *Safety property* states that the property must be true for all paths, informally, "Some bad thing never happens". A *Liveness property* ensures the progress of the workflow, informally, "Some good thing will eventually happen". *Time properties* refer to the properties that are related to time constraints. In the following, we articulate some norms described in [28] and their corresponding LTL formulas, the first two properties are *safety properties* and *liveness properties* respectively, the last four properties are *time properties*; 3 and 6 involve duration constraints, 4 and 5 involve both delay and duration constraints.

1. Limits of confidentiality are defined by the patient before information is shared.
   G !(confidentiality_not_defined ∧ information_shared)
2. End state is reached in all paths
   G F c_end

3. Any errors in therapy delivery are reported to supervisors immediately. The standard acceptable time allowed for such reports is two hours.
   G (start_error_in_therapy − > F (finish_report_to_supervisor ∧ timeRequiredToFinish2Hours)
4. Requests for initial evaluation are responded to within 48 hours.
   G (start_initial_evaluation_request − > F (finish_initial_evaluation_respond ∧ timeRequiredToFinish48Hours)
5. Care planning should not take more then 1 day in each therapeutic encounter.
   G (start_care_planning − > F (finish_care_planning ∧ timeRequiredToFinish1Day)
6. Interview with the family member should be done within 1 hour.
   G (start_interview − > F (finish_interview ∧ timeRequiredToFinish1Hour)

In the verification process, we are simulating the time by a *Tick* process which increments the *now* variable. Therefore, to identify a relative time distance between two non-consecutive tasks we have to store the start time of the preceding task and the end time of the subsequent task in the DVE model; the method is described in section 3.3.

Some requirements of the Palliative Care model norms cannot be represented due to the limitations of the modeling language and LTL. For example, an LTL property cannot represent that "the information is as accurate as possible". We are studying different methods to extend the language and the specification logic so that we can accurately specify and verify properties corresponding to real world requirements.

In our method, we are simulating time as states. *Delay* and *duration* can be expressed in time units, such as second, minute, hour, etc. While translating the YAWL model to the DVE code, we convert all the time units to the lowest one, which might blow up the state space to the workflow models where the time units of *delay* and *duration* vary substantially. To address this issue, we are incorporating the efficient EDM we proposed in [25], in which the *Tick* process may *leap* multiple time units in a tick.

Table 1. Experimental Results

Property	True/False	OWCTY/MAP	Time (s)	# of States	Memory (MB)
1	True	OWCTY	216.3	166914735	65062.6
2	True	OWCTY	1104.8	223439236	86953.3
3	False	MAP	6.7	957694	16262.5
4	True	OWCTY	303.9	217528767	80829.6
5	False	MAP	12.9	1557694	21246.3
6	True	OWCTY	312.4	218428214	81013.7

Table 1 gives the experimental results which shows that properties 1, 2, 4 and 6 holds in the model and properties 3 and 5 do not hold. The counter example for property 3 enables us to determine that the assigned duration for the task *Report to supervisor* is not at an acceptable level. The counter example for property 5 helps us to find an execution sequence for which the *Care Planning* takes more then 1 day, refactor the model and redo the model checking. All experiments are executed on the Mahone2 cluster of ACEnet [29], the high performance computing consortium for universities in Atlantic Canada. The cluster is a Parallel Sun x4100 AMD Opteron (dualcore) cluster equipped with Myri-10G interconnection. Parallel jobs are assigned using the Open MPI library. We have used 32 CPUs and 5G memory per CPU for all these experiments. In the cluster, there are 139 nodes, each containing 16G of memory. Future models will be larger and will require more resources. Current model utilizes approximately 30% of the resources of the cluster.

Two model checking algorithms in DiVinE 0.8.3 are used, namely, *One Way to Catch Them Young* (OWCTY) and *Maximal Accepting Predecessors* (MAP). If the property of a model is expected to hold and the state space can fit completely into the (distributed) memory, OWCTY is preferable as it is three times faster than MAP to explore the whole state space. On the other hand, MAP can generally find a counterexample (if it exists) much more quickly as it works on-the-fly. For each property, we only show the better result of these two algorithms.

5 Conclusion and Future Work

This research is a part of an ambitious research and development project, Building Decision-support through Dynamic Workflow Systems for Health Care [30] among researchers at StFX in a collaboration with the local health authority GASHA and an industrial partner, Palomino System Innovations INC. In prior work, Miller and MacCaull [31] developed a prototype tableau-based model checker based on timed BDI_{CTL} logic, Hao and MacCaull [25,32] developed several new Explicit-time Description Methods. These efforts facilitate the verification of properties written in an extended specification language involving information such as real time and agents' beliefs, goals and intentions, in large workflow models.

In this paper, we described an automated translator that translates time constrained workflow models into DVE code. Using an automated translator will greatly reduce the cost and time for the verification and will make the verification of real world models possible. We are developing a translator to the input language of SMV and other model checkers for CTL model checking. Other enhancements for model checking, like data aware verification techniques, reduction technique for the state space of the model and verification of compensable transactions for workflow systems are also in progress. Real world workflow processes can be highly dynamic and complex in a health care setting. Verification that the system meets its specifications is essential for such a safety critical process and can save time, money, or even lives.

Acknowledgment. This research is sponsored by Natural Sciences and Engineering Research Council of Canada (NSERC), by an Atlantic Computational

Excellence Network (ACEnet) Post Doctoral Research Fellowship and by the Atlantic Canada Opportunities Agency (ACOA) through the Atlantic Innovation Fund. The computational facilities are provided by ACEnet. We also like to thank Prof. Mary Heather Jewers from StFX School of Nursing, Jay Crawford, Keith Miller, Nazia Leyla, Zahidul Islam, Madonna MacDonald (VP, Community Service at GASHA) and numerous clinicians from GASHA.

References

1. Miller, K., MacCaull, W.: Toward web-based careflow management systems. Journal of Emerging Technologies in Web Intelligence (JETWI) Special Issue: E-health Interoperability 1(2), 137–145 (2009)
2. Wang, F.: Formal verification of timed systems: A survey and perspective. Proceedings of the IEEE 92, 1283–1305 (2004)
3. Marjanovic, O.: Dynamic verification of temporal constraints in production workflows. In: ADC '00: Proceedings of the Australasian Database Conference, Washington, DC, USA, pp. 74–81. IEEE Computer Society, Los Alamitos (2000)
4. Alur, R., Dill, D.L.: A theory of timed automata. Theor. Comput. Sci. 126(2), 183–235 (1994)
5. Merlin, P.M.: A study of the recoverability of computing systems. PhD thesis, Department of Information and Computer Science, University of California, Irvine, CA (1974)
6. Gruhn, V., Laue, R.: Using timed model checking for verifying workflows. In: Cordeiro, J., Filipe, J. (eds.) Computer Supported Activity Coordination, pp. 75–88. INSTICC Press (2005)
7. Abdeddaïm, Y., Maler, O.: Preemptive job-shop scheduling using stopwatch automata. In: Katoen, J. P., Stevens, P. (eds.) TACAS 2002. LNCS, vol. 2280, pp. 113–126. Springer, Heidelberg (2002)
8. Krcál, P., Yi, W.: Decidable and undecidable problems in schedulability analysis using timed automata. In: Jensen, K., Podelski, A. (eds.) TACAS 2004. LNCS, vol. 2988, pp. 236–250. Springer, Heidelberg (2004)
9. Foyo, P.M.G.D., Silva, J.R.: Using time petri nets for modeling and verification of timed constrained workflow systems. In: ABCM Symposium Series in Mechatronics, vol. 3, pp. 471–478 (2008)
10. Gardey, G., Lime, D., Magnin, M., Roux, O.H.: Roméo: A tool for analyzing time petri nets. In: Etessami, K., Rajamani, S.K. (eds.) CAV 2005. LNCS, vol. 3576, pp. 418–423. Springer, Heidelberg (2005)
11. Berthomieu, B., Vernadat, F.: Time petri nets analysis with tina. In: 3rd International Conference on The Quantitative Evaluation of Systems (QEST 2006), pp. 123–124. IEEE Computer Society Press, Los Alamitos (2006)
12. Barnat, J., Brim, L., Ročkai, P.: Scalable multi-core ltl model-checking. In: Bošnacki, D., Edelkamp, S. (eds.) SPIN 2007. LNCS, vol. 4595, pp. 187–203. Springer, Heidelberg (2007)
13. Barnat, J., Brim, L., Ročkai, P.: DiVinE 2.0: High-Performance model checking. In: International Workshop on High Performance Computational Systems Biology (HiBi 09), pp. 31–32. IEEE Computer Society, Los Alamitos (2009)
14. Leyla, N., Mashiyat, A., Wang, H., MacCaull, W.: Workflow verification with divine. In: 8th International Workshop on Parallel and Distributed Methods in verifiCation (PDMC '09) (2009) Work in progress report

15. Russell, N., Hofstede, A.T., Aalst, W.M.P.V.D., Mulyar, N.: Workflow control-flow patterns: A revised view. Technical report, BPMcenter.org (2006)
16. Rabbi, F., Wang, H., MacCaull, W.: YAWL2DVE: An automated translator for workflow verification. In: 4th IEEE International Conference on Secure Software Integration and Reliability Improvement, pp. 53–59. IEEE Computer Society, Los Alamitos (2010)
17. Aalst, W.M.P.V.D., Hofstede, A.T.: Yawl: yet another workflow language. Information Systems 30(4), 245–275 (2005)
18. DiVinE Project, http://divine.fi.muni.cz/ (last accessed June 2010)
19. Li, W., Fan, Y.: A time management method in workflow management system. In: Workshops at the Grid and Pervasive Computing Conference, pp. 3–10. IEEE Computer Society, Los Alamitos (2009)
20. WfMC: Workflow management coalition terminology and glossary. Technical Report (wfmc-tc-1011) v3.0. Technical report, Winchester, UK (1999)
21. Combi, C., Posenato, R.: Controllability in temporal conceptual workflow schemata. In: Dayal, U., Eder, J., Koehler, J., Reijers, H.A. (eds.) BPM 2009. LNCS, vol. 5701, pp. 64–79. Springer, Heidelberg (2009)
22. Combi, C., Gozzi, M., Juárez, J.M., Oliboni, B., Pozzi, G.: Conceptual modeling of temporal clinical workflows. In: TIME, pp. 70–81. IEEE Computer Society, Los Alamitos (2007)
23. Li, H., Yang, Y.: Verification of temporal constraints for concurrent workflows. In: Yu, J.X., Lin, X., Lu, H., Zhang, Y. (eds.) APWeb 2004. LNCS, vol. 3007, pp. 804–813. Springer, Heidelberg (2004)
24. Lamport, L.: Real-time model checking is really simple. In: Borrione, D., Paul, W. (eds.) CHARME 2005. LNCS, vol. 3725, pp. 162–175. Springer, Heidelberg (2005)
25. Wang, H., MacCaull, W.: An efficient explicit-time description method for timed model checking. In: 8th International Workshop on Parallel and Distributed Methods in verifiCation (PDMC 09), Eindhoven, The Netherlands, EPTCS, vol. 14, pp. 77–91 (2009)
26. Berg, L.V.D., Strooper, P.A., Winter, K.: Introducing time in an industrial application of model-checking. In: Leue, S., Merino, P. (eds.) FMICS 2007. LNCS, vol. 4916, pp. 56–67. Springer, Heidelberg (2008)
27. Henzinger, T.A., Manna, Z., Pnueli, A.: What good are digital clocks? In: Kuich, W. (ed.) ICALP 1992. LNCS, vol. 623, pp. 545–558. Springer, Heidelberg (1992)
28. Ferris, F.D., Balfour, H.M., Bowen, K., Farley, J., Hardwick, M., Lamontagne, C., Lundy, M., Syme, A., West, P.: A model to guide hospice palliative care: Based on national principles and norms of practice. Canadian Hospice Palliative Care Association, Ottawa (2002)
29. Atlantic Computational Excellence Network (ACEnet), http://www.ace-net.ca/ (last accessed, June 2010)
30. Centre for Logic and Information. St. Francis Xavier University, http://logic.stfx.ca/ (last accessed, June 2010)
31. Miller, K., MacCaull, W.: Verification of careflow management systems with timed BDI_{CTL} logic. In: 3rd International Workshop on Process-oriented Information Systems in Healthcare (ProHealth'09), in Conjunction with BPM'09. LNBIP, vol. 43, pp. 623–634. Springer, Heidelberg (2010)
32. Wang, H., MacCaull, W.: Verifying real-time systems using explicit-time description methods. In: Workshop on Quantitative Formal Methods: Theory and Applications, Eindhoven, The Netherlands, EPTCS, vol. 13, pp. 67–79 (2009)

Correctness of Sensor Network Applications by Software Bounded Model Checking

Frank Werner and David Faragó

Institute for Theoretical Computer Science
Karlsruhe Institute of Technology (KIT)
`werner@kit.edu, farago@kit.edu`

Abstract. We investigate the application of the software bounded model checking tool CBMC to the domain of wireless sensor networks (WSNs). We automatically generate a software behavior model from a network protocol (ESAWN) implementation in a WSN development and deployment platform (TinyOS), which is used to rigorously verify the protocol. Our work is a proof of concept that automatic verification of programs of practical size ($\approx 21\,000$ LoC) and complexity is possible with CBMC and can be integrated into TinyOS. The developer can automatically check for pointer dereference and array index out of bound errors. She can also check additional, e.g., functional, properties that she provides by `assume`- and `assert`-statements. This experience paper shows that our approach is in general feasible since we managed to verify about half of the properties. We made the verification process scalable in the size of the code by abstraction (eg, from hardware) and by simplification heuristics. The latter also achieved scalability in data type complexity for the properties that were verifiable. The others require technical advancements for complex data types within CBMC's core.

Keywords: Software Bounded Model Checking, CBMC, automatic protocol verification, embedded software, Wireless Sensor Networks, TinyOS, abstraction, simplification heuristics.

1 Introduction

We strongly rely on embedded systems, which are widely used in highly distributed as well as safety-critical systems, such as structural monitoring of bridges [22], intrusion detection [12], and many industrial use cases, e.g., using SureCross from Banner Engineering Corp. [19] or Smart Wireless from Emerson Electric Co [10]. Hence they must become more dependable and secure.

The application of formal methods to embedded systems could be the key to solve this. Although embedded devices carry only some hundred kilobytes of memory, their verification is neither simple nor easily automated (cf. related work below) because they run complex algorithms for the underlying protocols, distributed data management, and wireless communication. In the special domain of wireless sensor networks (WSNs), these techniques are all combined in

S. Kowalewski and M. Roveri (Eds.): FMICS 2010, LNCS 6371, pp. 115–131, 2010.

a single product, making it a challenging candidate for the application of formal methods. In this domain, powerful and extensible development and deployment frameworks are used, e.g., TinyOS [20]. By integrating formal methods seamlessly, i.e., fully automated, into such a framework, their usage by developers is most likely. This implies automatic generation of the model (cf. Section 4.2) for our verification process, which solves further problems:

- The development of manual artifacts is costly since the model is only required for verification.
- Since the verification model and the implementation must stay in conformance, the model must rapidly change, especially during the design phase. Hence additional work is required.
- There is a high danger to abstract from fault-prone details, e.g., due to missing constructs in the modeling language.

In this paper, we investigate a concast protocol [5] implementation called *ESAWN* [2] (*Extended Secure Aggregation for Wireless sensor Networks*). It is from the domain of WSNs and uses the development and deployment platform TinyOS. From this implementation, we automatically generate a software behavior model that fully comprises the protocol behavior of the sensor node. Then the model is used to rigorously verify the protocol using the software bounded model checking tool *CBMC* (*C Bounded Model Checking*) [6]. We used version 2.9, the most recent when we started, and implemented several heuristic simplifications and slicing rules (on a side branch of CBMC's repository) to make verification possible.

Related Work. Most approaches for protocol verification in WSNs use either a heavy abstraction from the actual implementation or only consider parts of the model behavior. The presented work is the first, as far as we know, to use software bounded model checking (SBMC) for verification.

The authors of [3] and [4] considers the application of verification techniques to software written in TinyOS, or more precisely, in the TosThreads C API. Instead on analyzing an integrative model with an operating system part and a protocol implementation, low level services are modeled and statistically verified against safety specifications. The verification tool employed was SATABS, which performs predicate abstraction using SAT and can handle ANSI-C and C++ programs. In this work the overall model size checked is at most 440 LoC. In our approach, we apply our abstraction to a more complex security protocol consisting of 21 000 LoC and obtain a model with about 4 400 LoC, which we subsequently check.

The T-Check tool [14] builds on TOSSIM and provides state space exploration and early detection of software bugs. The authors use a combination of model checking, random walks, and heuristics, to combat the complexity of nondeterministic branching. Also the results show the applicability of the tool and the fact that actual violated properties are found, this random search is not exhaustive and purely depends on the implemented heuristics [13] for finding liveness bugs, and the user's experience.

The Anquiro tool [15] is used for the verification of WSN software written for the Contiki OS using different levels of abstraction, which the user can select from. In comparison, our abstraction only eliminates direct function calls to the hardware and assembler constructs. Thereby, our abstraction is even able to detect erroneous packet fragmentations and reassembling errors. This is closer to the actual implementation - at the cost of complexity. In addition, since we use CBMC and its transformation mechanisms, we are able to directly point to the violating line of code.

The work in [3] considers the application of verification techniques to software written in TinyOS, or more precisely, in the TosThreads C API. Instead of analyzing an integrative model consisting of the operating system part and the protocol implementation, services are modeled and verified individually. The verification tool employed was SATABS, which performs predicate abstraction using SAT and can handle ANSI-C and C++ programs. In this work the overall model size checked is at most 440 LoC. In our approach, we apply our abstraction to a more complex protocol consisting of 21 000 LoC and obtain a model with about 4 400 LoC, which we subsequently check.

Insense [18] is a composition-based modeling language which translated models in a concurrent high-level language to Promela, to enable verification of WSN software by Spin. A complete model of the protocol under investigation has to be created, though, even if an implementation, e.g., in TinyOS, already exists. This is very time intensive and error prone. Though Spin is very well capable of analyzing concurrent and distributed settings, we experienced problems with state space explosion when checking a high-level behavior model in small topologies [21].

Structure of this paper. In Section 2, we introduce SBMC: in general, the SBMC tool CBMC, its capability to use nondeterminism, and the complexity of SBMC. Then we describe the heuristic improvements we contributed to make CBMC cope with our protocol. Section 3 explains the ESAWN protocol. Section 4 introduces the TinyOS platform in general and then the abstract behavior model we generate from its NULL platform. In Section 5, we specify the additional properties that we checked on the ESAWN protocol. The verification results are given in Section 6. Section 7 concludes this paper.

2   Bounded Program Verification

2.1   Software Bounded Model Checking

CBMC [6] is one of the most popular SBMC implementations for C programs. Before CBMC is described in detail, we will first review the technique SBMC. SBMC computes a solution to the following problem: For a program P, a bound k and a property f, does a path p within the bound k exist that violates the property f?

A *program state* can be characterized by the content of the heap, stack, all registers and a program counter. A *path* is a sequence of program states where a transition between states is triggered by the C statement at the program counter.

One interpretation of the *length* of a path in a program is the number of statements in a program. *Properties* declare some error states, or invalid sequences of program states, that shall never occur in any execution, e.g., certain values assigned to a variable.

A SBMC problem has three possible results [7]:

1. The property f holds for all paths.
2. The property f does not hold for at least one path p'.
3. The bound k is too small for at least one path p'.

In the two latter cases, a counter-example path p' is computed – a path having the form of a concrete program execution. For a program that contains a finite set of finite paths, k can always be set large enough such that a sound and complete verification of the property f can be achieved. If the bound is chosen too small, it can iteratively be increased.

Embedded systems (e.g., those following the MISRA C standard [1]) commonly use reactive systems that consist of an infinite outer loop, but within that loop, all possible paths are bounded.

We can usually show ultimate correctness for typical properties even when only considering these inner, finite functions (without the infinite loop around them), such that case 3 from above does not occur. This finitization might require underspecification (see Section 2.3 and 4.2).

2.2   CBMC

CBMC implements SBMC for C programs. Properties have to be specified by `assert(f)` statements. The semantics of such a statement is that whenever a program execution reaches the statement, the condition `f` must evaluate to `true`. CBMC also offers `assume(f)` statements, which we do not need. In CBMC, the positive integer *bound* denotes the maximum number of allowed loop body executions on a path and the maximum recursive depth. The *recursive depth* of a path is the number of stack frames it contains. For a given program, the bound limits the number of statements on any path. In CBMC the bound can be set individually for each loop occurring in the program.

The software behavior is encoded into a satisfiability (SAT) instance that is checked using a SAT solver (Minisat2 [9] in the case of CBMC). If the SAT problem is satisfiable, CBMC generates a concrete counter-example from the satisfying assignment produced by the solver. If the SAT problem is not satisfiable, the property holds for all program executions and the program always terminates.

2.3   Nondeterminism

In CBMC, we can set variables and return values of functions nondeterministically. Thus the model can subsume all possible behaviors of the implementation in a simple way. It usually contains even more behaviors than the implementation, i.e., the model is *over-approximated*, also known as *underspecified*. Then the verification can have false negatives, i.e., false error reports. But a successful verification implies a correct implementation, i.e., we do not have false positives.

2.4   Complexities

Covering all program states within the bound means that many values of the heap, stack, registers and program counter need to be considered (especially when nondeterminism is used). This leads to a combinatorial explosion of exponential size, called the *state space explosion*. The SAT problem encoding the SBMC problem has at least as many variables as the number of bits potentially addressed in the C program. Though the SAT problem is NP-complete, real world instances of SAT problems can be solved surprisingly fast. We found that the generated SAT instances of the investigated protocol posed a problem to Minisat2 simply because of their size. The problems were solved rather efficiently when we used preprocessing before calling Minisat2. For this, we engineered the following heuristic improvements into CBMC.

2.5   Extending CBMC Optimization Heuristics

Even for simple execution scenarios of our large scale program, e.g., one message shall be correctly processed, the size of the propositional formula that CBMC generates surpasses 4 GB. Therefore we extended CBMC with optimization heuristics, which respect non-simple types as arrays, pointers and structures and use slicing rules (enabled by the option -slice) and with simplifications that stem from the domain of compiler optimizations (enabled by the option -use-sd). They strongly reduce the problem size and complexity and are applied after the code is transformed into a more rudimentary, intermediate language (see below), but before it gets encoded into a SAT problem. The simplifications use the following steps, detailed in the following paragraphs:

- Constant propagation for arrays, pointers and structures, which can be computed efficiently in an unwound program.
- Expression simplification that uses the additional information generated by the constant propagation.
- Simplifying guards for statements by early satisfiability detection, using the above expression simplification.

SSA Encodings in CBMC. In order to solve the bounded software model checking problem, CBMC facilitates inlining (resp. unwinding of function calls and loops) up to an upper bound. CBMC also introduces single static assignments (SSA, see for example [17]) in the transformed program: Every assignment is replaced by a *versioned assignment* such that each identifier is assigned at most once. In order to transform a sequence of n assignments to a symbol, n new identifiers are introduced by appending a version number to the original identifier. Read accesses are replaced by read accesses to the currently active version. At program points where two control-flows join, e.g., the end of an IF block, a new

```
int x = 0;                                   x0 = 0;
if (x==0)                                    if (x0==0)
    x = x + 2;           becomes                 x1 = x0 + 2;
assert(x==0);                                // phi:
                                             x2 = (x0==0) ? x1 : x0;
                                             assert(x2==0);
```

Fig. 1. Exemplary SSA translation

phi assignment is introduced that determines which version should be used for the consecutive read accesses (cf. Figure 1).

In SSA form, use-definition chains are easily computed, which will in the following be used for constant propagation. In CBMC, the SSA statements have *guards*, i.e., necessary and sufficient conditions for the statements to be executed.

Field- and Array-Sensitive Constant Propagation. Many implementations (like the ESAWN protocol) rely on heavy use of arrays, pointers and structures. CBMC already contains many optimizations, but does not yet facilitate constant propagation for non-simple data types before the generation of the SAT problem: Hence sequences as a[0] = 0; if (a[0] == 0) are not simplified. In contrast to the built-in approach, we have implemented the propagation on the level of the SSA representation of the program by flattening these complex data types.

Expression Simplifier. Using the additional information generated by the constant propagation, we have added an expression simplifier. Any expression that can be simplified by one of the three following rules is replaced by its simplified expression. It has to be noted that all expressions are side-effect free at this level of encoding:

- Boolean expressions with Boolean operands: If an expression has Boolean type and any Boolean operand must evaluate to a constant true or false, the expression is simplified, e.g., expr && false becomes false and false? expr1:expr2 becomes expr2. Additional cases where more than one operand evaluates to a constant are also simplified.
- Boolean comparisons: Cases where Boolean operands have non-Boolean type operands are also simplified, e.g., c <= c becomes true, with c being a constant or versioned identifier.
- Integer expressions with constant integer or Boolean operands: Arithmetic expressions $+, -, *, /, <<, >>$ where all operands are constants are simplified according to their C semantics.

The last rule can be extended to float and double type variables. As the ESAWN implementation does not use such types, they are not yet implemented. As we will show later, the above rules provide necessary simplifications for the verification of the ESAWN implementation.

Early Satisfiability Detection. The above simplifier can be effectively used to simplify guards for statements. If a guard always evaluates to `false`, a statement can be removed from the encoding as it cannot be executed anyway. If a reachable guard evaluates to `true` and the statement expresses an `assert` statement that evaluates to `false`, the program cannot be verified. The heuristic can often detect the reachability and stops further encoding with an according message. If the `assert` statement is always true it can be removed.

The effectiveness of early satisfiability detection lies in the fact that the unwinding bounds for loops are unknown and can only be determined by many runs of CBMC. For loops that are executed a fixed number of times, i.e., most of the ESAWN loops, the heuristic detects that loop bounds are chosen too small. Hence the overall process of finding the correct loop bounds is greatly improved.

We have 32 loops in total. For one loop, we were able to infer the required unwindings: It belongs to a `memset` function, which has to be iterated very often when duplicating memory locations. Consequently, we set the required unwindings to a sufficiently high and safe value of 20. The unwindings for the other loops were determined iteratively by automatically running the unwinding check provided by CBMC, and incrementing the unwinding setting if the unwinding-assertion failed.

3   The ESAWN Protocol

The protocol under investigation is called ESAWN [2]. It offers means to handle the transportation and aggregation of messages in sensor networks from many senders to one receiver, so called *concasts*. By using an end-to-end authenticity, the transport of sensible data is possible even in the presence of multiple malicious nodes under the control of an adverse acting entity. The protocol runs in two phases: First an initialization is necessary, before the actual probabilistic concast can be performed in the second phase.

We first consider the second phase, in which the actual sensor data is passed around and aggregated all along the way to the sink, the root node. In this phase, packets of type ESAWN are used. Since the packets are relayed down the aggregation tree via intermediate nodes, their entries are encrypted such that only the destination can decode its contents (see Section 5.2).

For the concast with probability, each node checks the authenticity of each received aggregate only with a fixed probability p. Otherwise it just assumes that the aggregate is authentic. Since authentication is costly, this is a trade-off between low energy consumption (low p) and high probability of authenticity (high p).

To be able to check for authenticity, a node sends its information to a fixed number w of additional child nodes, called *witnesses*. The employed concast saves additional energy by buffering packets and sending them all together later on using an aggregation function f_{agg}.

An example setup is given in Figure 2 where 5 nodes are used. The leaf node n_0 triggers the probabilistic concast by sending a packet (with its data value D_0)

to its successor on the aggregation path n_1. Since this node could be cheating, additional packets are sent to node n_2 and n_3, which act as witnesses to assure the proper behavior of node n_1. The nodes n_i ($i \in \{1,..3\}$) are collecting all incoming packets, then check authenticity with probability p and finally, if all incoming packets were authentic, send out packet $agg_i = f_{agg}(agg_{i-1}, D_i)$ (with D_i being the new data value from n_i and $agg_0 := D_0$). The root node n_4 finally collects all data. It is located at the base station and accessible by the user.

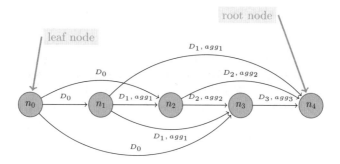

Fig. 2. ESAWN scenario of an aggregation tree with $w = 2$ witnesses

In the initialization phase, the parameter settings and the aggregation tree are made known to all nodes in the network. For this task, the ESAWN protocol uses $STATUS$ packets, which are also encrypted (see Section 5.1). So the number of nodes (num_nodes), probability p and the number of witnesses w are sent around in the network using SET packets. In addition, the aggregation tree is spread using packets of type $SETAGG$ which contain the $parent\_ids$ for each node. Finally, a packet of type GO triggers the second phase of the protocol. The GO packet contains a value specifying the frequency at which nodes send their data (0 means only one concast). Further packet types exist, which we do not consider since they play only a minor role for the verification of relevant global properties.

4   TinyOS Platform and Model Abstraction

4.1   The TinyOS Platform

TinyOS is an open source operating software for embedded devices and widely used for programming embedded devices. Its component based architecture and event driven execution model make it very suitable for resource constrained hardware systems with respect to memory, computation power and energy shortness.

TinyOS is an operating system and a software development platform that offers means to deploy the implementation on various hardware platforms through a modular design. So once a protocol, e.g., ESAWN, is implemented, it can be deployed automatically to the desired sensor type. With many possible combinations of interacting components, automatic verification within TinyOS is the solution for checking that the resulting composition behaves as expected.

In more detail, software in TinyOS is initially written in nesC, a C dialect having special constructs for embedded devices. Before the software can be deployed on sensor nodes, it is firstly translated from the modular description in nesC into an intermediate ANSI C representation, which includes specific constructs for interaction with the hardware. The C code could theoretically be used as model for the verification process already. But an abstraction is required when considering the size and complexity of the C code: Essentially, the hardware part, which includes register assignments and interrupt handling, would inhibit a successful verification process because of state space explosion. Due to this reasons another approach – described in the following section – is required. It abstracts appropriately from the hardware part by generating an *abstract behavior model*.

4.2   A Behavior Model Abstraction

The NULL Platform. The *NULL* platform is a hardware model included in the TinyOS environment. It can be used to generate a hardware independent software behavior model. In particular the platform can be understood as a skeletal structure containing only the functionality of the protocol plus some overhead in form of the *scheduling* functions for jobs and the *job queue*. But all hardware specific functions (e.g., for the UART and LEDs) are removed, i.e., empty function bodies are generated. Since this abstraction exactly comprises the pure protocol behavior under investigation, it is safe. Besides strongly reducing complexity, this abstraction has the major advantage that we do not have to take hardware platforms into account when specifying properties.

Abstract behavior model. We made four modifications to the NULL platform for our verification: instrumentation with `assert()` statements, a so-called autostart function, rudimentary packet transportation functionality and a task loop finitization:

The *autostart* function imitates some of the omitted hardware functionality, most of all the input from the environment. The function makes parameters known to a node by inserting them in its receive queue. Tasks can be enqueued to the *task queue* to let the node perform certain actions like sleep, start the processing of packets, etc. Essentially the autostart function brings us in the favorable position to bring the nodes in any state.

Since the NULL platform is hardware independent, also functionality that transports packets to the transceiver chip is lost. Since all protocols for WSNs depend excessively on packet sending and receiving, our generation rudimentarily inserts this into the function bodies of the sending and receiving functions that are empty in the NULL platform.

Task loop finitization changes the scheduler which periodically executes the task loop: The protocol usually does not terminate because of its controller-like nature: As long as the sensor nodes are active, new packets are generated and processed. The original task loop is hence infinite. By limiting the execution number of the task loop, a bounded model is obtained that is well suited for verification since its complexity is limited. In consequence, the model will run either until all tasks from the task queue are processed or an upper bound is reached, which we compute with injected code and check via assertions. If finished, it simply stops the node. In the course of this finitization, we are also able to further reduce the scheduler's complexity by replacing the complex functions for initializing the scheduler queue and the assignment of the empty task element by the necessary core functionality in the autostart function. With the help of nondeterminism for our correctness proofs, it is sufficient to show that individual packets are transported and processed in accordance with the protocol. Hence regarding the finite task loop is sufficient. Having only finitely many terminating paths, CBMC's verification is sound and complete. An overview of the generated model is depicted in Figure 3.

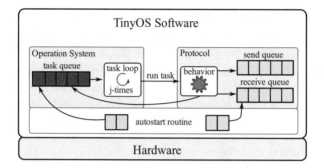

Fig. 3. Abstraction from TinyOS

Sensors are also not present in the NULL platform. But the implementation of the ESAWN protocol was using the node's IDs as sensor data to be transmitted, anyways, for clarity reasons. Since the IDs are unique, this approach also reduces the verification complexity.

We modified the NULL platform with manual intervention, but the modifications for the task loop finitization and packet transportation can be automated straightforwardly, e.g., by introducing a verification platform into TinyOS. The autostart function cannot be completely automated, since the initialization depends on the protocol and contains the configuration we want to consider.

With these modifications to the NULL platform, we get our *abstract behavior model*. From originally 21 000 lines of C code, as in the example of a real hardware platform (MicaZ nodes), the abstract behavior model only contains 4 400 lines of C code and CBMC statements.

Simulation. Besides verification, the abstract behavior model can also be used for simulation: We enriched the abstract behavior model with debugging statements and executed it. A few internal variables of TinyOS that were set nondeterministically in the model were now set to various specific values. This simulation can be strengthened by setting these variables automatically (e.g., randomly) until a desired coverage is reached, to even better complement the verification process.

5   Specification

After acquiring the abstraction in Section 4.2, we start specifying properties. These properties need to be local, since we only have a limited scope of a single node since the original code is intended for deployment. This means we cannot specify properties that include two or more nodes, only the behavior of one node at a time can be verified. Correctness is shown with local properties by non-deterministically setting the network into all relevant states using our powerful autostart function and then checking the according desired behavior at a single node (cf. the exemplary REQ4 below). This is achieved using `assert()` statements incorporated into the sources, to be able to check additional properties, i.e., monitor the behavior and stop the execution in case of an error. In Section 5.3 we will show a solution for global properties. We formulate the desired functional behavior as requirements (REQ), which are all translated into properties that are verifiable by CBMC using CBMC's `assert` functions. These assertions check whether the corresponding variables (e.g., a node's locally stored parameter w or outgoing packet queue) are set correctly. The assertions are either located after a node's computation or within the alarm function that is built into the protocol. This instrumented function is then able to indicate wrong behavior of the protocol, potential attacks and also erroneous packets.

5.1   STATUS Packets

The entries of the $STATUS$ packets are encrypted with an RC5 cipher. To avoid state space explosion, the encryption procedure was automatically removed for the abstract behavior model without changing the underlying protocol, i.e., nodes send their data as plain text.

For the autostart function, we chose an initialization of the network as described in Section 3 (cf. Figure 2), so $w = 2$ and $num\_nodes = 5$. p was set to 1, so we check with the strictest possible authentication and can fully avoid the complexity caused by probability, i.e., the random variables and the function computing the seed. Whether the values are set correctly by the autostart function is checked via the assertions for the following three requirements, which are categorized by packet type.

The first requirement covers packets of type SET, which are sent initially by the base station to make protocol parameters known to the network. The following property states that a node processes this type of packet correctly:

$$SET(num\_nodes, w, p) \text{ sets variables correctly} \qquad (REQ1)$$

The second requirement considers packets that make the aggregation tree public using $SET\,AGG$ packets. For this reason each node is informed about its successor nodes that it will send packets to. The $SET\,AGG$ packets contain the fields $node\_id$ and $parent\_id$ and must be sent to every node in the network.

$$SET\,AGG(node\_id, parent\_id) \text{ sets variables correctly} \qquad (REQ2)$$

The following requirement is about protocol conform behavior after receiving a *GO* packet: Only leaf nodes initiate concasts and the frequency value f in the *GO* packet (cf. page 122) must be respected.

$$\text{correct action upon reception of } GO(f) \qquad \text{(REQ3)}$$

We omit the trivial requirements for the packet type *RESET*, which causes a hard reset of the node, and *ALARM*, which is simply forwarded.

5.2   ESAWN Packets

Entries of ESAWN packets are encrypted using symmetric keys (cf. SKEY [23]). Again, we consider unencrypted packets instead. Similarly to *STATUS* packets, we also split the correct handling of ESAWN packets into several requirements.

Firstly, we require that ESAWN packets are correctly transported. This also implies that packets have been correctly aggregated and are correctly forwarded (e.g., correct computation of the relay count). As aggregation function f_{agg} the sum is used ($f_{agg}(a, b) = a +_{int} b$). We check this requirement exemplary for the packet P that contains D_1, agg_1 sent to n_2:

$$\text{correct reception of packet } P \qquad \text{(REQ4)}$$

Secondly, we require that ESAWN packets are correctly authenticated (which also implies correct aggregation). For this, a node n_i has to alarm if any of the last w aggregates is incorrect (n_0 to n_w can only check fewer aggregates):

$$(\exists j \in \{1, .., w\} : agg_{i-j} - D_{i-j} \neq agg_{i-j-1}) \iff alarm_i \qquad \text{(REQ5)}$$

Finally, we must also check that this $alarm_i$, a certain alarm function built into n_i, behaves correctly, i.e., issues an *ALARM* packet to be sent. We do this by checking whether *ALARM* packets are put in the outgoing packet queue out_{n_i} of n_i:

$$alarm_i \implies ALARM \text{ packets in } out_{n_i} \qquad \text{(REQ6)}$$

5.3   Global Properties

Global properties can achieve stronger and more comfortable formulations, for instance: if some node alarms, then eventually the sink will receive an ALARM packet. Since we are verifying the derived code that can be deployed on a sensor node, the verification process cannot handle multiple nodes so far, i.e., it does not consider distributed settings where messages are interchanged. To imitate this, we implemented simple multitasking between nodes: When the current node sends out a packet, a switch between nodes takes place. For this, we modified TinyOS' send routine: The local variables of the current node are saved and the local variables of the destination node are loaded. The packet being sent is enqueued into the receive queue. With this, a distributed network behavior can be imitated to some degree, with packets being sent to their destination without delay.

The trade-off of using global properties is an increased complexity. Therefore, we successfully verified only very simple ones and will use more powerful global properties only in future work after local properties no longer cause problems (cf. next section).

6   Verification Results

For the verifications, we used CBMC version 2.9 with our additional heuristics (cf. Section 2.5), some bug fixes related to complex data types and compiled for 64bit processors because some verifications required a lot of memory (see below).

Table 1. Verification results for *STATUS* packets for a valid loop unwinding of 4

SET packets			SETAGG packets			GO packets		
check	passes	|claims|	check	passes	|claims|	check	passes #	|claims|
REQ1	yes	6	REQ2	no	4	REQ3	yes	4
unwinding	yes	37	unwinding	yes	37	unwinding	yes	37
bounds	yes	60	bounds	yes	60	bounds	yes	59
pointer	no	181	pointer	no	177	pointer	no	175

As described in the previous section, the generated code is manually instrumented with the assertions that specify REQ1 to REQ6. All other assertions are inserted automatically by CBMC. The first verification step is finding the required number of loop unwindings using the according assertions to be sure the verification of the other properties is complete.

Table 1 displays the performed verifications for the *STATUS* messages, their results and number of required claims, which are CBMC's internal assertions. For the verification, we fixed node n_2, which exhibits all the behavior relevant to our verification. An unwinding depth of 4 is sufficient. The properties for code safety detect array index out of bounds and bad pointer dereferences. All checks had to be performed for each REQ since the autostart function was adjusted to each REQ. The pointer checks failed for every packet type. Debugging the source code of CBMC showed that this is not a failure of the protocol, but CBMC does not find correct symbols during its pointer-analysis.

For REQ1 and REQ3, all other checks are successful. The assertions for REQ2 are violated: The cause seems to be that CBMC is unable to handle arrays of structures, which are heavily used for the queues. This is one example where CBMC does not scale related to data type complexity.

Besides verifying these properties, we raised our confidence in the correctness of ESAWN by successful simulation (cf. 4.2) and fault injections in the code and in the assertions, all of which CBMC found.

Unfortunately, we were not able to verify REQ4 to REQ6 because the unwinding checks were problematic: At first we had difficulties setting the loop unwindings just as high as necessary, which is crucial. For instance, when we set the unwindings to 11 for all loops, CBMC requires 30GB of RAM (and over 3 hours) to detect that not enough unwindings were made. For 12 unwindings, CBMC gives segmentation faults because 32GB are exceeded. We solved the difficulty of finding the smallest possible unwinding value for each loop by searching automatically. But as the search is very time consuming, it is important to start with sensible values. When we used `--unwind 6 --unwindset 1:20`, i.e., unwindings 20 for the first loop (`memset`, which needs to be able to copy values sufficiently often) and unwindings 6 for all others, verification came much further with much less memory: With 2.5GB, CBMC reached the stage `passing to decision procedure`. Unfortunately, CBMC then halts with the error message `unexpected array expression: typecast`. Because CBMC aborted with a typecast exception, we tested whether the unwindings might be sufficient by injecting a fault into one of our assertions for REQ4 to REQ6. But these verifications also caused typecast exceptions. This shows again that CBMC does not scale with data type complexity.

CBMC offers two possibilities when enough unwindings cannot be reached efficiently: Firstly, paths with more unwindings can simply be ignored. But this leads to a bad testing coverage: In our case, a lot of packets in the queue need to be processed for initialization. Thus the processing of the ESAWN packets – and therefore their bugs – would not be reached. Secondly, we could have used nondeterminism at points where the maximum unwindings are reached, and possibly over-approximate (cf. Section 2.3). In our case, we would need to generate packets nondeterministically. Because of CBMCs difficulties with complex data types, it cannot create them nondeterministically. Hence the only solution would be the cumbersome manual implementation of nondeterministically generating a protocol-conform sequence of packets whenever maximum unwindings are reached. But that would counteract our intent of a fully automatic verification process. We also tried the current CBMC version 3.6. Since it does not include our heuristics (cf. Section 2.5), we encountered segmentation faults, e.g., when passing the problem to propositional reduction, already with 4 unwindings. We alternatively tried VCC [8], a SBMC tool similar to CBMC and currently developed at Microsoft Research. We experienced similar problems as in the first steps with CBMC: Pointer constructs present in the generated model could not be handled correctly and resulted in a syntax error while parsing. This shows that handling complex data types in SBMC tools is currently problematic, but a necessary improvement for verifying realistically complex programs.

7   Conclusion

7.1   Summary

We have described a proof of concept for an automatic verification process for realistically large and complex sensor network applications that can be integrated into the software design process. To be able to handle such large scale programs, the process must be automatic and requires the abstractions and heuristics we provided. It generates an abstract behavior model that is then verified by CBMC. We were able to prove correctness for the *SET* and *GO* packets, but not for the *SET AGG* and ESAWN packets, due to technical difficulties in CBMC, e.g., unsupported arrays of structures, pointer bugs and typecast exceptions. It shows that, in our case, CBMC does not scale well with the complexity of data types. Since we learned from our case study that this is very important for the successful verification of programs of practical size, CBMC (and VCC) can improve by not only supporting flat C data types, such as a single struct or array, but also their closure, i.e., nested types. A different solution is using a simpler intermediate language, e.g., LLVM (see Section 7.2).

Many of the technical difficulties in CBMC were caused by large function parameters ($\approx$ 500 byte) in the source code of ESAWN. In some cases, this can be considered a design flaw in ESAWN since frequent, unnecessary copying (because of C's call-by-value evaluation) is inefficient. We have informed the developer of ESAWN about this.

Our heuristics (cf. Section 2.5) improved the scalability in data type complexity, and even more the scalability in the size of the code: Without them, state space explosion prevents verification of even the simplest instances for the ESAWN protocol. A general lesson learned is that recent advances in compiler optimizations for the generation of runtime code can also improve static analysis mechanisms in real world settings, which is another argument for LLVM.

Our abstractions (cf. Section 4.2) also improve scalability in the size of the code and additionally allow hardware independence. Using our heuristics and abstractions, we have seen that, in general, CBMC is powerful enough to be employed in the verification process for large scale programs.

7.2   Future Work

As further SBMC tools emerge and improve, we can use our case study as benchmark for them, e.g., for NEC's VeriSol via F-Soft [11]. We can also consider unbounded model checking tools, e.g., use our generation of the abstract behavior model and apply SATABS afterwards, in the line of the recently published paper [3]. If this approach is infeasible, a combination of SBMC and predicate abstractions (cf. [16]) might be able to cope with our large protocol. At our institute, we are currently developing a new SBMC tool which will be based on the LLVM compiler toolkit. We expect that with this new tool, many of the technical difficulties can be avoided, and also better scalability can be achieved.

Promising enhancements in our abstract behavior model are: Firstly, improving multitasking between nodes for verifying global properties. We can reduce the large memory requirement by not storing the local variables (e.g., w, p and the whole aggregation tree) of all simulated nodes independently, but compactly or even only once. We can also implement a more general multitasking that allows several leaf nodes and delayed transmission of packets. This is achieved by using one extended scheduling function that comprises all jobs of all simulated nodes. With these improvements, all distributed properties we have verified with the tool Spin in [21] using hand-written models will be verifiable automatically.

Secondly, we can use an alternative to setting $p = 1$: By settling for a quantitative instead of a qualitative inspections, i.e., by using CBMC's nondeterminism instead of probabilistic choices, we are able to avoid the complexity of using probability and still investigate all possibilities of the probabilistic concast. The trade-off in this approach is the loss of quantitative results and the additional complexity that nondeterminism might cause.

Thoroughly investigating the protocol's robustness is another important research direction, made possible by the powerful autostart function. Since it can set all state variables to arbitrary values, also hazardous situations can be constructed.

Incorporating our generation scheme (simulation features inclusive) as a verification platform into TinyOS will enable many developers of WSN protocols to easily check correctness of their implementations.

References

1. Motor Industry Research Association. MISRA-C 2004: Guidelines for the Use of the C Language in Critical Systems. Motor Industry Research Association (September 2004)
2. Blaß, E.-O., Wilke, J., Zitterbart, M.: Relaxed Authenticity for Data Aggregation in Wireless Sensor Networks. In: 4th International Conference on Security and Privacy in Communication Networks (SecureComm 2008), Istanbul, Turkey (September 2008)
3. Bucur, D., Kwiatkowska, M.: Ambient Intelligence. In: Tscheligi, M., de Ruyter, B., Markopoulus, P., Wichert, R., Mirlacher, T., Meschterjakov, A., Reitberger, W. (eds.) AmI 2009. LNCS, vol. 5859, pp. 101–105. Springer, Heidelberg (2009)
4. Bucur, D., Kwiatkowska, M.: Towards Software Verification for TinyOS Applications. In: Proc. 9th ACM/IEEE International Conference on Information Processing in Sensor Networks (IPSN 2010), Computing Laboratory, Oxford University, UK, pp. 400–401. ACM, New York (April 2010)
5. Calvert, K.L., Griffioen, J., Sehgal, A., Wen, S.: Concast: Design and implementation of a new network service. In: Proceedings of 1999 International Conference on Network Protocols (1999)
6. CBMC: Bounded Model Checking for ANSI-C, http://www.cprover.org/cbmc/ (March 2010)
7. Clarke, E.M., Kroening, D., Lerda, F.: A Tool for Checking ANSI-C Programs. In: Jensen, K., Podelski, A. (eds.) TACAS 2004. LNCS, vol. 2988, pp. 168–176. Springer, Heidelberg (2004)
8. Cohen, E., Moskal, M., Schulte, W., Tobies, S.: A practical verification methodology for concurrent programs. Technical Report MSR-TR-2009-15, Microsoft Research (February 2009)
9. Eén, N., Sörensson, N.: An Extensible SAT-solver. In: Giunchiglia, E., Tacchella, A. (eds.) SAT 2003. LNCS, vol. 2919, pp. 502–518. Springer, Heidelberg (2004)
10. Emerson Smart Wireless, http://www2.emersonprocess.com/en-us/plantweb/wireless/pages/pages/wirelesshomepage.aspx
11. Gupta, A.: From hardware verification to software verification: Re-use and re-learn. In: Yorav, K. (ed.) HVC 2007. LNCS, vol. 4899, pp. 14–15. Springer, Heidelberg (2008)

12. Ioannis, K., Dimitriou, T., Freiling, F.C.: Towards intrusion detection in wireless sensor networks. In: Proceedings of the 13th European Wireless Conference (2007)
13. Killian, C., Anderson, J.W., Jhala, R., Vahdat, A.: Life, death, and the critical transition: Detecting liveness bugs in systems code. In: Proc. of the 4th Symposium on Networked Systems Design and Implementation (NSDI), Cambridge, MA, USA (2007)
14. Li, P., Regehr, J.: T-Check: Bug Finding for Sensor Networks. In: Proc. 9th ACM/IEEE International Conference on Information Processing in Sensor Networks (IPSN 2010), School of Computing, University of Utah, USA, pp. 174–185. ACM, New York (April 2010)
15. Mottola, L., Voigt, T., Österlind, F., Eriksson, J., Baresi, L., Ghezzi, C.: Anquiro: Enabling Efficient Static Verification of Sensor Network Software. In: Proc. 1st International Workshop on Software Engineering for Sensor Networks (SESENA - Colocated with 32nd ACM/IEEE International Conference on Software Engineering ICSE), ACM, New York (2010)
16. Post, H., Sinz, C., Kaiser, A., Gorges, T.: Reducing false positives by combining abstract interpretation and bounded model checking. In: ASE '08: Proceedings of the 2008 23rd IEEE/ACM International Conference on Automated Software Engineering, Washington, DC, USA, pp. 188–197. IEEE Computer Society, Los Alamitos (2008)
17. Rosen, B., Wegman, M., Zadeck, F.: Global value numbers and redundant computations. In: 15th ACM Symposium on principles of Programming Languages, pp. 12–27 (1988)
18. Sharma, O., Lewis, J., Miller, A., Dearle, A., Balasubramaniam, D., Morrison, R., Sventek, J.: Model Checking Software. In: Păsăreanu, C.S. (ed.) SPIN Workshop. LNCS, vol. 5578, pp. 223–240. Springer, Heidelberg (2009)
19. SureCross Wireless Industrial I/O Sensor Network Applications, http://www.bannerengineering.com/en-us/wireless/surecross_web_appnotes
20. TinyOS: An open-source OS for the networked sensor regime (March 2010), http://www.tinyos.net
21. Werner, F., Steffen, R.: Modeling Security Aspects of Network Aggregation Protocols. In: 8. GI/ITG KuVS Fachgespräch Drahtlose Sensornetze, Hamburg, pp. 83–86 (August 2009)
22. Xu, N., Rangwala, S., Chintalapudi, K.K., Ganesan, D., Broad, A., Govindan, R., Estrin, D.: A wireless sensor network for structural monitoring. In: SENSYS, pp. 13–24. ACM, New York (2004)
23. Zitterbart, M., Blaß, E.-O.: An Efficient Key Establishment Scheme for Secure Aggregating Sensor Networks. In: ACM Symposium on Information, Computer and Communications Security, Taipei, Taiwan, pp. 303–310 (March 2006) ISBN 1-59593-272-0

Model Checking the FlexRay
Physical Layer Protocol

Michael Gerke, Rüdiger Ehlers, Bernd Finkbeiner, and Hans-Jörg Peter

Reactive Systems Group
Saarland University
66123 Saarbrücken, Germany
{gerke,ehlers,finkbeiner,peter}@cs.uni-saarland.de

Abstract. The FlexRay standard, developed by a cooperation of leading companies in the automotive industry, is a robust communication protocol for distributed components in modern vehicles. In this paper, we present the first timed automata model of its physical layer protocol, and we use automatic verification to prove fault tolerance under several error models and hardware assumptions.

The key challenge in the analysis is that the correctness of the protocol relies on the interplay of the bit-clock alignment mechanism with the precise timing behavior of the underlying asynchronous hardware. We give a general hardware model that is parameterized in low-level timing details such as hold times and propagation delays. Instantiating this model for a realistic design from the Nangate Open Cell Library, and verifying the resulting model using the real-time model checker UPPAAL, we show that the communication system meets, and in fact exceeds, the fault-tolerance guarantees claimed in the FlexRay specification.

1 Introduction

The safety-critical functionality of modern cars is increasingly implemented in distributed embedded components that connect through a robust communication system. Since delays or communication errors in such X-by-wire applications can cause serious harm, fault tolerance is a key consideration in the design of the communication protocols.

In this paper, we study the physical layer of the FlexRay protocol [7]. Developed by the FlexRay Consortium, a cooperation of leading companies including BMW, Bosch, Daimler, Freescale, General Motors, NXP Semiconductors, and Volkswagen, FlexRay was first employed in 2006 in the pneumatic damping system of BMW's X5, and fully utilized in 2008 in the BMW 7 Series. The FlexRay specification was completed in 2009 and is widely expected to become the future standard for the automotive industry.

The role of the physical layer is to compensate for low-level communication errors such as *glitches*, i.e., incorrect transmissions due to electromagnetic interference and similar effects, and *jitter*, resulting from clock drift between asynchronous components. For this purpose, the protocol includes a complicated

S. Kowalewski and M. Roveri (Eds.): FMICS 2010, LNCS 6371, pp. 132–147, 2010.

voting and *bit-clock alignment* mechanism, which analyzes a stream of samples, identifies the boundaries of the individual bit transmissions, and computes the correct value of the bits.

How robust is the resulting protocol? The FlexRay standard states, somewhat vaguely, that "the decoding function attempts to enable tolerance of the physical layer against presence of one glitch in a bit cell when the length of the glitch is less than or equal to one channel sample clock period," adding in a footnote that "there are specific cases where a single glitch cannot be tolerated and others where two glitches can be tolerated" [7, Sect. 3.2.7]. Clearly, a more precise characterization of the fault tolerance is desirable. The challenge is, however, that the correctness of the protocol relies on the interplay of the bit-clock alignment mechanism with the timing behavior of the asynchronous hardware. A careful analysis of the fault tolerance must therefore include a detailed timing model of the underlying hardware.

Previous efforts [4,13,12,9,1] to analyze FlexRay have been based on manual or semi-automatic verification methods, which make it very difficult to determine the robustness of the protocol under different error models and hardware configurations. We present a new formalization of the FlexRay physical layer protocol, parameterized in several low-level timing details such as hold times and propagation delays, that is based on *timed automata*. Because timed automata can be analyzed fully automatically using model checkers such as UPPAAL [3], we can quickly analyze the model for different settings and track the dependence of the protocol on hardware and design parameters.

Our analysis provides a detailed picture of the robustness of the FlexRay physical layer protocol. We show that, for typical hardware parameters, such as those of a realistic design from the Nangate Open Cell Library [11], FlexRay tolerates one glitch every four samples. In fact, this tolerance is robust under variations of the hardware. For example, the protocol tolerates a clock drift of up to 0.46%, which significantly exceeds the limit of 0.15% described in the FlexRay standard. While fault tolerance thus holds for a wide range of hardware configurations, it strongly depends on design parameters like the size of the voting window: for example, the voting window of five samples, specified in the standard, allows for up to one glitch every four samples, while an alternative voting window of three samples would allow for one glitch every three samples.

In the following sections, we give a detailed presentation of the model and the results of our analysis.

2   Overview

We present a model of the physical layer protocol of the FlexRay coding/decoding unit (CODEC). As illustrated in Fig. 1, our model is structured into a model of the protocol and a model of the underlying hardware. The *protocol model*, which is given in Sect. 3, consists of a sender and a receiver.

We regard the message *frames*, which are obtained from the next-higher FlexRay layer and contain data to be transferred as well as protocol related

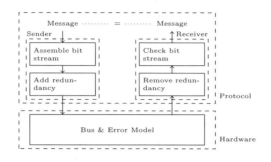

Fig. 1. The structure of the model

information, as simple byte strings independent of their format and content and call these *messages* in the following. The *sender* embeds the message in a structured *bit stream*. To introduce redundancy, every bit of this stream is sent as a *bit cell* in which the bit value is held for eigth clock cycles.

The *receiver* in turn reads one value in every clock cycle from the bus (the so-called *samples*), removes the redudancy and transmits the message received to the next-higher layer of the FlexRay protocol. If the received message is not the same as the message sent, the receiver goes into a designated error state.

The *hardware model*, which will be described in Sect. 4, describes the underlying hardware, including the communication bus and the error model describing the effects of glitches and jitter.

The scenario considered in our model is the reception of a message from a sending CODEC of a FlexRay controller that is directly connected to the receiving CODEC. It is sufficient to consider the scenario of one sending and one receiving *controller*, as the number of receiving controllers does not influence the message transfer process. According to the FlexRay standard [7, Chap. 5], FlexRay uses a time division multiple access (TDMA) scheme, which excludes collisions [1]. The correctness of higher protocol levels and the ability of FlexRay to deal with errors outside the error model are beyond the scope of this work.

2.1   The Error Model

In our model, we consider two types of erroneous behavior: *glitches* induced by influences from the environment, and *jitter* induced by the asynchronous nature of physical layer protocols.

Glitches. Environmental interferences can always disturb electronic communication, but smaller disturbances should be compensated in a fault-tolerant physical layer protocol. A sample taken from the bus might have been replaced by an arbitrary value. Simply said, it is possible that something different from the bit that has been sent is received. We model this by nondeterministically flipping samples in the receiver process. Such a flip is called a *glitch* [7, Sect. 3.2.2]. If too many glitches occur, the message might be compromised. However, the FlexRay physical layer protocol compensates for infrequent glitches. Our error model is parameterized in the *error distance*, which gives a lower bound on the number of correct samples between any pair of samples affected by glitches.

Jitter. In addition to glitches, the communication protocol must deal with several undesired effects due to the displacement of pulses in the signal. Since sender and receiver do not share a common oscillator, there may be a drift between the local oscillators. Additionally, the transition between voltage levels takes varying amounts of time. All undesired behavior caused by these effects is called *jitter*.

2.2   Timed Automata

We describe our model as a *network of timed automata* [2]. We assume familiarity with timed automata and refer the reader to a UPPAAL tutorial [3] for more background. Each automaton consists of a set of locations, representing discrete control points, which can be labeled with *invariants* over clock variables indicating the condition under which the system can stay at that location. Transitions can be labeled with *broadcast synchronization channels* over which a sender (identified by "!") can force receivers (identified by "?") to take a transition. Also, each transition can have an *update expression* to set clock or integer variables, and a *guard* determining its enabledness. Furthermore, a location can be marked as *committed* to force the system to immediately leave the location before time can pass. To improve the readability of complex models, we cut large automata into smaller ones.

2.3   Related Work

There are several previous formalizations of the FlexRay physical layer protocol. Beyer et al. [4] gave the first manual deductive correctness proof. In [12,13], Schmaltz presented a semi-automatic correctness proof in which the proof obligations are discharged using Isabelle/HOL and the NuSMV model checker. This proof has also been integrated into larger verified system architectures [9,1].

Vaandrager et al. [14] use UPPAAL to derive invariants of the Biphase Mark physical layer protocol, which are used for semi-automatically proving the formal correctness with the proof assistant PVS. Brown and Pike [6] follow an alternative approach, where they use the verification tool SAL to increase the degree of automation in the correctness proofs of the Biphase Mark and the 8N1 protocols. Unlike the FlexRay physical layer protocol, these protocols are not designed for an unreliable physical environment.

In contrast to all the semi-automatic approaches mentioned above, this paper presents a *fully automatic* correctness proof of the FlexRay physical layer protocol only using the real-time model checker UPPAAL [3]. Furthermore, we consider a more realistic *unreliable* physical environment to study the fault tolerance of the protocol.

In addition to protocol verification, there are several related works in the more general setting of hardware verification. Bozga et al. [5] verify asynchronous circuits with the real-time model checker KRONOS, where the low-level timing behavior of the individual gates is modeled by timed automata. A hierarchical approach to the verification of asynchronous circuits is described in [15]. By translating the system model together with a scheduler restricting the temporal evolution of the system into a communicating sequential processes (CSP) model, the possible timing behavior of the system is over-approximated to allow the efficient verification using a CSP model checker. The focus of this line of research is the analysis of asynchronous circuits on a chip, not the communication protocols considered in this paper.

3   The Protocol Model

We model a scenario in which the sender transmits a formatted bit stream, and the receiver checks if the format of the stream complies with the standard described in [7, Sect. 3.2.1.1] and if all message bits are received correctly. To avoid unnecessary counter variables that keep track of the current position within the message, we abstract from the concrete message length: after each transmitted byte, we let the sender nondeterministically determine whether a further message byte should follow, thus allowing an arbitrary message length.

3.1   The Sender

The Bit Stream Format. A message is transmitted as a structured stream [7, Sect. 3.2.1.1] of bit cells as shown in Fig. 2. As stated in Sect. 2.1, in every bit cell, the bit value is held for eight clock cycles (not shown in the figure).

The start of the stream is the so-called *transmission start sequence* (TSS), which consists of a sequence of low bits. It precedes every transmission.

After the TSS, the *frame start sequence* (FSS) signals the start of a message transmission. The FSS consists of a single high bit. The receiving controller accepts a transmission even if the FSS is received zero or two times.

Each message byte is prefixed with a *byte start sequence* (BSS). The BSS consists of one high bit followed by one low bit. The high to low transition in the middle of the BSS is used as a trigger for the bit clock alignment.

At the end of the message, a *frame end sequence* (FES) is appended. The FES consists of one low bit followed by one high bit.

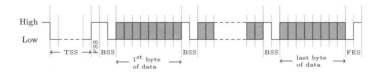

Fig. 2. Format of a message bit stream

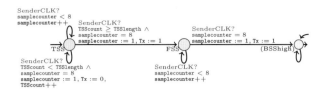

Fig. 3. Model of the start of the transmission

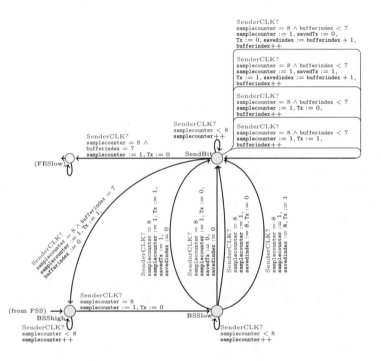

Fig. 4. Model of the transmission of the message bytes

Sending the Bit Stream. The sending of the bit stream is modeled by the automaton shown in Fig. 3. The message is generated nondeterministically as shown in Fig. 4. Also, the sender nondeterministically determines whether a particular bit should be verified by the receiver. In this case, the value of the chosen bit is stored in `savedTx` and its offset within the current byte is stored in `savedindex`[1]. In our model, the variable `End` is used to signal to the receiver that that the bit stream is about to end (shown in Fig. 5).

3.2   The Receiver

Voting. In order to reconstruct the bit stream sent by the sender, the receiver takes several samples from each bit cell. The five most recent samples always form

---

[1] The inital value `savedindex = 8` means "no bit to test".

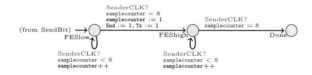

Fig. 5. Model of the end of the transmission

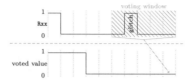

Fig. 6. Correction of a glitch through majority voting

the so-called *voting window*.[2] In each clock cycle, a *voted value*, i.e., the value of the majority of the five samples in the voting window, is computed from these. As the size of the voting window is odd, there will always be a clear majority.

As depicted in Fig. 6, infrequently occurring glitches are mostly filtered out directly. However, if a glitch occurs close to a change in the sample sequence, it leads to a premature or delayed change of the voted value. More precisely, if the glitch inverts one of the samples of the new value, it takes one more cycle until the new value becomes the majority in the voting window. On the other hand, if the glitch inverts one sample of the old value, the value will change one cycle too early. Such untimely changes of the voting value may also be the result of jitter, as described in Sect. 4.2. The errors can also occur in combination, as shown in Fig. 7.

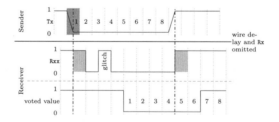

Fig. 7. Combination of jitter and glitch

Our receiver model always maintains the respective previous four samples and the sample obtained in the current clock cycle. The variable `window0` always holds the newest value. In every cycle, the values of the `window` variables are

---

[2] According to the FlexRay standard [7, Sect. 3.2.6], one sample is taken in one *sample clock period*, which is derived "from the oscillator clock period directly or by means of division or multiplication". Here, a *sample clock period* of one clock cycle is assumed in accordance with [4,13,12,1,9].

Fig. 8. Model of the voting process

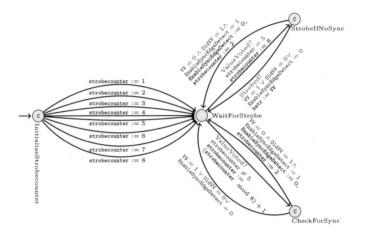

Fig. 9. Model of the strobing process

shifted accordingly, as shown in Fig. 8. If the majority of the `window` variables contains a 1, `VV` is set to 1, and to 0 otherwise. The respective previous value of `VV` is stored in `OldVV`.

Strobing. From each bit cell, only one voted value is used to reassemble the bit stream. To avoid choosing values that are affected by glitches, the fifth voted value (computed from samples from the middle of the bit cell) is taken as the so-called *strobed value*.

Bit Clock Alignment. In order to identify the (approximate) boundaries of the bit cells and thus the strobed values, the receiver keeps the variable `strobecounter` synchronized to the stream of received voted values.

The bit clock alignment mechanism makes use of the bit stream format. At the beginning of the transmission and during the *byte start sequences*, the first transition of the voted value from high to low is detected and `strobecounter` is reset to 2 for the next voted value. Thus, the second recognized voted value of the bit cell is considered the second voted value of the cell.

If a combination of clock drift and a glitch interferes with the bit clock alignment mechanism by delaying the recognition of the high to low transition, `strobecounter` will be off by more than 1, thus parts of the next bit cell are also

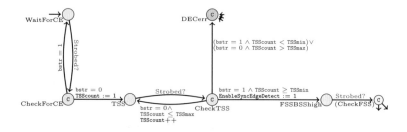

Fig. 10. Model of the start of the reception

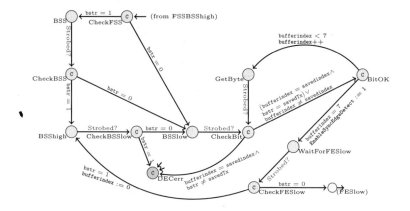

Fig. 11. Model of the reception of the message bytes

taken into account when computing the strobed value. This situation is shown in Fig. 7; recall the delay of two cycles introduced by the voting process. The bit clock alignment can analogously also happen too early.

As shown in Fig. 9, `strobecounter` has no default value, but is initialized nondeterministically. When the new voted value, `VV`, is 0 and the voted value from the cycle before, `OldVV`, is 1, and `EnableSyncEdgeDetect` enables the bit clock alignment mechanism, `strobecounter` is reset to 2, as the received 0 is the first bit of the new bit cell, and the bit clock alignment mechanism is deactivated using `EnableSyncEdgeDetect`.

When `strobecounter` has a value of 5 and channel `ValueVoted` signals that the voted value for this cycle of the receiver's clock is reached, `VV` is chosen as the value for `bstr`. Channel `Strobed` allows other automata to synchronize on this event in order to use the new `bstr` value.

Receiving the Bit Stream. When channel `Strobed` signals that a new value has been strobed, the receiver checks if it is consistent with the expected format of the bit stream, as shown in Fig. 10. As soon as a received value is not the expected one, the error state `DECerr` is entered.

The received TSS is accepted if it contains at least `TSSmin` bits. A further bit of the TSS is accepted if not more than `TSSmax` bits have been received before.

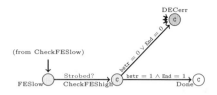

Fig. 12. Model of the end of the reception

During the reception of the TSS or after the reception of a message byte, the variable `EnableSyncEdgeDetect` is used, as shown in Fig. 11, to enable the bit clock alignment mechanism. During the reception of a message byte, the number of bits received so far within this byte is counted using variable `bufferindex`. When `savedindex` indicates that the current message bit is to be verified, the received value (stored in `bstr`) is compared to `savedTx`. The variable `End` is checked to prohibit entering the location `Done` too early, as shown in Fig. 12.

4   The Hardware Model

In FlexRay networks, each controller has a local *oscillator* that clocks all local circuits. The individual controllers run asynchronously and communicate via a shared *bus*. In our model, we use *registers* (standard circuits used to persist values) to simulate the low-level timing behavior of transmitting bit values from sender to receiver.

Figure 13 gives an overview. The sender begins a transmission of a bit by storing its value in a register `Tx`. The bus content is represented as the output of register `Tx`, which is connected to a register `Rx` on the receiver's side. Following [4,13,12,9,1], as proposed by [10], we forward the output of register `Rx` through a consecutive register `Rxx` to suppress metastability problems.

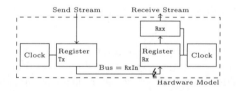

Fig. 13. Overview of the hardware sub-architecture

4.1   Oscillators

We model the local oscillators of the sender and the receiver as automata that emit *tick*-events (SenderCLK and ReceiverCLK) which, in turn, are received by other automata modeling connected circuits. According to the specification, distributed oscillators may deviate from the standard rate up to a certain bound [7, Appendix A.1]. Furthermore, as these oscillators are not started at the same

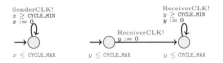

Fig. 14. Oscillators for sender and receiver

time, their periods can be shifted arbitrarily. This is modeled by not specifying a minimum length for the first cycle of the receiver's oscillator in Fig. 14. Here, x and y are continuous-valued clock variables.

In our model, we parametrize the length of an ideal clock cycle (which is the same for each controller) by CYCLE. To model the deviation, we use a parameter DEVIATION. This gives us a lower and an upper bound for tick-events:

$$\texttt{CYCLE\_MIN} = \texttt{CYCLE} - \frac{\texttt{DEVIATION}}{2} \quad \text{and} \quad \texttt{CYCLE\_MAX} = \texttt{CYCLE} + \frac{\texttt{DEVIATION}}{2}.$$

4.2   Registers

Following the setting of [4,13,12,9,1], we assume a *register semantics* to model the timing behavior of the bus which connects the sender and the receiver. Before we come to the actual transmission of bit values via the bus, we first give a general description of the low-level timing behavior of registers.

Register Semantics.   The behavior of a particular register hardware is described in terms of the following parameters:

- SETUP (HOLD) is the *setup (hold) time*, i.e., the time that the value on the input of a register is required to be stable before (after) the occurrence of a tick-event;
- PMIN (PMAX, where PMIN $\leq$ PMAX), is the *minimal (maximal) propagation delay*, i.e., the minimal (maximal) time after which a register changes its output to an undefined value (to the new value) after the occurrence of a tick-event.

The register content represents a particular Boolean value using voltage levels: A value below a certain voltage level is considered as 0 and a voltage above a certain level is considered as 1. However, there is a certain range of voltage levels between the two thresholds that cannot be interpreted as any Boolean value.

Fig. 15 illustrates a scenario in which first a register's input I and, after a tick-event, also its output R changes from X to Y. Here, τ refers to the time between two consecutive tick events and Ω indicates an undefined state of the register's output.

We assume that the unknown value is stable before $\tau - \texttt{SETUP}$, i.e., before it could violate the setup times of connected registers in the next cycle. In the FlexRay context, for a particular controller, all inputs of registers are connected to circuits that use the same oscillator as the registers. Hence, according to [8, Sect. 5.2], we assume that all local inputs are stable.

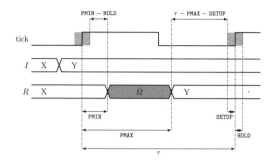

Fig. 15. Value change scenario of a register R

More generally, let $R(t)$ and $I(t)$ be a register's output and input at a point of time t, respectively, and let T be the point of time of a tick event, $t_{old} = T - \tau + \texttt{PMAX}$, and $t_{next} = T + \tau + \texttt{PMIN}$. Furthermore, let there be a point of time t' where the register's input changes, i.e., $T - \texttt{SETUP} \leq t' \leq T + \texttt{HOLD}$ such that $I(t') \neq R(t_{old})$. Then, the output of a register at time t, $t_{old} \leq t \leq t_{next}$, is formally defined as

$$R(t) = \begin{cases} R(t_{old}) & t_{old} \leq t \leq T + \texttt{PMIN}, \\ \Omega & T + \texttt{PMIN} < t < T + \texttt{PMAX}, \\ X & T + \texttt{PMAX} \leq t \leq t_{next}, \end{cases}$$

where
$$X = \begin{cases} I(T) & \text{if } \forall t'.(T - \texttt{SETUP} \leq t' \leq T + \texttt{HOLD}) \Rightarrow (I(t') = I(T)), \\ \Omega & \text{otherwise.} \end{cases}$$

Model of the Bus. Figure 16 shows the automaton modeling the transmission of a bit value according to the register semantics defined in the beginning of this section. Recall the structure of the hardware sub-architecture shown in Fig. 13. In our model, we represent register Tx's content by a variable Tx, and register Rx's input (which also represents the bus' content) by a variable RxIn. As the bus value is high whenever it is idle [7, Sect. 3.2.4], RxIn is initialized with 1.

At every tick of the sender's clock, the variable Tx is checked: if the sender is still writing the same value to the bus, nothing changes, but if the sender tries to write a different value to the bus, RxIn changes its value. Here, we represent an undefined bus content by a value of 2 for RxIn, and use the parameters HLMIN, HLMAX, LHMIN, and LHMAX to model the delays induced by the hardware: As a conservative approximation, we assume

$$\texttt{HLMIN} = \texttt{LHMIN} = \texttt{PMIN} \quad \text{and} \quad \texttt{HLMAX} = \texttt{LHMAX} = \texttt{PMAX}.$$

Model of the Receiving Register. Figure 17 shows the automata modeling the sampling process on the receiver's side. The receiver samples a value from

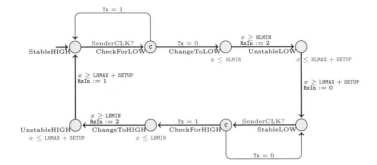

Fig. 16. Model of the bus

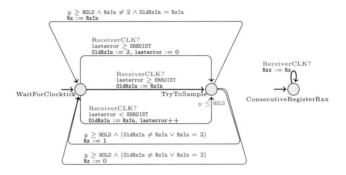

Fig. 17. Model of the sampling process

the bus using the register Rx. After exactly HOLD time units following a tick-event, we update Rx either (1) nondeterministically with 1 or 0 if Rx's input RxIn changes or is undefined, or (2) with RxIn otherwise.

Furthermore, for modeling glitches, we introduce a variable lasterror that counts the number of samples without a glitch. Whenever lasterror $\geq$ ERRDIST, the sampling process nondeterministically decides whether the current sample is affected by a glitch.

5   Model Checking the FlexRay Physical Layer Protocol

In our analysis, we fix values for the model parameters and check several correct-ness properties (shown in Table 1) using the real-time model checker UPPAAL [3]. In a first analysis, we use conservative approximations based on [7,11], which are listed in Table 2(a). We globally assume a CPU frequency of 80 MHz[3].

We initially assume an error distance of four which corresponds to one glitch in a voting window. This intuitive choice is overly pessimistic: in fact, the exper-

---

[3] Note that 80 MHz corresponds to an *ideal* clock cycle. Recall that every actual clock cycle of a CPU may deviate up to a certain rate, defined by DEVIATION.

Table 1. Satisfied correctness properties and corresponding running times of UPPAAL on a computer with an AMD Opteron 2.6 GHz and 4 GB RAM

Property	MC Time
`A<> Receiver_Control.TSS`	0.65 sec
It is always the case that the reception of the bit stream eventually starts.	
`A<> Receiver_Control.CheckFESlow`	7624.90 sec
It is always the case that the first byte of a message is eventually correctly received.	
`A[] !Receiver_Control.DECerr`	73.08 sec
Invariantly, the received bit stream is in the correct format and the received message is correct.	
`A[] (!Deadlock || Receiver_Control.Done)`	136.47 sec
Invariantly, there is no deadlock before the message is completely received.	

Table 2. Standard values based on conservative approximations of the parameters taken from the FlexRay standard [7] and the Nangate Open Cell Library [11], as well as the impact of changed parameters on the tolerable glitches. Here, "1 out of x" stands for "at most 1 glitch in x consecutive samples" and thus an error distance of $x - 1$, and "at most y" means "at most y glitches in the overall stream at arbitrary positions".

(a) Standard parameter values.

Parameter	Value	Corresponds to
CYCLE	10000	$\frac{1}{80\,MHz} = 12.5\,ns$
DEVIATION	30	$\pm 0.15\,\%$
SETUP	368	$460\,ps$
HOLD	1160	$1450\,ps$
PMIN	12	$15\,ps$
PMAX	1160	$1450\,ps$
ERRDIST	4	1 out of 5

(b) Changed parameter values.

Changed parameter	Tolerable glitches
PMAX − PMIN ≤ 6086	1 out of 4
PMAX − PMIN ≤ 6086	at most 2
PMAX − PMIN ≤ 9616	at most 1
DEVIATION ≤ 92	1 out of 4
DEVIATION ≤ 92	at most 2
DEVIATION ≤ 218	at most 1
DEVIATION ≤ 348	none
Voting window size = 3	1 out of 3
Voting window size = 5	1 out of 4
Voting window size = 7	1 out of 5
Voting window size = 9	1 out of 6

iments show that for the standard parameters, we can tolerate an error distance of three without violating any correctness property.

The impact of changing the hardware parameters `PMIN`, `PMAX`, or `DEVIATION` on the amount of tolerable glitches (such that the properties from Table 1 are still preserved) is shown in Table 2(b). Interestingly, this analysis demonstrates the robustness of the FlexRay physical layer protocol even for more pessimistic hardware assumptions: beyond our conservative choice of the parameters, there is still a comfortable safety margin for reasonable error models.

With slightly more elaborate adjustments to the automaton from Fig. 17, we also investigate an error model with two arbitrary glitches within every sequence of samples of a certain length. For instance, assuming the standard parameters from Table 2(a), it turns out that two glitches in a sequence of up to 82 samples lead to a violation of the correctness properties. The impact of changing the size of the voting window is shown in the last four rows of Table 2(b). Here, the error distance increases linearly in the size of the window.

6   Conclusion

In this paper, we have demonstrated the use of automatic verification to analyze the fault tolerance of a complex real-time protocol under variations of the design parameters, the error model, and the hardware parameters. Beyond proving that the physical layer protocol *meets* the fault tolerance requirements claimed in the FlexRay specification, our analysis gives a detailed picture of the *impact* the different parameters have on the robustness of the protocol.

An *a posteriori* analysis, as carried out in this paper, is helpful to understand the importance of individual design choices and hardware requirements in an established protocol, and to identify requirements that are too conservative and can therefore be relaxed. An interesting direction for future research might be to carry out the analysis *a priori*, exploring the design space of an as yet unfinished protocol: model checking variations of the protocol on a parameterized hardware model, like the one presented in this paper, can help the designer make safe and robust choices.

Acknowledgment. This work was supported by the German Research Foundation (DFG) as part of the Transregional Collaborative Research Center "Automatic Verification and Analysis of Complex Systems" (SFB/TR 14 AVACS). The authors want to thank Matthew Lewis for pointing out the Nangate Open Cell Library [11] and the anynomous reviewers for their helpful comments.

References

1. Alkassar, E., Böhm, P., Knapp, S.: Formal correctness of an automotive bus controller implementation at gate-level. In: Kleinjohann, B., Kleinjohann, L., Wolf, W. (eds.) 6th IFIP Working Conference on Distributed and Parallel Embedded Systems (DIPES 2008), International Federation for Information Processing, vol. 271, pp. 57–67. Springer, Heidelberg (2008)
2. Alur, R., Dill, D.L.: A theory of timed automata. Theo. Comp. Sci. 126(2) (1994)
3. Behrmann, G., David, A., Larsen, K.G.: A tutorial on UPPAAL. In: Bernardo, M., Corradini, F. (eds.) SFM-RT 2004. LNCS, vol. 3185, pp. 200–236. Springer, Heidelberg (2004)
4. Beyer, S., Böhm, P., Gerke, M., Hillebrand, M., Rieden, T.I.d., Knapp, S., Leinenbach, D., Paul, W.J.: Towards the formal verification of lower system layers in automotive systems. In: ICCD '05: Proceedings of the 2005 International Conference on Computer Design, pp. 317–326. IEEE Computer Society, Los Alamitos (2005)
5. Bozga, M., Jianmin, H., Maler, O., Yovine, S.: Verification of asynchronous circuits using timed automata. Electr. Notes Theor. Comput. Sci. 65(6) (2002)

6. Brown, G.M., Pike, L.: Easy parameterized verification of biphase mark and 8N1 protocols. In: Hermanns, H., Palsberg, J. (eds.) TACAS 2006. LNCS, vol. 3920, pp. 58–72. Springer, Heidelberg (2006)
7. FlexRay Consortium: FlexRay Communications System Protocol Specification Version 2.1 Revision A (2005)
8. Keller, J., Paul, W.J.: Hardware design: Formaler Entwurf digitaler Schaltungen, vol. 15. Teubner-Texte zur Informatik (1995)
9. Knapp, S., Paul, W.: Realistic worst case execution time analysis in the context of pervasive system verification. In: Reps, T., Sagiv, M., Bauer, J. (eds.) Wilhelm Festschrift. LNCS, vol. 4444, pp. 53–81. Springer, Heidelberg (2007)
10. Männer, R.: Metastable states in asynchronous digital systems: Avoidable or unavoidable? Microelectronics Reliability 28(2), 295–307 (1998)
11. Nangate Inc.: Nangate 45nm Open Cell Library Databook (2009)
12. Schmaltz, J.: A Formal Model of Clock Domain Crossing and Automated Verification of Time-Triggered Hardware. In: Baumgartner, J., Sheeran, M. (eds.) 7th International Conference on Formal Methods in Computer-Aided Design (FMCAD'07), November 11-14, pp. 223–230. IEEE Press Society, Los Alamitos (2007)
13. Schmaltz, J.: A formal model of lower system layers. In: Formal Methods in Computer Aided Design (FMCAD'06), pp. 191–192. IEEE Computer Society, Los Alamitos (2006)
14. Vaandrager, F., Groot, A.d.: Analysis of a biphase mark protocol with Uppaal and PVS. Formal Aspects of Computing Journal 18(4), 433–458 (2006)
15. Wang, X., Kwiatkowska, M.Z., Theodoropoulos, G.K., Zhang, Q.: Towards a unifying CSP approach to hierarchical verification of asynchronous hardware. Electr. Notes Theo. Comp. Sci. 128(6), 231–246 (2005)

SMT-Based Formal Verification of a *TTEthernet* Synchronization Function

Wilfried Steiner[1] and Bruno Dutertre[2]

[1] TTTech Computertechnik AG, Chip IP Design
A-1040 Vienna, Austria
wilfried.steiner@tttech.com
[2] SRI International, Computer Science Laboratory
Menlo Park, CA 94025, USA
bruno@csl.sri.com

Abstract. *TTEthernet* is a communication infrastructure for mixed-criticality systems that integrates dataflow from applications with different criticality levels on a single network. For applications of highest criticality, *TTEthernet* provides a synchronization strategy that tolerates multiple failures. The resulting fault-tolerant timebase can then be used for time-triggered communication to ensure temporal partitioning on the shared network.

In this paper, we present the formal verification of the compression function which is a core element of the clock synchronization service of *TTEthernet*. The compression function is located in the *TTEthernet* switches: it collects clock readings from the end systems, performs a fault-tolerant median calculation, and feedbacks the result to the end systems. While traditionally the formal proof of these types of algorithms is done by theorem proving, we successfully use the model checker `sal-inf-bmc` incorporating the `YICES` SMT solver. This approach improves the automatized verification process and, thus, reduces the manual verification overhead.

1 Introduction

Modern networked systems host a multitude of applications often with varying criticality levels. In an on-board network of an airplane, for example, highly critical flight-management and control applications are implemented as well as less critical video applications. To ensure independence between these applications, traditionally a federated network approach is realized in which different applications use private networks. However, with the increasing number of applications the federated approach becomes costly and, as a consequence, there is a tendency throughout many industries to converge from a multitude of heterogeneous federated networks to an integrated communication infrastructure.

TTEthernet (Time-Triggered Ethernet [1,2]) is such a communication infrastructure for mixed-criticality systems. For traffic of highest criticality, *TTEthernet* provides time-triggered communication. Time-triggered communication, also

S. Kowalewski and M. Roveri (Eds.): FMICS 2010, LNCS 6371, pp. 148–163, 2010.

known as time-division multiple-access (TDMA), is a communication paradigm in which the local clocks of the communication participants are synchronized, and frames are dispatched and relayed according a communication schedule defined *a priori*. Hence, as the local clocks in the participants are synchronized, the communication schedule is executed synchronously and contentions at the network are avoided. Time-triggered communication provides therefore strong temporal partitioning because the possibility that two or more communication participants access the network at the same point in time can be excluded by design and enforced by simple guardian mechanisms. The synchronized local clocks are the fundamental prerequisite for time-triggered communication, and the correctness of the synchronization algorithms is therefore essential.

The main contribution of this paper is the discussion and formal verification of the compression function which is a core element of the *TTEthernet* fault-tolerant synchronization strategy. We present the verification of several properties of different characteristics (membership and clock synchronization) and discuss their different computational overhead.

The subject of clock synchronization is very well understood, with a broad academic foundation developed as early as in the nineteen-eighties (e.g. [3], [4]). Our work proves the correctness of a particular implementation of these fundamental results. Still, there is also a certain novelty in the compression function: the compression function runs unsynchronized to the synchronized timebase; its core functionality is the collection of local views of the global synchronized timebase and the generation of a consolidated new reference point. The approach presented in this paper can easily be applied to enhance master-slave based clock synchronization systems to multi-master systems, in which the compression function operates as proxy for fault-tolerant clock synchronization.

Formal proofs of this kind of algorithms have been traditionally done by theorem proving [5], [6]. In this paper we discuss the application of the SMT-based verification approach introduced in [7] and [8] to fault-tolerant clock synchronization problems. To our knowledge this is the first time that model-checking has been applied to the verification of a convergence function such as the fault-tolerant median.

The formal models are free for download from the SAL wiki[1] to foster cooperation in the current ongoing standardization process of *TTEthernet* (SAE AS6802) as well as for upcoming inter-operability and conformance tests. While this paper discusses the *TTEthernet* low-level synchronization functions, the higher-level synchronization strategy focusing on startup/restart is presented in [9]. Because of space limitations, we present and discuss only parts of the formal model. The full model and a more detailed verification report are described in [9].

This paper is structured as follows: we give an overview of *TTEthernet* and an informal description of the compression function in the next section. Section 3 provides an overview of the formal model. We present the verification procedure and results in Section 4. Finally, we conclude in Section 5.

---

[1] http://sal-wiki.csl.sri.com

2   *TTEthernet* Informal Discussion

2.1   Communication of Synchronization Information

Figure 1 depicts an example *TTEthernet* network consisting of five end systems and two redundant communication channels. Channel 1 consists of three switches, where one of the switches is configured as *Compression Master* (CM) and the other switches are configured as *Synchronization Clients* (SC). Channel 2 consists of a single switch configured as CM. All end systems are configured as *Synchronization Masters* (SM). The synchronization procedure is initiated by the SMs which send synchronization messages, called *Protocol Control Frames* (PCF), to the CMs. The CMs process the proposed PCFs and relay new PCFs back to the SMs and SCs. SCs will relay the PCFs from the SMs to the CMs and vice versa but use only the PCFs from the CMs for their own synchronization.

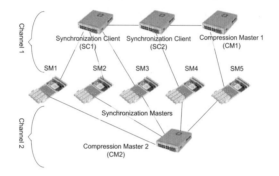

Fig. 1. Example TTEthernet network

TTEthernet implements a so called "permanence function" that compensates for network jitter of PCFs: as a PCF flows through the network, all devices that relay the frame add their delay imposed on the PCF into a dedicated field of the frame. Hence, a receiver can determine the actual latency of a PCF through the network with negligible error. The permanence function is then a simple method executed in the receiver to transform network jitter into network latency: (a) we calculate offline the maximum network latency considering all PCFs; (b) upon reception of a PCF the receiver artificially delays the PCF for the remaining difference between this maximum network latency and the actual latency as transported in the PCF. Hence, the "transmission" of each PCF will always take the maximum network latency.

To highlight the difference between the point in time of physical reception and the point in time when the frame is actually used in the CM, we use the term *"permanence point in time"* for the latter (see Figure 2). The permanence function allows us to abstract from network jitter and to treat the network latency as a constant. Without loss of generality we assume a zero network latency in the formal proofs: at the point in time when a PCF is dispatched by a SM it is immediately *"permanent"* at the CM. The negligible error of the permanence functions are covered by the modelling of the clock drift. The automatized formal proof of the permanence function using `sal-inf-bmc` can be found in [9].

2.2 Compression Function Informal Description

During synchronized operation mode, the SMs dispatch their PCFs at the same nominal point in time to the CMs. Due to drifts in the oscillators, the actual dispatch points in the SMs and the resulting permanence points in time in the CMs will deviate. Therefore, the CMs implement a so called *"compression function"* that runs unsynchronized to the synchronized global time. The compression function collects the PCFs from different SMs and produces a new PCF which is sent back to the SMs. The dispatch point in time of this new PCF is calculated as a function of the relative permanence points in time of the PCFs from the SMs. This dispatch point in time from the CM is called the *"compressed point in time"*. The focus of this paper is to verify the correct relation between the permanence points in time and the compressed point in time.

The compression function runs unsynchronized to the synchronized timebase. It is started upon the reception of a PCF, rather than upon the synchronized local clock in the CM reaching a particular point in time. Therefore, it has to be guaranteed that faulty SMs that may send early or late will not cause the compression function to recognize only a subset of PCFs from correct SMs in the generation of the new PCF.

Figure 2 depicts an example execution of the compression function. In this example three end systems that are configured as SMs dispatch PCFs, in particular a special type called Integration Frame (IN), to a switch that is configured as CM. The depicted deviation of the dispatch points in time stem from the relative differences in the oscillators of the end systems; in a perfect world, these dispatch points in time would be perfectly aligned.

CM will use the permanence function discussed previously to derive the permanence points in time of the PCFs. The first permanence point in time (p_1) will cause the compression function to start the collection phase. As successive PCFs become permanent, the CM records their offsets relative to the first permanence point in time ($p_i - p_1, i > 1$) and stores these offsets in a local data structure that we call the *clock synchronization stack*. The duration of the collection phase is given by the following rules, where "observation window" specifies the maximum deviation of two correct local clocks in the system as measurable by a clock within the network:

- The first permanence point in time will cause the compression function to collect the following permanent PCFs for one observation window.
- When the compression function collects at least a second permanent PCF during the first observation window, the collection phase is prolonged for a second observation window.

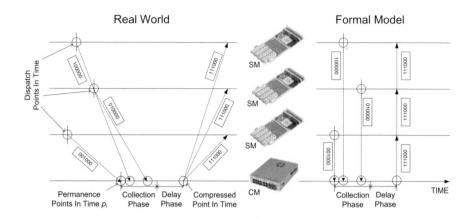

Fig. 2. Compression function overview, three end systems configured as SM provide their local clock readings to a switch configured as CM. In the real world the network jitter is compensated by the permanence function.

- The collection phase will end when the number of permanent PCF collected during observation window i is equal to the number of permanent PCFs collected during observation window $i-1$ (hence, when no new PCF became permanent for the duration of one observation window). Otherwise collection will be continued for another observation window.
- The collection phase will stop at the latest after the $(k+1)^{th}$ observation window, where k is the configured number of faulty SMs to be tolerated.

After the collection phase the relative permanence points in time of the collected PCFs are used to determine a correction value for the following delay phase. In order to minimize the impact of the faulty SMs we use a variant of the fault-tolerant median (where $p_i, i \geq 1$ represent the permanence points in time):

- 1 permanence point in time: $correction\_value = 0$
- 2 permanence points in time: $correction\_value = \frac{p_2 - p_1}{2}$
- 3 permanence points in time: $correction\_value = p_2 - p_1$
- 4 permanence points in time:
  $correction\_value = \frac{((p_2 - p_1) + (p_3 - p_1))}{2}$
- 5 permanence points in time: $correction\_value = p_3 - p_1$
- more than 5 permanence points in time: take the average of the $(k+1)^{th}$ largest and $(k+1)^{th}$ smallest inputs, where k is the number of faulty SMs that have to be tolerated.

In the delay phase, the compression function will wait for

$$delay = correction\_value +$$
$$(k+1) * observation\_window -$$
$$collection\_phase\_duration$$

where *collection_phase_duration* is the length of the preceding collection phase.

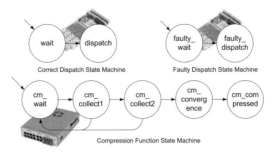

Fig. 3. State machines for the faulty and the correct dispatch processes as well as for the compression function

Figure 3 depicts the state machines of the dispatch processes in the SMs and the state machine for the compression function in the CMs.

The dispatch process is described by a very simple state machine consisting of only two states: `wait` and `dispatch` (or `faulty_wait` and `faulty_dispatch` for faulty components). The dispatch process maintains a local timer variable that identifies the dispatch point in time. When this dispatch point in time is reached the dispatch process dispatches the PCF and enters the `dispatch` state (or `faulty_dispatch`). Once in `dispatch` or `faulty_dispatch`, a dispatch process will remain in that state forever.

The state machine of the compression function consists of the following states: `cm_wait`, `cm_collect1`, `cm_collect2`, `cm_convergence`, and `cm_compressed`. The compression function starts in the `cm_wait` state and enters the `cm_collect1` state when the first PCF becomes permanent. The `cm_collect1` and `cm_collect2` represent the collection phase and `cm_convergence` represents the delay phase of the compression function as described above. Finally, the compression function enters the `cm_compressed` state.

We are interested in verifying the correctness of the collection phase as well as the delay phase in the compression function, which results in the following four properties:

- `agreement`: when the compression function collects one permanence point in time of a PCF sent from a correct SM it will also collect permanence points in time from all other correct SMs within the same collection phase.
- `window`: the compressed point in time will be within the interval $[k *\ observation\_window, (k + 2) * observation\_window]$.
- `correction`: all correct SMs will perceive the compressed point in time not more than $observation\_window$ from when they expect the compressed point in time.
- `termination`: the compression function process will produce a result.

3   Formal Model

Figure 4 gives an overview of the formal model used to verify the compression function. It consists of N modules that represent a dispatch process and the

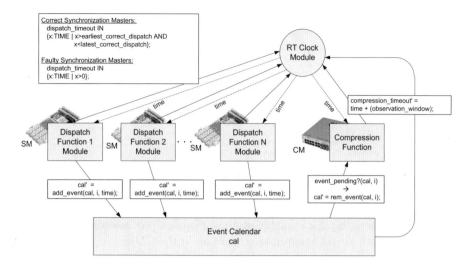

Fig. 4. Compression function model overview

compression function. An additional RT (Real-Time) Clock Module manages the timing in the model: the dispatch and compression modules receive the current time as an input from the RT Clock module. Furthermore, these modules each maintain a timeout output reflecting the next point in time when the module will produce its next event. The RT Clock module receives all timeout outputs as input and advances time to the smallest timeout value.

Clock drifts resulting in deviations of the local clocks and therefore different dispatch points in time are modelled by uncertainty intervals, which means that the end systems will set their new timeout to a non-deterministic position within parameterizable bounds.

The global data structure "Event Calendar `cal`" is used to model the flow of a PCF from the dispatch processes to the compression function. The transmission of a PCF by a SM is done by adding an event to the event calendar; likewise the reception of the PCF by the CM is modelled by the consumption of this event.

More detail on the progress of time using calendars as well as the exchange of messages can be found in [7].

The faulty SMs are simulated by allowing their dispatch points in time to occur at an arbitrary instant, while a correct SM dispatches its PCF within the specified uncertainty interval.

In the following we describe some parts of the model in the SAL notation. It starts with some general definitions.

```
k: NATURAL = 3;
N: NATURAL = 3*k + 1;
OBSERVATION_WINDOW_ID : TYPE = [1..k+1];
```

k defines the number of faulty SMs that have to be tolerated and N, the number of overall SMs required to tolerate the defined number of failures, is then given by N=3*k+1. The SMs are represented by the dispatch functions described by the state machines above. DISPATCH_ID identifies the SMs in the system by numbering them [1..N]. Similarly, OBSERVATION_WINDOW_ID labels the observation windows from [1..k+1].

```
observation_window: REAL = 5;
earliest_correct_dispatch: REAL= (k+1)*observation_window;
latest_correct_dispatch: REAL = earliest_correct_dispatch + observation_window;
end_of_time: REAL = latest_correct_dispatch + ((k+1)+2)*observation_window;
```

Besides the number of faulty SMs to be tolerated, the length of the observation window is the only other parameter that has to be assigned by hand. All other parameters in the system are derived from those two. In this setup we set observation_window=5. As observation_window is the only temporal parameter that we assign a particular value, it does not matter what this value is: 5 represents $5\mu sec$ as well as $5sec$ or any $\frac{x*5}{y}sec, x, y > 0$. The earliest_correct_dispatch and the latest_correct_dispatch define the uncertainty interval when a correct SM dispatches its PCF. The definition of this interval contributes to the hypothetical worst case, in which the faulty SMs would send their PCFs in such a way that the collection phase in the compression function (which lasts $k + 1$ observation windows at most) could complete without collecting any PCF stemming from a correct SM. By definition, all correct SMs will dispatch their PCF within an interval of length observation_window. end_of_time is used to initialize the timeout variable of the reactive modules. The compression function is the reactive module that initially waits for the reception of PCFs. In order to prevent the compression function module from blocking the progress of time, we initially set its value to the point in time when execution of the compression function would be finished in the worst case.

Real-time is modelled analogously to [7] using a dedicated real-time clock module. For the compression function we need additional data structures and functions in order to collect the permanence point in times of PCFs and to calculate their fault-tolerant median.

```
clock_readings: TYPE =
 [# valid: ARRAY DISPATCH_ID OF BOOLEAN, value: ARRAY DISPATCH_ID OF TIME #];
```

clock_reading defines the clock synchronization stack, the data-structure that we use for storing the relative permanence points in time of PCFs that the compression function receives during its collection phase. empty_clock_readings defines the empty clock synchronization stack.

```
add_clock_reading(cr: clock_readings, i: DISPATCH_ID, v: TIME): clock_readings =
                 ((cr WITH .valid[i] := TRUE) WITH .value[i] := v);
```

add_clock_reading specifies a function for collecting values in the clock readings data-structure. The values are added in a stack-like fashion, so the relation between clock reading entry to SM will be lost. Whenever a new value is added, valid is set to TRUE and the value field holds the relative difference to the first permanence point in time p_1. The fault-tolerant median calculation is specified according to the requirements given in the informal discussion.

```
ft_median(cr: clock_readings): TIME = % for k=2, N=7
 IF    cr.valid[7] THEN (cr.value[3] + cr.value[5])/2
 ...
 ELSIF cr.valid[4] THEN (cr.value[2] + cr.value[3])/2
 ...
 ELSE cr.value[1]  ENDIF;
```

The algorithms are modelled as guarded commands of following form:

```
guard --> list of commands
```

The correct SMs dispatch their PCF within the uncertainty interval; faulty SMs may dispatch their PCF at any time. An example guarded command for a correct SM is given below.

```
dispatch_state = wait AND dispatch_timeout = time
-->
dispatch_state' = dispatch; dispatch_pit' = time;
cal'           = add_event(cal, i, time); dispatch_timeout' = time+end_of_time;
```

When SM is in `wait` state and the RT Module signals that time has reached its dispatch event, the SM will dispatch its PCF by adding an event to the calendar. Furthermore, it locally stores the current point in time, which we use in the formal proof, and sets its timeout output to a high value such that it does not block time progress.

We describe some core transitions of the compression function module next. The first transition describes the reception of the first PCF, which starts the collection phase.

```
[([] (i:DISPATCH_ID):
   event_pending?(cal, i) AND event_time(cal, i) = time AND compression_state = cm_wait
-->
compression_state' = cm_collect1;
compression_timeout' = time + (observation_window);
reading_index' = 2; last_reading_index' = 2;
membership_new'=[[index:DISPATCH_ID] IF index=i THEN TRUE ELSE membership_new[index] ENDIF];
pit_0' = time;
clock_stack'=add_clock_reading(clock_stack,reading_index,0);
cal' = rem_event(cal, i);)
```

When the compression function is in the `cm_wait` state and a new entry is added to the calendar, the transition to `cm_collect1` state is triggered. Note that we abstract from the transmission delays that would naturally occur in the *TTEthernet* network. We justified this abstraction in Section 2.

`reading_index` is used both for counting the number of permanent PCFs and as an index in the clock synchronization stack, where it points to the next free entry. `last_reading_index` is used to store the number of permanent PCFs collected until the latest observation window has been started. When the collection phase is started, the `reading_index` and the `last_reading_index` are updated and the entry in the `membership_new` bitvector for the SM that triggered the transition is set. `pit_0` is used to store the current point in time when the transition is triggered (which is p_1). Note, that in a real implementation this timestamp would be taken from an internal clock in the CM, rather then the current point in real-time, which naturally is not present in any component. However, as we do not use pit_0 directly, but only relative offsets to it, we conclude that our modelling does not introduce invalid additional information. Finally, 0 is added as the first entry to the clock synchronization stack and the entry to the calendar that triggered the transition is removed from the calendar.

The next transition is triggered at the end of an observation window i ($i \geq 2$).

```
[] compression_state = cm_collect2 AND time = compression_timeout
AND reading_index >  last_reading_index AND window_counter < k+1
-->
compression_state' =  cm_collect2; compression_timeout' = time + observation_window;
last_reading_index' = reading_index;
window_counter' = IF window_counter=N THEN window_counter ELSE window_counter+1 ENDIF;
```

In this transition we check whether the number of permanence points in time has increased during the last observation window. If so, and it was not the last observation window yet, we continue the collection for another observation window. window_counter is used to keep track of the number of observation windows.

The next transition is taken when the number of permanence points in time is equal to the number collected during the previous collection window (hence, no new PCF has become permanent during the latest observation window), and at least $k + 1$ PCFs have been received. The state machine proceeds then to the cm_convergence state. The duration of the delay phase is calculated based on the relative permanence points in time, and the timeout is set accordingly to simulate the delay phase.

```
compression_state=cm_collect2 AND reading_index=last_reading_index
AND time=compression_timeout AND window_counter<k+1 AND reading_index>k+1 %proof only
-->
compression_state' =  cm_convergence; window_counter' = window_counter;
compression_timeout'= time+ft_median(clock_stack)+(k+1-window_counter)*observation_window;
```

The compression function will stay in the cm_convergence state for the duration of the delay value.

```
compression_state = cm_convergence AND time = compression_timeout
-->
compression_state' = cm_compressed; compressed_true' = TRUE;
```

When real-time indicates the timeout of the delay value, the compression function transitions to the cm_compressed state and sets compressed_true to TRUE.

Once in the cm_compressed state, the compression function will stay in this state forever, setting the compressed_true flag to FALSE immediately after entering. Hence, compressed_true marks exactly one instant in real-time, which is used as the reference for clock correction in the higher-layer synchronization protocol. This instant marks the compressed point in time (cm_compressed_pit).

For the proof of termination of the compression function we define two transitions:

```
[] compression_state=cm_wait AND time=compression_timeout --> compression_state'=cm_error;
[] compression_state=cm_error --> compression_state' = cm_error;
```

The first transition says that, when the compression function is in `cm_wait` state for too long it will enter the dedicated error state `cm_error`. The second transition is there to avoid a deadlock in the error state.

4   Verification Procedure and Results

The proof of the compression function builds on the abstraction method introduced in [7]. In our assessment, we extend this approach to allow a configurable number of faulty dispatch processes. Furthermore, we add a dedicated error state that is entered when the compression function is not finished in time. This allows us to also verify a termination property of the compression function. For the abstraction, we first define abstract system states and the abstract transitions between them: the composition of the SMs and the CM results in the product automata of their respective state machines. An abstract system state is a subset of states in the product automata and the abstract transitions are between these subsets. We prove the correctness of the abstraction (lemma *abstract_inv*), which is then used in the verification of our properties of interest. The proofs are done by k-induction.

`sal-inf-bmc` provides assistance in the construction of the abstraction via counterexamples. Given that we defined an abstraction consisting out of two abstract states $A1, A2$ and an abstract transition from $A1$ to $A2$ a typical counterexample during the design phase could be as follows: SAL shows how a transition in one of the original state machines, say in an SM, imposes an abstract transition from $A1$ to an abstract state $A2'$ other than $A2$ which may be undefined yet. Resolving this situation can be done by either restricting $A1$, extending $A2$, or introducing a new $A2'$ with the respective abstract transition.

4.1   Abstraction Description

The system abstraction is depicted in Figure 5.
A 1: This is the initial abstract state when all dispatch functions and the compression function have assigned their local variables as well as the global calendar to the initial values.
A 2: In this abstract state, at least one of the dispatch functions has dispatched a PCF modelled by adding the respective entry in the calendar.

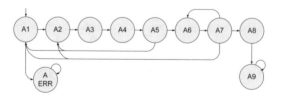

Fig. 5. System-Level Abstraction

A 3: In the A 3 abstract state, the compression function has consumed at least one of the permanent PCFs from the calendar and has started the first observation window of the collection phase.

A 4: This is the abstract state representing the first observation window of the collection phase of the compression function.

A 5: In the A 5 abstract state the collection phase has completed the first observation window. In this state we check whether to continue the collection of values or to restart the compression function.

A 6: This abstract state, again, represents the collection phase throughout one particular observation window for observation window $i \in 2..(k+1)$.

A 7: The A 7 abstract state is used to check at the end of each observation window $i \geq 2$, whether more PCFs have become permanent during the latest observation window $i - 1$ and whether the collection phase operated already for $(k+1)$ observation windows. If the number of permanent PCFs has increased and the number of observation windows collected so far is below $k + 1$ then the abstract state A 6 is entered again. If the number of permanent PCFs has not increased and the number of permanent PCFs is smaller than $k + 1$, then the compression function is restarted. If the number of permanent PCFs has not increased, but the number of permanent PCFs so far is higher than $k + 1$ then the abstract state A 8 is entered. Also, when the collection phase has reached the end of the $(k+1)^{th}$ observation window the abstract state A 8 is entered.

A 8: In this abstract state the compression function waits for the duration of the delay value calculated from values on the clock synchronization stack and the duration of the collection phase.

A 9: This is the final abstract state.

A ERR: This is the error state entered, when the compression function fails to terminate within a given timeout.

4.2   Key Disjunctive Invariants and Related Functions

The key in verification of the agreement and timing properties is in relating the individual states of the SMs to the state in the CM. For the agreement property this relation is a simple count of those SMs that have dispatched their PCF to the counter used in the CM. For the timing properties the relation is more complex as we not only have to formulate the relation based on the number, but also on the sequence in which the SMs dispatched their PCF.

4.2.1   Invariant for the Agreement Property.
The agreement property can be verified using an invariant that describes the equality: the *number* of SMs that have dispatched their PCF is equal to the counter in the CM (reading_index).

```
reading_index =
IF count_msg(1, cal, list_dispatch_states, list_dispatch_pits,
            pit_0, window_counter, old_values)< N
THEN count_msg(1, cal, list_dispatch_states, list_dispatch_pits,
             pit_0, window_counter, old_values)+ 1
ELSE N ENDIF
```

The `count_msg` function counts those dispatch functions `idx` that have already dispatched their PCF (`list_dispatch_states[idx]` = `dispatch`) and which have been consumed by the compression function (`NOT cal.signal[idx]`).

4.2.2 Invariant for the Timing Properties. The verification of the window and correction property is more challenging than for the agreement property. Here we not only have to relate the number of SMs to the CM state, but the *sequence* in which the SMs dispatched their PCF. Analogously to the `reading_index` used above, the CM uses the clock synchronization stack `clock_stack` to locally store the relative differences of the frame permanence points in time. On the other hand we store the individual dispatch points in time in the `list_dispatch_pits[i]`, where `i` is the index of the SMs.

For the invariant we now have to define how the `clock_stack` relates to the `list_dispatch_pits[i]`:

```
(FORALL (i:DISPATCH_ID):
IF    i = 1 THEN clock_stack.value[i]=0
ELSIF i <= count_memb(1, membership_new)
   THEN  clock_stack.value[i] =  list_dispatch_pits[observed_order[i]]
                              - list_dispatch_pits[observed_order[1]]
ELSE clock_stack.value[i]=0 ENDIF)
```

We know that the first entry on the clock synchronization stack will always be 0. Furthermore, the number of values on the clock synchronization stack is determined by the number of PCFs received by the SM so far. This number can be obtained from the membership vector `membership_new`, using a simple count function (`count_memb`). The ith value on the clock synchronization stack will be the temporal distance between the ith PCF and the first PCF that has become permanent.

To determine the first and the ith PCF requires some type of sort procedure on `list_dispatch_pits[i]`. As it turns out, this is a little tricky in our formalism as an explicit sort algorithm works only for a very small number of values. To overcome this limitation we use a declarative approach: we introduce `observed_order` as a new array and `observed_order[i]` shall be assigned the index of the SM that provided the ith PCF. Hence, `observed_order` is not the sorted version of `list_dispatch_pits`, but rather a sorted array of pointers to `list_dispatch_pits`. In SAL this can be done via a non-deterministic selection (using the `IN` construct) and a predicate:

```
observed_order IN {x: ARRAY DISPATCH_ID OF DISPATCH_ID | sort([[i:DISPATCH_ID]
   IF NOT membership_new[i] THEN time+1 ELSE list_dispatch_pits[i] ENDIF], x)};
```

Here we say, that `observed_order` is some array x spanning over the SMs, which satisfies the `sort` predicate. The sort predicate simply takes a modified version of `list_dispatch_pits` and x as input. Note that the modification of `list_dispatch_pits` is necessary to exclude PCFs that have become permanent in a collection phase prior to the latest one.

```
sort(unsorted_list: ARRAY DISPATCH_ID OF TIME,
     sorted_list: ARRAY DISPATCH_ID OF DISPATCH_ID): BOOLEAN =
  (FORALL (i:DISPATCH_ID): i<N =>
     unsorted_list[sorted_list[i]] <= unsorted_list[sorted_list[i+1]]) AND
  (FORALL (i,j:DISPATCH_ID): sorted_list[i]=sorted_list[j] => i=j);
```

Finally, sort returns true when its second parameter is an ordered pointer list.

4.3 Verification Properties and Results

```
agreement: LEMMA system |- G(compression_state=cm_compressed =>
                            (FORALL (i:DISPATCH_ID): i<=k OR membership_new[i]));
```

agreement says that once the compression function has reached the cm_compressed state, all correct SMs are present in the membership_new vector.

```
window: LEMMA system |- G(compression_state=cm_compressed AND compressed_true =>
  (FORALL (i:DISPATCH_ID): i<=k OR
   (list_dispatch_pits[i]+k*observation_window<=time_out[COMPRESSION_FUNCTION_ID] AND
    time_out[COMPRESSION_FUNCTION_ID]<=list_dispatch_pits[i]+(k+2)*observation_window)));
```

window says that the cm_compressed_pit occurs in a window of size 2*observation_window.

```
correction: LEMMA system |- G(compression_state=cm_compressed AND compressed_true =>
(FORALL (i:DISPATCH_ID): i<=k OR
(time_out[COMPRESSION_FUNCTION_ID] - list_dispatch_pits[i] + (k+1)*observation_window
   <= observation_window) OR
(list_dispatch_pits[i]+ (k+1)*observation_window-time_out[COMPRESSION_FUNCTION_ID]
   <= observation_window)));
```

In a perfect world all sm_dispatched_pit would occur at the same point in time resulting in a nominal cm_compressed_pit of (k+1)*observation_window later. correction says that all SMs will observe the actual cm_compressed_pit with a maximum deviation of one observation_window from the nominal cm_compressed_pit. Hence, all correct SMs will have to correct their local clocks for a maximum of one observation_window.

Note that the window and correction properties do not account for the network latency and jitter (as these are abstracted by the permanence function). Hence in the real world the nominal cm_compressed_pit will occur *max_transmission_delay* later than reflected in the properties above.

```
termination: LEMMA system |- G(compression_state/=cm_error);
```

The termination property says that the cm_error state will never be reached. Hence, termination ensures that eventually the cm_compressed state is reached and trivial solutions to the previous properties are excluded.

The results of our model-checking assessment are presented in Table 1, where N is the number of SMs of which k are faulty. For each scenario we also give the number of SMT variables and SMT assertions.

Table 1. Verification results for the compression function properties

Property	k	N	Verif. Time	#var	#assert	k	N	Verif. Time	#var	#assert
agreement	1	4	1.65 sec	633	606	2	7	2.58 sec	964	955
window	1	4	1.81 sec	633	720	2	7	7.49 sec	964	1136
correction	1	4	1.80 sec	633	721	2	7	4.07 sec	964	1036
termination	1	4	1.72 sec	633	723	2	7	2.67 sec	964	1134
abstract_inv	1	4	6.51 sec	633	727	2	7	2,227.38 sec	964	1036

As depicted, the main computation time is consumed in the verification of the abstract invariant, while the verification time of the actual properties is small. Verification runs for $k = 3$ have been aborted after several hours. Although, the approach is not scalable for high k, it is sufficient for the verification of dual fault-tolerance as required in the original *TTEthernet* specification. The main reason for this computational complexity is the non-deterministic selection construct used in the definition of the observed_order array, as this results in a quadratic number of SMT constraints. Table 2, shows the verification results for a restricted compression function model that only models the membership part.

Table 2. Verification results for membership only

Property	k	N	Verif. Time	#var	#assert	k	N	Verif. Time	#var	#assert
agreement	1	4	0.97 sec	509	454	2	7	1.51 sec	766	663
agreement	3	10	2.02 sec	1023	872	4	13	2.51 sec	1280	1081
agreement	5	16	3.13 sec	1537	1290	6	19	3.57 sec	1794	1499
abstract_inv	1	4	1.27 sec	509	490	2	7	2.57 sec	766	840
abstract_inv	3	10	6.92 sec	1023	1113	4	13	75.35 sec	1280	1386
abstract_inv	5	16	508.57 sec	1537	1659	6	19	10,056.97 sec	1794	1932

Again, we see that the main computational complexity is in the verification of the abstract invariant. Indeed, the membership-only verification allows us to increase the system size quite significantly from seven to nineteen SMs (with $k = 6$).

5   Conclusion

In this paper, we discussed the formal verification of the *TTEthernet* compression function, which is essential for its application in safety-critical and mixed-criticality systems.

We have shown how `sal-inf-bmc` can be applied to the formal verification of fault-tolerant convergence functions. Though the overall number of concurrent processes and in particular the number of faulty processes is limited, our results are sufficient to argue dual fault tolerance as required by *TTEthernet*. A crucial aspect preventing better scalability is the number of SMT constraints generated which grows quadratically with the number of network components.

For the verification of complex problems, SAL provides guidance in the development of the proof by producing counterexamples. This is a practical and powerful feature that allows systematically strengthening of the invariant.

Although the formal verification of the full-blown *TTEthernet* clock synchronization service as a whole is outside the scope of this paper, the compression function as a core element will be used as a basic building block in future studies.

Acknowledgments

The research leading to these results has received funding from the European Community's Seventh Framework Programme (FP7/2007-2013) under grant agreement $n°236701$ (*CoMMiCS*). The second author was supported in part by NSF grant CSR-0917398 and by NASA Cooperative Agreement NNX08AC59A.

References

1. Steiner, W.: TTEthernet Specification, TTA Group (2008),
   http://www.ttagroup.org
2. Kopetz, H., Ademaj, A., Grillinger, P., Steinhammer, K.: The time-triggered ethernet (tte) design. In: 8th IEEE International Symposium on Object-oriented Real-time Distributed Computing (ISORC), Seattle, Washington (May 2005)
3. Kopetz, H., Ochsenreiter, W.: Clock synchronization in distributed real-time systems. IEEE Trans. Comput. 36(8), 933–940 (1987)
4. Lundelius, J., Lynch, N.: An upper and lower bound for clock synchronization. Information and Control 62, 190–204 (1984)
5. Pfeifer, H.: Formal Analysis of Fault-Tolerant Algorithms in the Time-Triggered Architecture. Ph.D. dissertation, Universität Ulm, Germany (2003),
   http://www.informatik.uni-ulm.de/ki/Papers/pfeifer03-diss.pdf
6. Pike, L.: Formal verification of time-triggered systems. Ph.D. dissertation. Indiana University (2006)
7. Dutertre, B., Sorea, M.: Modeling and Verification of a Fault-Tolerant Real-Time Startup Protocol Using Calendar Automata. In: Lakhnech, Y., Yovine, S. (eds.) FORMATS 2004 and FTRTFT 2004. LNCS, vol. 3253, pp. 199–214. Springer, Heidelberg (2004)
8. Brown, G.M., Pike, L.: Easy parameterized verification of biphase mark and 8N1 protocols. In: Hermanns, H., Palsberg, J. (eds.) TACAS 2006. LNCS, vol. 3920, pp. 58–72. Springer, Heidelberg (2006)
9. Steiner, W.: TTEthernet Executable Formal Specification, Marie Curie Technical Deliverable RO_A (2009), Available via TTA Group, http://www.ttagroup.org/

Embedded Network Protocols for Mobile Devices

Despo Galataki[1,2], Andrei Radulescu[2], Kees Verstoep[1], and Wan Fokkink[1]

[1] VU University, Dept. Computer Science, Amsterdam, The Netherlands
[2] ST-Ericsson, Eindhoven, The Netherlands

Abstract. Embedded networks for chip-to-chip networks are emerging as communication infrastructure in mobile devices. We present three novel embedded network protocols: a sliding window protocol, a protocol for opening and closing connections, and a bandwidth reservation protocol. The design of these protocols is tailored to the low power and low cost requirements of mobile devices. The model checker SPIN played an important role in the design and analysis of these protocols. Large instances of the protocols could be analyzed successfully using the distributed model checker DiVinE.

1 Introduction

For certain (e.g., mobile) applications there is too little physical space on the chip packages to accommodate all the necessary traditionally-parallel interfaces. Therefore, there is a shift from parallel interfaces towards high-speed serial interfaces. This trend is visible in, e.g., computer chips [12,16,18], FPGA chips [1,28], and mobile device chips [23,15].

High-speed serial links, while very efficient in terms of energy per bit, have transmission errors which need to be resolved by the protocols above. Moreover, these links are intrinsically point-to-point, which implies that if multiple devices need to be connected together, a network topology must be used.

The trade-offs for designing a chip-to-chip network are different from computer networks [7,22], which are often designed for scalability and throughput, or on-chip networks [4,6,13], which tend to be designed for low cost and power, but have a much higher throughput due to wires being relatively inexpensive. A chip-to-chip network is also designed for low cost and power. Moreover, it must cope with relatively large latencies caused by the transmission serialization, which puts pressure on buffering, one of the most important cost factors. Chip-to-chip interconnects are thus typically designed to offer reliable, in-order communication at the Data Link layer. Additionally, due to the small-scale and controlled environment, and to avoid retransmission buffers at the Transport layer, routers do not drop data when their buffers fill up, but apply backpressure instead.

In computer chip networks, the high-level protocols are memory-based and host-centric to cope with the existing legacy [12,16,18]. In mobile devices, a

S. Kowalewski and M. Roveri (Eds.): FMICS 2010, LNCS 6371, pp. 164–179, 2010.

different approach has been taken, in which, due to the trend towards multi-host systems, the chip-to-chip networks are emerging as flat and non-hierarchical, offering services similar to those in computer networks, such as TCP-like connection-oriented communication [8,15,21]. A connection-oriented service involves the ability to open connections, which are then used to transfer data, and close connections, such that ports can be reused by the same application to communicate to other nodes, or by a different application. Another aspect when designing chip-to-chip networks for mobile devices is native support for bandwidth reservation to enable correctness by a composable system design [8,21]. This is similar to some approaches for on-chip networks [10,14]. However, instead of a tightly coupled system-wide time-division-multiplexing approach, which is less suitable in an intrinsically asynchronous network, bandwidth is assumed to be allocated at each link. Consequently, it needs to be allocated and deallocated as part of the connection opening and closing stages.

We report on the design and analysis of three core protocols for communication and connection management. We focus on these protocols because their design had to be tailored to the low power and low cost requirements, and model checking played an important role in the design process. We first present a sliding window protocol for the Data Link layer that has been optimized for the target domain. We then present a protocol for opening and closing connections, which takes advantage of in-order delivery in chip-to-chip networks within mobile devices. As a result, the protocol does not use sequence numbers and maximum segment lifetime as in TCP [19]. Finally, we discuss an extension of this connection management protocol that includes in-band link-bandwidth reservations. Due to space restrictions, we cannot explain the protocols in full detail. The reader is referred to [9] for detailed descriptions of the protocols.

During their design, the protocols were analyzed using the SPIN model checker, as well as with DiVinE, which distributes the workload of a verification among multiple compute nodes. DiVinE could verify larger problems than SPIN, while SPIN's detailed error trails were used to find flaws in a particular design and correct them. The use of model checking was crucial in the protocol design. Notably, through verification we learned that an extra phase is needed for the connection management protocol, in contrast to TCP's three-phase connection protocol. Additionally, verification guided us in the design of an optimization of bandwidth (de)allocation to reduce memory overhead.

The protocols were developed in the context of UniPro[SM], a serial high-speed interface for interconnecting integrated circuits in mobile phones; it is bound to become part of millions of mobile phones world-wide. It should be noted that UniPro[SM] is still under development, and the protocols described in this paper will undoubtedly be adapted and extended in the near future, or be replaced by alternative designs, to meet the requirements of the different industrial partners.

2   UniPro[SM]

The diversity and complexity of the development of mobile phones has created a need for standardization, which is addressed by the Mobile Industry Processor

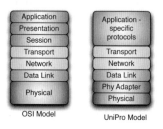

Fig. 1. OSI and UniPro^{SM} network layers

Interface (MIPI®). MIPI®, which is supported by an alliance of most mobile industry companies, defines the interface standards for mobile phones features, like audio, displays and cameras. In particular, there is a need for a general protocol that is responsible for the communication among applications and devices. This is the responsibility of the UniPro^{SM} [15] layer stack. UniPro^{SM} can support networks of up to 128 devices (integrated circuits, camera processor, displays, baseband, etc). It is a generic hardware- and software-friendly technology, which can support a diversity of applications. UniPro^{SM} offers low-power modes through the physical layer underneath to minimize power consumption. Other important requirements are low memory consumption, high speed, reliability and robustness, even in the face of failures in mobile devices, message loss and crashing applications. Inspired by the new era of multitasking, UniPro^{SM} is ready for upcoming innovations of parallel processing on mobile devices as well.

UniPro^{SM} is largely based on the OSI Reference Model. ¿From Fig. 1, one can observe some differences between the two models. UniPro^{SM} partitions the physical layer in two. The lowest layer is in charge of electrical signaling, line encoding, etc. (like the physical layer in the OSI model), while the intermediate layer (Phy Adapter) is responsible for abstracting the different technologies and combining them in a heterogeneous environment. The Data Link layer ensures that there is a reliable link between two modules in one hop distance, and that a frame can be arbitrated and multiplexed corresponding to the specified priorities. Similar to OSI, the Network layer deals with routing and addressing packets. The Transport layer defines the quality of a connection and is responsible for the flow and congestion control of the network. The UniPro^{SM} model combines the three upper layers of the OSI model – Session, Presentation and Application – into a single one, because it is responsible for connecting the diversity of applications and modules together rather than for implementing applications. The interface of the Transport layer has to be simple, so that applications can be easily adapted to it.

3   Sliding Window Protocol

Errors may occur on the links and routers may get overflowed, so messages can get lost. As a result, a continuous flow of communication between a sender and a receiver (data packets and acknowledgments providing feedback that they have been received) has to be established by dedicated protocols. Sliding window protocols (see, e.g., [22]) offer reliable data transmission and control the flow of messages, accommodating differences in link and processing speeds. Sliding window variations are used at both the Data Link layer (HDLC) and in the Transport layer (TCP) of the OSI model.

The data being transferred from a sender to a receiver is fragmented into packets. The packets carry sequence numbers, which can be seen as a running index into the buffered packets at the sender, with an extra bit to avoid confusion between old and new fragments. The receiver sends as acknowledgment (ACK) the sequence number of a received packet to the sender. It may also send a negative acknowledgment (NAC) in case of a failure. Sliding window protocols are typically enhanced with optimizations, e.g., to hide latency of transmission and increase the network utilization by pipelining techniques. An example is TCP [5], which in addition uses the maximum packet lifetime and an estimate of the round trip time [24]. Variations of sliding window protocols have been studied and formally verified in different ways (see, e.g., the related work section in [2]).

There are two generic sliding window protocols in the literature [22]. One version, called *go-back-N*, is that the receiver ignores all packets after an error until it receives the correct one; the sender resends *all* packets that have not been acknowledged, after a timeout. The second version, called *selective repeat*, is that only failed packets are resent; the receiver informs the sender if there is a failure and on which packet. Go-back-N wastes time, compared to selective repeat, because the sender needs a timeout to learn about failed packets. On the other hand, it is simpler and gives less memory overhead at the receiver. The sliding window protocol (SWP) we developed for the Data Link layer is a mixture of go-back-N and selective repeat. When the receiver notices a failure, as in selective repeat, it sends NAC_i with i the sequence number of the last correct packet it received. The sender thus gets to know about the failure earlier than if it had to wait for a timeout. As in go-back-N, the receiver ignores all packets after an error until it receives the correct one.

The sender's flow chart is shown in Fig. 2. In general, the sender can send up to N packets to the network, and it can only send the next one when some of the packets that it sent are acknowledged by the receiver. It will resend a packet only if it receives a NAC or after a timeout. The sender needs to store any two out of three predicates, *beginning*, *on_post* and *current*. These are the basic variables defining the sender's *window* of packets which have been sent but not acknowledged. By maintaining two of these variables for a connection, the sender can easily derive the third one, because *beginning* = *current* − *on_post*.

- *beginning*: Indicates the first packet that was sent but not acknowledged.
- *on_post*: Indicates the number of the packets waiting for an acknowledgment; it can be no more than the maximum window size.
- *current*: Indicates the next packet that will be sent.

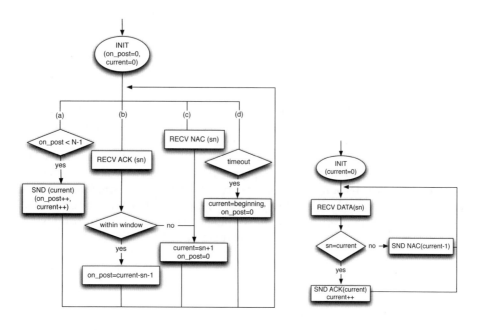

Fig. 2. SWP sender   **Fig. 3.** SWP receiver

Fig. 3 shows a flow chart of the receiver's algorithm. The protocol starts with *current* = 0, where *current* indicates the identity of the expected packet. When the receiver receives a packet, it checks if it is the expected one; if so, it sends back an acknowledgment ACK_i, and waits for the next packet to arrive by incrementing *current*. In case an unexpected or garbled packet arrives, it sends NAC_{i-1} with the identity of the last correct packet which arrived in order.

The resulting protocol has the advantage of little memory overhead (the same as go-back-N), while giving a significant recovery time gain compared to go-back-N. For further details, the reader is referred to [9, Sect. 3].

4   Connection Management Protocol

The connection management protocol (CMP) presented here is based on the well-known TCP connection protocol, with its *three-way handshake*, which works as follows. A client initiates a connection by sending a synchronization request (SYN) to a server. The server, if readily available, acknowledges the request. Finally the client sends an acknowledgment back. The client repeats sending a SYN and the server repeats sending an ACK when a timeout occurs. After reception of a client's ACK, both end nodes are connected and ready to exchange data. If a node wants to leave, it informs the other party by sending a finalization request (FIN), and waits for an acknowledgment. If this acknowledgment is delayed, then after a timeout it resends the FIN. After receiving a FIN, a node can continue to send data until it is also ready to close the connection.

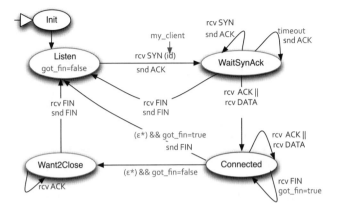

Fig. 4. Server's state machine with its current client

To improve power and memory consumption, we make a number of adaptations to TCP's connection management protocol. We aim at minimizing the number of exchanged messages, memory overhead and completion time. Tables that hold history information and interpretations whether a delayed message has become obsolete are excluded. Session identification of a connection and timing variables are kept to a minimum. Messages may be dropped due to resource contention, if there is a shortage of buffer space or processing power. However, the network is designed to deliver messages in order.

Part of the state machine of a server is displayed in Fig. 4 (for the interplay of a server with a node that is not its client, see [9, Fig. 22]). The initial state is Listen. The received messages are from its client. The states are as follows:

- Listen: The server is free to accept a new connection and is not busy with a client. When it receives a SYN from a new client, it sends back an ACK and proceeds to WaitSynAck.
- WaitSynAck: The server can receive an ACK or a DATA (a message containing data), indicating its client received its ACK and is connected. The server then moves to Connected. If it receives a FIN, it replies with FIN and goes back to Listen. The FIN may indicate that the client does not want to use the connection anymore. The server stays in the same state if it receives another SYN or a timeout; in both cases it sends ACK to its client.
- Connected: The server is participating in a data exchange. It stays in the same state if it receives an ACK, DATA or FIN; they are not answered. At reception of a FIN, it sets $got\_fin = true$; (ε^*) means that the server closes the connection. If the server already received a FIN from its client, it can reply with FIN and move to Listen. Otherwise, it just moves to Want2Close.
- Want2Close: The server can receive an ACK in case there was a repeated and delayed ACK from the client. Then the server stays in the same state. When a FIN arrives, the server answers with FIN and moves to Listen.

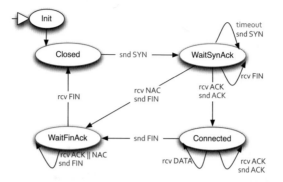

Fig. 5. Client's state machine with its current server

If the server receives a FIN or (except for state Listen) SYN from a node that is not its client, it replies with FIN or NAC, resp., and stays in the same state.

Fig. 5 shows a client's interaction with its server (for the interplay of a client with a node that is not its server, see [9, Fig. 24]). The initial state is Closed.

- Closed: The client chooses a server and tries to connect to it by sending SYN and moving to WaitSynAck.
- WaitSynAck: The client expects to receive an ACK, which it answers with ACK. It may receive a NAC, indicating the server is busy. It is important that in this case, the client replies with FIN and moves to WaitFinAck (this will be explained in detail below). SYN is replayed after a timeout. If the client receives a FIN, this means the server replied to a FIN of an old connection.
- Connected: The client can receive another ACK, after which it sends ACK back to its server. As this is the state where data exchange is done, the client generally receives some DATA too. When it does not want to send more data, it informs the server with a FIN and moves to WaitFinAck. Notice that the client should not receive any FIN from its server before it sends its own FIN.
- WaitFinAck: The client waits for a FIN, after which it goes to Closed. Apart from a successful request (through Connected), the client also reaches this state after it receives a NAC. That means it can receive multiple ACKs and NACs before it gets a FIN from the server.

In every state a FIN can arrive, as a delayed repeated message from a server of an old connection. The client ignores such messages.

We explain why the client should send FIN after the server answers with NAC to a SYN. The other option would be that the client simply stops trying to connect and moves to Closed. The server is not affected, as at the moment it answered to the SYN, it was busy with another client and it did not initiate any new connection. This is a fast and simple way to close the connection. However, by means of the model checker SPIN, we found a flaw in this idea, depicted by the scenario in Fig. 6. The client sends two SYNs to the server. While receiving the first one, the server is busy with another client, and thus answers with NAC.

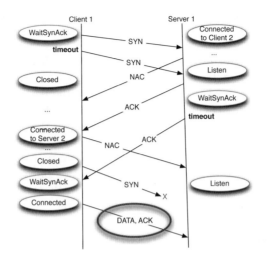

Fig. 6. An example where the client closes immediately after a server's NAC without going through WaitFinAck

By the second SYN, the server is ready to set up a new connection and replies with ACK. Then it moves to WaitSynAck, where a timeout occurs, and as a result it replays ACK. In the meantime, the client has received a NAC and has moved to the Closed state. As a result, the client may follow up connecting to another server. Consequently, when the client receives teh first ACK from the first server, it responds with NAC. As a result, the server moves to Listen (in the correct version of the protocol this NAC to the server cannot happen, therefore it is not considered in Fig. 4). The client decides to reconnect to the server, and receives an ACK from it. However, the received ACK is from the first connection attempt, and the server is not aware of this new connection, because the corresponding SYN was lost, due to resource contention. The client incorrectly assumes it has a connection, and starts sending data to the server.

If we can distinguish SYN messages from different sessions (replayed SYNs are considered to be in the same session), the problem is solved. A trivial solution is to keep track of the last session of all servers at the client side and all clients at the server side. This solution, however, does not scale. Trying to keep track of all different sessions with only one extra bit is not possible, because servers and clients can connect to each other multiple times.

By asking the client to close the connection via WaitFinAck, we prevent it from connecting to another server until it receives the server's FIN. The main idea is that the client can only move to the next session when it is certain it will not receive any more ACKs and NACs from the server for this session. Once the server sends ACK, it moves to WaitSynAck, and after that, it can only send ACKs after a timeout, until it gets an answer from the client. Hence the client receives at least one of the NACs or ACKs before it goes to the next session. Once it receives an ACK, it can only receive ACKs until it moves to the next session. If none of the NACs arrive at the client, it sends SYNs until it gets an ACK, and then moves to Connected. If a NAC arrives at the client, it answers ACKs and NACs with a FIN, until it gets a FIN from the server, and then it moves to Closed. Thus we make sure that both ends absorb all the SYNs, ACKs and NACs for this session before moving to the next session.

We have simplified the closing of connections by enforcing that the client is always the first to send a FIN to the server. The server thus always closes before the client. In addition, the client is the one who requests a new connection. Therefore, there is no way to mix one session with another. One could claim that having the client always close first is a limitation of the protocol. This can be hidden, however, as we could give the server (in Want2Close) the option to piggyback a flag that it wants to close the connection.

5   Router Management Protocol

We now turn to the router management protocol (RMP) for congestion avoidance, on top of CMP. The protocol is able to avoid overloading paths in the network by making explicit bandwidth allocations at the routers for every segment of the path. First we sketch how it works when the bandwidth allocation succeeds; see Fig. 7 for an illustration of this procedure. The client starts by sending SYN to the server. To this message it attaches the bandwidth ($bw1$) that needs to be reserved. Routers do not make a reservation on receiving this SYN, but just forward it to the next router or the server. The server sends an ACK with an aggregate value ($bw1 + bw2$) of the client's and its own bandwidth.

A router, when receiving an ACK from server to client, first searches if the triple (client, server, bandwidth) already exists in its memory. If not, and if the router has sufficient remaining bandwidth, it creates a triple with bandwidth $bw1 + bw2$, which reserves this bandwidth to the connection. The connection is established by the subsequent ACK from client to server, and then data can be exchanged. The routers wait until they receive a FIN from the server to the client, indicating the end of the connection on both sides. Then the router checks if a corresponding triple exists in memory. If so, it reclaims the bandwidth for this connection and removes the triple from memory.

Suppose a router, when receiving an ACK from server to client, finds it has insufficient remaining bandwidth. As illustrated in Fig. 8, the router then sends ERR in the client's direction without storing the triple. If this ERR gets lost, the client replays SYN or the server replays ACK after a timeout, invoking another ERR at the router. When the client finally receives the ERR, it closes the connection exactly as when it receives a NAC (by sending a FIN and waiting for the server's FIN). When a second ACK arrives at the router, the router may in the meantime have freed adequate bandwidth to serve the connection. Then the connection can still get established, if the ERR never arrived at the client.

When a connection is being closed, routers must be able to distinguish the first FIN received from a client and repeated FINs for closing this same connection. Otherwise routers could reclaim bandwidth for the same closing connection

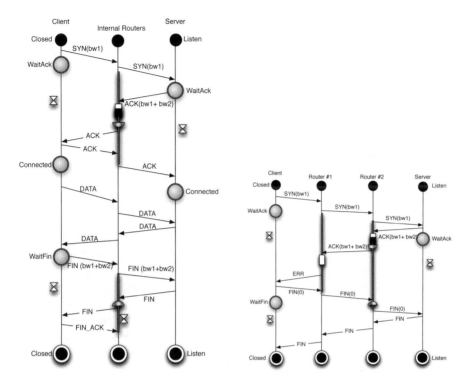

Fig. 7. Bandwidth allocation succeeds   **Fig. 8.** Bandwidth allocation fails

multiple times. An easy solution is to let routers store triples (client, server, bandwidth) until the end of a connection. However, since there can be hundreds of active connections, this imposes a relatively heavy memory load. Therefore, in the final version of the protocol we introduced an optimization in which such triples are only kept in the routers' memory while setting up and closing the corresponding connection, and not during data exchange.

When a router receives an ACK from client to server, it looks if there is a corresponding triple in its memory, and if so, removes this triple. On the other hand, when a client closes a connection, it attaches the bandwidth of this connection to FIN, so that routers can restore the triple. To remove this triple from the routers' memory again, we add an extra message at the very end of CMP. After a client has received a FIN from its server, finalizing the closure of the connection, it sends one extra message back, to inform intermediate routers that they can remove the corresponding triple.

6   Model Checking Analysis

We applied the model checker SPIN [11] during the design of the SWP, CMP and RMP protocols. SPIN is widely used to analyze real-life communication protocols. The tool can discover potential deadlocks, livelocks or invalid states. In addition, properties written in LTL (Linear Time Logic) can be checked.

SPIN has a wide range of analysis options, e.g., live simulation, and full scale or approximate state space analysis. An important characteristic of SPIN specifications are the dimensions of the various model state variables. These maximum dimensions need to be chosen carefully, or the corresponding state space will very quickly grow such that full scale analysis is no longer feasible.

To reduce the relevant state space to a managable size, a wide range of techniques is reported on in the literature [20], but applying them successfully may require significant expertise and often some amount of experimentation while "tuning" the model. As a result, memory requirements are frequently the bottleneck in being able to analyze larger protocol instances. It can thus be beneficial to employ analysis tools using a large distributed memory, provided that both data and computation can be distributed effectively.

A prominent example in the category of distributed LTL model checkers is the DiVinE [3] system. As shown in [25], the DiVinE model checker has good scalability on clusters with a fast interconnect, but can also be applied successfully in a high-bandwidth computational grid environment. Unlike sequential model checkers, which typically use depth-first search, DiVinE uses breadth-first search (which parallellizes well) and employs a hashing function to evenly spread the state space and work load over the compute nodes. To facilitate LTL model checking, which requires a cycle detection algorithm, DiVinE implements various distributed algorithms. In this paper we used the "OWCTY" algorithm, which is based on a distributed version of Topological Sort.

DiVinE supports both a native modeling language "DVE" and codes written in SPIN's modeling language Promela. Promela specifications are handled by DiVinE using the embedded "NIPS" module. NIPS is a complete reimplementation of the original SPIN tool, by means of a specially developed model-checking *virtual machine* [27]. An interesting aspect of this SPIN reimplementation effort is that the resulting model checking byte code can be optimized off-line by additional tools, which can significantly reduce the resulting state space. Practical examples of these reductions will be discussed below. Instead of using Promela, the protocols discussed might also have been modeled in DVE, giving an additional performance gain. However, for pragmatic reasons we chose Promela.

We ran DiVinE on 64 compute nodes of the DAS-3 cluster (`www.cs.vu.nl/das3/`) at VU University. The 2.4 GHz AMD Opteron-based nodes are interconnected by a fast Myri-10G network, and have 4 Gigabyte of memory each.

6.1   Model Checking SWP

For SWP, we checked a number of LTL properties that together assert the required behavior of the protocol, i.e., it should eventually deliver all messages, in order, without duplication, despite possibly loosing packets. In particular, we looked at the following LTL properties:

Table 1. States in the SWP LTL=1 for SPIN and DiVinE/NIPS

Window	SPIN states	DiVinE/NIPS states				
		PR/DVR/SCR	PR	DVR	SCR	Base
2	$1.38 * 10^5$	$1.00 * 10^5$	$1.56 * 10^5$	$1.47 * 10^6$	$1.75 * 10^6$	$1.75 * 10^6$
3	$3.19 * 10^6$	$2.00 * 10^6$	$3.62 * 10^6$	$3.55 * 10^7$	$4.44 * 10^7$	$4.44 * 10^7$
4	$5.11 * 10^7$	$2.95 * 10^7$	$5.78 * 10^7$	$5.82 * 10^8$	$7.43 * 10^8$	$7.43 * 10^8$

- LTL 1: no message is duplicated
- LTL 2: messages are not reordered
- LTL 3: every data message sent is eventually received

We also included LTL 4, which is a combination of LTL 2 and 3, and LTL 5, which is an alternative formulation of LTL 3. We will focus on LTL 1 and 5, being representative for the model checking effort required (e.g., the size of the resulting state space). For the formulation of these properties, see [9].

With sequential SPIN, we could indeed check all properties. However, the state space growth when gradually increasing the maximum window size (the most important model parameter) was considerable. As illustrated in Table 1, the growth rate is over an order of magnitude for every increment of the window size. As a result, analyzing the properties for a window size of 4 is already becoming difficult, as the state space exceeds available memory (we determined the largest state space on a special DAS-3 node equipped with more memory than the 4 GByte available by default). By enabling SPIN's state compression methods, the state space capacity can be extended, but the most efficient compression technique comes at a significant runtime cost – potentially further increasing the high runtime by a factor of ten of more. It is worth mentioning that the SWP specification discussed is already optimized using most well-known SPIN state space reduction techniques available; unoptimized initial versions of the SWP specification could in fact only be analyzed up to a window size of 2. On the other hand, a full-scale analysis for a window size of 4 appears reasonable, given the target setting.

Table 1 also shows the sizes of the state spaces using the SPIN support in DiVinE. The unoptimized NIPS bytecode (the "Base" version in the table) induces a much larger state space than SPIN. However, successive bytecode optimizations by means of the SARN [17] toolset reduce the effective state space to somewhat below the state space reported by SPIN with its default partial order optimization enabled. The SARN tools applied are Path Reduction (PR), Dead Variable Reduction (DVR) and Step Confluence Reduction (SCR). PR appears to be the optimization with the largest impact, since it most effectively reduces the number of synchronization points in the model checking byte code.

Fig. 9 shows the effects of state space reduction on the DiVinE running time. Note that the figure is log-log scaled to account for the wide range in state spaces (due to static optimization discussed above) and parallel running times. The figure indicates that DiVinE is able to achieve almost linear speedup up to 32 compute nodes, and for the larger problem sizes up to 64 compute nodes. A

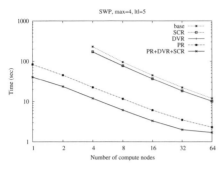

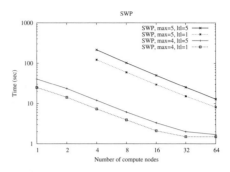

Fig. 9. SWP state space reduction impact on DiVinE runtime

Fig. 10. SWP model scaling and LTL impact on DiVinE runtime

Table 2. SPIN and DiVinE SWP run times in sec. for large instances (note that state space volumes are not identical)

Problem	Instance	SPIN 1 node	DiVinE 1 node	DiVinE 4 nodes	DiVinE 16 nodes	DiVinE 64 nodes
SWP	max=4,ltl=1	8.8	24.9	7.3	2.1	1.5
	max=4,ltl=5	18.2	40.6	11.9	3.3	1.7
	max=5,ltl=1	158	448	122	29.5	8.1
	max=5,ltl=5	324	819	214	49.9	12.8

similar pattern can be seen in Fig. 10, where the state space variation is induced by scalings in the maximum window size (and the LTL formula). Finally, Table 2 shows the running times of SPIN and DiVinE, the latter on 1, 4, 16 and 64 nodes.

6.2   Model Checking CMP

For the analysis of CMP, the state machines for the client and server shown in Sect. 4 were transformed into Promela code. Assertions were added regarding messages that should be impossible to be received in particular states. The protocol was instantiated with a configuration of two clients making a sequence of arbitrary connections to two servers. For the initial analysis we used SPIN in default mode, i.e., checking for possible deadlocks, unreachable code, invalid end states and assertions. As explained in Sect. 4, this SPIN analysis led to the detection of a flaw in our original CMP, where the server answered with NAC to a SYN. The rest of this section discusses the analysis of the corrected CMP.

As an additional CMP model parameter we varied the capacity of the channels between the client and server processes. Asynchronous communication with the channel size set to one found no errors, but detected some unreachable code, which indicates that some valid scenarios may not have been analyzed with a channel size this small. Parallel performance of the DiVinE analysis of CMP using channel capacity between two and five is shown in Fig. 11.

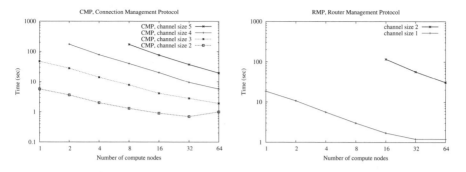

Fig. 11. CMP analysis time using DIVINE

Fig. 12. RMP analysis time using DIVINE

Table 3. SPIN and DIVINE run times for CMP and RMP in sec. for large instances (note that state space volumes are not identical)

Problem	Instance	SPIN 1 node	DIVINE 1 node	DIVINE 4 nodes	DIVINE 16 nodes	DIVINE 64 nodes
CMP	cap=2	103	5.7	2.0	0.9	1.0
	cap=3	N/A	47.3	14.1	4.1	1.9
	cap=4	N/A	291.7	78.1	20.1	5.7
RMP	cap=1	18.4	18.5	5.6	1.7	1.2
	cap=2	1470	N/A	N/A	116.2	30.6

Table 3 compares the running times of SPIN and DIVINE. The entries marked *N/A* could not be completed due to memory shortage. The state space corresponding to the CMP protocol is again very effectively reduced by the SARN toolset, in particular by its Step Confluence Reduction (SCR) tool. By merging equivalent sets of states based on program location, SCR here reduces the state space almost by a factor of 60, allowing DIVINE with NIPS and SARN to outperform SPIN even on a single compute node, which is rather uncommon.

6.3 Model Checking RMP

For the analysis of RMP, the model of CMP was extended with explicit routing nodes between a client and server. A fixed configuration of three routing nodes was used to represent arbitrary setups involving an initial, intermediate, and final routers. State regarding remaining bandwidth described by the (client, server, bandwidth) triples was modeled for every router explicitly, and referred to in assertions for particular states. We used an LTL expression to verify that the router bandwidth allocation does not exceed capacity (no duplicated bandwidth allocation) and does not become negative (no duplicated bandwidth releases).

Parallel performance of a DiVinE analysis of RMP is shown in Fig. 12. As the figure shows, RMP displays quite extreme effects on the state space when the model parameter for the channel capacity is scaled up, making a distributed analysis with DiVinE attractive.

7 Conclusions

In this paper we discussed the design of three embedded networking protocols that were tailored to the specific resource requirements of novel mobile devices. We investigated a sliding window protocol, a protocol for connection establishment and a related bandwidth reservation protocol. In designing the protocols, the SPIN model checking tool was very helpful in preventing errors in the protocol descriptions at a very early stage. This should be contrasted with scenarios where a design is already mostly pinned down or an actual implementation exists, which first has to be reformulated back into a different modeling language.

In the models we checked deadlock freeness, various assertions on states, as well as more general properties formulated in LTL. As the protocol designs became more mature, the checking of larger model instances was attempted. The state space explosion phenomenon forced us to apply a range of SPIN model "optimization" techniques to significantly reduce the effective protocol state space. Unfortunately, this forces a modeler to focus on low-level SPIN implementation aspects which are mostly irrelevant to the abstract model as such.

Despite extensive state space reductions achieved on the models, several realistic instances still were infeasible for analysis with SPIN, due to the limited memory capacity. These larger instances were then checked with the distributed DiVinE tool, which also supports SPIN specifications. This should be weighed against the limited support for error tracing in the SPIN version of DiVinE; for effective work with Promela specifications, use of SPIN itself is currently indispensible. Though DiVinE sequentially runs slower than the highly optimized SPIN tool, given a fast cluster network it exhibits excellent scalability on large problems, making it a useful option for cluster environments with a large distributed memory capacity.

An additional advantage of large-scale distributed model checking is that it can make an approach where model checking is applied to the *target* application language (e.g., as in Java PathFinder [26]) able to efficiently deal with realistic instances, despite the larger state space.

References

1. Altera Corp. and Innocor Ltd. SerialLite Protocol Specification, Rev. 1.0 (2003)
2. Badban, B., Fokkink, W.J., van de Pol, J.C.: Mechanical Verification of a Two-way Sliding Window Protocol. In: Proc. CPA, pp. 179–202. IOS Press, Amsterdam (2008)
3. Barnat, J., Brim, L., Černá, I.: Cluster-Based LTL Model Checking of Large Systems. In: de Boer, F.S., Bonsangue, M.M., Graf, S., de Roever, W.-P. (eds.) FMCO 2005. LNCS, vol. 4111, pp. 281–293. Springer, Heidelberg (2006)

4. Benini, L., De Micheli, G.: Networks on Chips: Technology and Tools. Morgan Kaufmann, San Francisco (2006)
5. Comer, D.E.: Internetworking with TCP/IP, Principles, Protocols, and Architecture, vol. 1. Prentice-Hall, Englewood Cliffs (2006)
6. Dally, W.J., Towles, B.: Route Packets, Net Wires: On-Chip Interconnection Networks. In: Proc. DAC, pp. 684–689. ACM Press, New York (2001)
7. Dally, W.J., Towles, B.P.: Principles and Practices of Interconnection Networks. Morgan Kaufmann, San Francisco (2004)
8. Desoli, G., Filippi, E.: An Outlook on the Evolution of Mobile Terminals: From Monolithic to Modular Multiradio, Multiapplication Platforms. IEEE Circuits and Systems Magazine 6(2), 17–29 (2006)
9. Galataki, D.: Design and Analysis of UniPro Protocols for Mobile Phones. Master's thesis, VU University Amsterdam (2009)
10. Goossens, K., Dielissen, J., Rădulescu, A.: The Æthereal Network on Chip: Concepts, Architectures, and Implementations. IEEE Design and Test of Computers 22(5), 414–421 (2005)
11. Holzmann, G.J.: The SPIN Model Checker. Addison-Wesley, Reading (2004)
12. HyperTransport Technology Consortium. HyperTransport I/O Link Specification, Revision 3.10b (2009)
13. Jantsch, A., Tenhunen, H. (eds.): Networks on Chip. Kluwer, Dordrecht (2003)
14. Millberg, S.M., Nilsson, E., Thid, R., Jantsch, A.: Guaranteed Bandwidth Using Looped Containers in Temporally Disjoint Networks within the Nostrum Network on Chip. In: Proc. DATE, pp. 890–895. IEEE, Los Alamitos (2004)
15. MIPI® Alliance. Specification for Unified Protocol (UniPro^{SM}), 2010. Version 1.10
16. PCI-SIG. PCI Express® Base Specification, Revision 2.1 (2009)
17. Quirós Araya, G.: Static Byte-Code Analysis for State Space Reduction. Master's thesis, RWTH University, Aachen (2006)
18. RapidIO Trade Association. RapidIO® Interconnect Specfication, Rev. 2.1 (2009)
19. RFC 793: Transmission Control Protocol, Edited by Jon Postel (1981)
20. Ruys, T.C.: Low-Fat Recipes for SPIN. In: Havelund, K., Penix, J., Visser, W. (eds.) SPIN 2000. LNCS, vol. 1885, pp. 287–321. Springer, Heidelberg (2000)
21. Suoranta, R.: New Directions in Mobile Device Architectures. In: Proc. DSD, pp. 17–26. IEEE, Los Alamitos (2006)
22. Tanenbaum, A.S.: Computer Networks. Prentice Hall, Englewood Cliffs (2002)
23. MIPI® Alliance. Specification for D-PHY, Version 1.00.00 (2009)
24. Udaya Shankar, A.: Verified Data Transfer Protocols with Variable Flow Control. ACM Transactions on Computer Systems 7(3), 281–316 (1989)
25. Verstoep, K., Bal, H.E., Barnat, J., Brim, L.: Efficient Large-Scale Model Checking. In: Proc. IPDPS. IEEE, Los Alamitos (2009)
26. Visser, W., Havelund, K., Brat, G.P., Park, S., Lerda, F.: Model Checking Programs. Autom. Softw. Eng. 10(2), 203–232 (2003)
27. Weber, M.: An Embeddable Virtual Machine for State Space Generation. In: Bošnački, D., Edelkamp, S. (eds.) SPIN 2007. LNCS, vol. 4595, pp. 168–186. Springer, Heidelberg (2007)
28. XILINX®. Aurora Protocol Specification, SP002, v1.2 (2003)

A Study of Shared-Memory Mutual Exclusion Protocols Using CADP

Radu Mateescu and Wendelin Serwe

INRIA Grenoble – Rhône-Alpes, Inovallée, 655, av. de l'Europe,
Montbonnot, F-38334 Saint Ismier, France
{Radu.Mateescu,Wendelin.Serwe}@inria.fr

Abstract. Mutual exclusion protocols are an essential building block of concurrent systems: indeed, such a protocol is required whenever a shared resource has to be protected against concurrent non-atomic accesses. Hence, many variants of mutual exclusion protocols exist in the shared-memory setting, such as Peterson's or Dekker's well-known protocols. Although the functional correctness of these protocols has been studied extensively, relatively little attention has been paid to their non-functional aspects, such as their performance in the long run. In this paper, we report on experiments with the performance evaluation of mutual exclusion protocols using Interactive Markov Chains. Steady-state analysis provides an additional criterion for comparing protocols, which complements the verification of their functional properties. We also carefully re-examined the functional properties, whose accurate formulation as temporal logic formulas in the action-based setting turns out to be quite involved.

1 Introduction

Mutual exclusion is a long-standing problem in concurrent programming, formulated initially by Dijkstra almost half a century ago [10]. It consists in controlling the access of concurrent processes to a shared resource such that at most one process can use the resource at a time and that the execution of the system is guaranteed to progress. In the shared-memory setting, in which processes communicate by atomic read and write operations on shared variables, a large number of protocols implementing mutual exclusion were proposed and studied in the literature (see, e.g., the surveys in [37,2,42]). Most of the effort has been concentrated on analyzing the functional correctness of these protocols, either by hand-written proofs [10,26,5,35,27,40,2,41] or by applying automated reasoning and model checking techniques [29,24,9,4]. However, much less attention has been given to the model-based performance evaluation of these protocols, most of the existing works dealing with performance measurements of protocol implementations on specific architectures [43,45].

In this paper, we show how Interactive Markov Chains (IMC) [19] and their implementation in the CADP verification toolbox [17] can be applied to the performance analysis of shared-memory mutual exclusion protocols. We assume

S. Kowalewski and M. Roveri (Eds.): FMICS 2010, LNCS 6371, pp. 180–197, 2010.

that only the mean values of actual durations are known, which can be modeled conveniently using exponentially distributed durations in the IMC setting. If more concrete duration information is available, this can be encoded using IMCs by means of phase-type distributions [21], which can be employed as precise approximations of arbitrary (discrete or continuous) probability distributions.

As high-level specification language for IMCs, we use LOTOS NT [6,18], a process-algebraic language with imperative flavor accepted as input by CADP. We study the stochastic behavior of these protocols in the long run by further transforming the IMCs generated from LOTOS NT specifications into continuous-time Markov chains (in which nondeterminism is solved by a uniform scheduler) and analyzing them using the BCG_STEADY [20] tool of CADP, which computes the throughputs of various actions at steady-state. This allows to compare the performance of various protocols and to study the impact of certain parameters (e.g., relative speed of processes, fraction of time taken by critical sections, etc.) on the performance of the system and/or of individual processes. Another useful measure that can be obtained from steady-state analysis is the mean number of accesses to shared variables performed by each process [7]. For cache-coherent, distributed shared memory architectures, this enables to enhance the locality of a mutual exclusion protocol by making each shared variable local to the process that accesses it most often.

One advantage of IMCs is that the *same* specification of a protocol can be used for both performance evaluation and functional verification [15]. Although mutual exclusion protocols serve traditionally as basic examples to illustrate the use of model checkers, it is not obvious to find an accurate description of their correctness properties in the action-based setting. We revisit these properties and specify them concisely using MCL [32], an extension of alternation-free modal μ-calculus with data-handling constructs and fairness operators accepted as input by the EVALUATOR 4.0 on-the-fly model checker. We observe that certain important properties are of linear-time nature, requiring formulas of $L\mu_2$ (the μ-calculus of alternation depth two) [12] or ACTL* [34]. Using MCL formulas parameterized by data values, we apply model checking also to determine some non-functional parameters of the protocols, such as the degree of overtaking between processes. The results of model checking (e.g., about the starvation of certain processes) are corroborated by the results of performance evaluation.

The paper is organized as follows. Section 2 defines the terminology, shows the encoding of mutual exclusion protocols using LOTOS NT and how the stochastic aspects are incorporated to yield IMC models. Section 3 presents the analysis of the protocols by means of model checking and performance evaluation. Finally, Section 4 gives some concluding remarks and directions for future work.

2   Background

After recalling the mutual exclusion problem in the shared-memory setting, we present in this section the modeling of the behavioral and stochastic aspects of mutual exclusion protocols using LOTOS NT.

2.1   Shared-Memory Mutual Exclusion Protocols

We briefly present here the mutual exclusion problem in the shared-memory setting as formulated in [2]. Concurrent processes communicate and synchronize only by means of atomic read/write operations on shared variables. Each process consists of four parts of code, executed cyclically in the following order: non-critical section, entry section, critical section, and exit section. The shared resource can be accessed only in the critical section, and the shared variables can be accessed only in the entry and exit sections. Processes are allowed to stop in their non-critical section but must leave their critical section in a finite amount of time. The entry and exit sections must manipulate the shared variables in such a way that at most one process at a time is in its critical section and the execution of processes is guaranteed to progress (see Sec. 3.1 for a more precise formulation of these properties). For simplicity, we consider in this study shared-memory protocols involving only two processes; as pointed out in [3], any mutual exclusion protocol for two processes can be generalized to $n \geq 2$ processes.

2.2   Modeling Mutual Exclusion Protocols Using LOTOS NT

We specified the mutual exclusion protocols formally using LOTOS NT [6,18], a variant of the E-LOTOS [23] standard implemented within CADP. LOTOS NT tries to combine the best of process-algebraic languages and imperative programming languages: a user-friendly syntax, common to data types and processes; constructed type definitions and pattern-matching; and imperative statements (assignments, conditionals, loops, etc.). LOTOS NT is supported by the LNT.OPEN tool, which translates LOTOS NT specifications into labeled transition systems (LTSs) suitable for on-the-fly verification using CADP.

Figure 1 shows the LOTOS NT specification of the protocol proposed by Burns & Lynch [5], instantiated for two processes. This protocol uses two shared bits, which we represent as the cells $A[0]$ and $A[1]$ of a two-bit array, in the same way as [3]. The original pseudo-code of the protocol (see Fig. 1(a)) contains conditional jump statements, which are translated in LOTOS NT using "**break**" statements (see Fig. 1(b)). The non-critical and critical sections are modeled using the (non-synchronized) actions NCS and CS. The read/write operations on a shared variables are modeled as rendezvous synchronizations on gate A with a process Var, which models a cell of the two-bit array (see Fig. 1(d)). Note that process Var is parameterized by a natural number instead of merely a boolean value; this will allow Var to be reused also for other protocols involving shared natural numbers.

As in LOTOS, emission and reception of values on a gate can take place simultaneously, as in the action "A (Read, 0, $?a_0$, j)" (where the values Read, 0, and j are emitted and a value is received in variable a_0), except that the variables holding the received values must be previously declared using a "**var**" statement. Unlike LOTOS, gates are typed in LOTOS NT: in process P, the types Pid, Access, and Operation denote the communication profiles (i.e., number and types of the exchanged values) of gates NCS, CS, and A, respectively. To facilitate the

```
loop
    non-critical section;
L0: A[j] := 0;
    if j = 1 and A[0] = 1 then
       goto L0
    end if;
    A[j] := 1;
    if j = 1 and A[0] = 1 then
       goto L0
    end if;
L1: if j = 0 and A[1] = 1 then
       goto L1
    end if;
    critical section;
    A[j] := 0
end loop                              (a)
```

```
process P [NCS:Pid, CS:Access,
           A:Operation] (j:Nat) is
   loop var a0, a1:Nat in
    NCS (j);
    loop L in
      A (Write, j, 0, j);
      A (Read, 0, ?a0, j);
      if j == 0 or a0 == 0 then
        A (Write, j, 1, j);
        A (Read, 0, ?a0, j);
        if j == 0 or a0 == 0 then
          break L
        end if
      end if
    end loop;
    A (Read, 1, ?a1, j);
    while j == 0 and a1 == 1 loop
      A (Read, 1, ?a1, j)
    end loop;
    CS (Enter, j); CS (Leave, j);
    A (Write, j, 0, j)
   end var end loop
end process                           (b)
```

```
par A, CS, NCS in
  par A in
    par
      P [NCS, CS, A] (0)
      ||
      P [NCS, CS, A] (1)
    end par
    ||
    par
      Var [A] (0,0) || Var [A] (1,0)
    end par
  end par
  ||
  L [A, CS, NCS, MU]
end par                               (c)
```

```
process Var [A:Operation] (ind, val:Nat) is
   loop
     select
       A (Read, ind, val, ?any Nat)
       []
       A (Write, ind, ?val, ?any Nat)
     end select
   end loop
end process                           (d)
```

```
process L [A:Operation, CS:Access, NCS:Pid, MU:Latency] is
   loop var ind, pid:Nat in select
     A (Read, ?ind, ?any Nat, ?pid); MU (Read, ind, pid)
     []
     A (Write, ?ind, ?any Nat, ?pid); MU (Write, ind, pid)
     [] ...
     CS (Enter, ?pid); MU (Enter, pid)
     []
     NCS (?pid); MU (Work, pid)
   end select end var end loop
end process                                                   (e)
```

Fig. 1. Burns & Lynch protocol [5] for two processes: (a) Unstructured pseudo-code of process P_j ($j \in \{0,1\}$); (b) LOTOS NT code of process P_j; (c) LOTOS NT code of the systems' architecture; (d) LOTOS NT code of the cell $A[ind]$ of the shared array; (e) LOTOS NT code of the auxiliary process L for inserting Markov delays.

specification of temporal properties (see Sec. 3.1), the critical section is split in two actions and each read/write operation carries the identifier of the underlying process. The LOTOS NT specification of process P_j follows very closely the pseudo-code of the protocol, but makes explicit all read operations on shared variables before each evaluation of an expression containing these variables. The architecture of the system (see Fig. 1(c)) shows the interconnection of processes and shared variables. For all protocols considered, all shared variables are initialized to 0. The additional process L (see Fig. 1(d)) serves to insert Markov delays at appropriate places in the model (see Sec. 2.3).

We specified 23 mutual exclusion protocols in LOTOS NT following the scheme shown in Figure 1: Burns & Lynch [5], Craig and Landin & Hagersten (CLH) [8,28], Dekker [11], Dijkstra [10], Peterson [35], Knuth [26], Lamport [27], Kessels [25], Mellor-Crummey & Scott (MCS) [33], Szymanski [40], the black-white bakery protocol of [41], and twelve protocols generated automatically in [3]. Additionally, we also specified a trivial (incorrect) one-bit protocol for benchmarking purposes. The total size of the specifications (including comments, and after factoring common datatypes and processes in separate modules as much as possible) is about 2850 lines of LOTOS NT.

2.3   Transformation to Interactive Markov Chains

The LOTOS NT specification of each protocol is transformed into an Interactive Markov Chain (IMC) by adding Markov delays in a constraint-oriented style [15]. Precisely, we add a concurrent process L to the system consisting of the two processes and the shared variables. A skeleton of process L is shown in Figure 1(e).

Because process L is synchronized on all actions A, CS, and NCS, L enforces that each of these actions is followed by a MU action, which can be renamed into a stochastic transition once the LTS corresponding to the LOTOS NT specification has been generated. The parameters of action MU allow to distinguish, for each process, between a read access, a write access, a stay in the critical section, and a stay in the non-critical section. We exploit these parameters to experiment with different rates for all of these actions.

Unfortunately, although each process taken separately is deterministic and never blocks (but rather enters a busy-wait loop), the obtained IMCs contain nondeterministic choices whenever two concurrent read/write accesses to shared variables are possible in the same state. To resolve this nondeterminism, we assume the presence of a uniform scheduler, which chooses equiprobably one of the two actions (see Sec. 3.2 for details). This assumption is based on the fact that an uniform scheduler provides the best choice (in the sense of maximising entropy [38]) when no additional information is available about the choice of actions performed by the physical system. A more general solution, inspired by a technique used in the context of Markov decision processes [36], would be to consider all possible schedulers to identify the interval (minimum and maximum) of possible throughput values at steady state (an effective procedure for this analysis in the IMC setting was proposed very recently [44], but is not yet available as an implementation).

3   Analysis of Mutual Exclusion Protocols Using CADP

This section is devoted to the automated analysis of the mutual exclusion protocols using the CADP toolbox [17]. The protocols were analyzed by model checking and performance evaluation, both kinds of analysis being automated using SVL [16] scripts.

3.1   Model Checking

We expressed the correctness properties of the mutual exclusion protocols as formulas in the MCL language [32], which extends the alternation-free μ-calculus [12] with regular expressions over transition sequences similar to those of PDL [13], data-handling constructs inspired from functional programming languages, and a (generalization of) the infinite looping operator of PDL-Δ [39]. MCL allows a concise formulation of temporal properties, especially when these properties are parameterized by data values, such as the index of processes in mutual exclusion protocols. The EVALUATOR 4.0 model checker [32], built using the OPEN/CÆSAR [14] graph exploration environment of CADP, implements an efficient on-the-fly model checking procedure for MCL, by translating MCL formulas into boolean equation systems and solving them on-the-fly using the algorithms of the CÆSAR_SOLVE library [31]. The model checker also exhibits full diagnostics (examples and counterexamples) as subgraphs of the LTS illustrating the truth value of MCL formulas.

MCL is roughly built from three kinds of formulas. First, *action formulas* A characterize actions (transition labels) of the LTS, which contain a gate name G followed by a list of values $v_1, ..., v_n$ exchanged during the rendezvous on G. An action formula is built from action patterns and the usual boolean connectors. An action pattern of the form "$\{G ?x:T !e$ where $b(x)\}$" matches every action of the form "$G v_1 v_2$" where v_1 is a value of type T that is assigned to variable x, v_2 is the value obtained by evaluating the expression e, and the boolean expression $b(v_1)$ evaluates to true. Arbitrary combinations of value matchings ("$!e$") and value extractions ("$?x:T$") are allowed, all variables assigned by value extraction being exported to the enclosing formula. Second, *regular formulas* R characterize sequences of transitions in the LTS. A regular formula is built from action formulas and (extended) regular expression operators: concatenation ("$R_1.R_2$"), choice ("$R_1|R_2$"), unbounded iterations ("R^*" and "R^+"), and iterations bounded by counters ("$R\{n\}$"). Third, *state formulas* F characterize states of the LTS by specifying (finite or infinite) tree-like patterns going out from these states. A state formula is built from boolean connectors, possibility ("$<R>F$") and necessity ("$[R]F$") modalities containing regular formulas, minimal ("mu $X.F$") and maximal ("nu $X.F$") fixed point operators, quantifiers over finite domains ("exists $x:T.F$" and "forall $x:T.F$"), and the infinite looping operator ("$<R>@$"). An informal explanation of the semantics of MCL state formulas will be given by means of the examples below.

Mutual exclusion. This essential safety property of mutual exclusion protocols states that two processes can never execute simultaneously their critical section code. It can be expressed in MCL by a single box modality containing a regular formula that characterizes the undesirable sequences:

```
[ true* . { CS !"ENTER" ?j:Nat } . (not { CS !"LEAVE" !j })* .
  { CS !"ENTER" ?k:Nat where k <> j }
] false
```

This modality forbids the existence of sequences containing the entry of a process j in the critical section followed by the entry of another process $k \neq j$ in the critical section before process j has left its critical section. Note how the process index j is extracted from a transition label by the first action predicate "{ CS !"ENTER" ?j:Nat }" and is used subsequently in the formula.

Livelock freedom. This liveness property[1] states that each time a process is in its entry section, then *some* process will eventually execute its critical section. A direct formulation of this property in MCL yields the formula below:

```
[ true* . { NCS ?j:Nat } . (not { ?any ?"READ"|"WRITE" ... !j })* .
  { ?any ?"READ"|"WRITE" ... !j }
] mu X . (< true > true and [ not { CS !"ENTER" ?any } ] X)
```

The minimal fixed point formula binding the X variable expresses the inevitable execution of some critical section after process P_j executed the first read or write operation of its entry section. However, this formula is violated by all the protocols considered, because each time some process decides to stop its execution (an unrealistic hypothesis if we assume a fair scheduling of processes by the underlying operating system) the other process can spin forever on reading shared variables. Figure 2(b) illustrates the counterexample of this formula exhibited by EVALUATOR 4.0 for Peterson's protocol. This protocol uses three shared variables, two of which being encoded as array cells $A[0], A[1]$ and the third one by a separate variable B. The lasso-shaped diagnostic in Figure 2(b) shows that after process P_1 has executed its entry section and is ready to enter the critical section (because variable B has value 0) but does not do so, process P_0 may spin forever in the while loop of its entry section.

In fact, a livelock situation occurs when both processes are executing cyclically at least one operation but none of them is able to progress towards its critical section. Therefore, an accurate formulation of livelock freedom in MCL must forbid the existence of such cycles:

```
[ true* . { NCS ?j:Nat } . (not { ?any ?"READ"|"WRITE" ... !j })* .
  { ?any ?"READ"|"WRITE" ... !j }
] not < (not { CS ... })* . { ?G:String ... ?k:Nat where G <> "CS" } .
        (not { CS ... })* . { ?G:String ... !1 - k where G <> "CS" }
      > @
```

---

[1] Although some authors [3] use the term *deadlock* for this property, we prefer the term *livelock* used in [2]. Indeed, in the shared-memory setting involving only atomic read and write operations, the behavior of the system cannot contain deadlocks (i.e., sink states in the LTS), since each process can at any time execute some instruction.

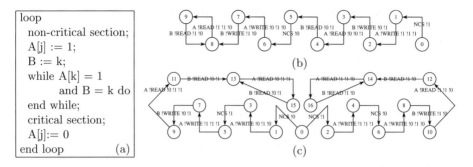

loop
non-critical section;
A[j] := 1;
B := k;
while A[k] = 1
and B = k do
end while;
critical section;
A[j]:= 0
end loop   (a)

Fig. 2. (a) Peterson's protocol for process P_j ($k = 1 - j$); (b) Livelock produced by spinning of process P_0 when process P_1 "has decided to stop"; (c) Livelocks produced after P_0 or P_1 crashed while executing their entry sections.

The < ... > @ operator, which is the MCL counterpart of the infinite looping operator of PDL-Δ, expresses the existence of an infinite sequence consisting of the concatenation of subsequences satisfying a regular formula. Note that the formula above, when translated to plain modal μ-calculus, belongs to the fragment $L\mu_2$ of alternation depth two [12], because the regular formula inside the infinite looping operator (which denotes a maximal fixed point) contains star operators (which denote minimal fixed points). Nevertheless, this formula is evaluated in linear-time by the algorithm proposed in [32], which generalizes the detection of accepting cycles in Büchi automata.

We can also observe that (a state-based version of) this formula cannot be specified in LTL [30], because it expresses the existence of sequences (denoted by the < ... > @ operator) starting from various states of the LTS (the states at the end of the subsequences captured by the [...] modality) and not only from the initial state of the LTS. However, as it was pointed out in [3], livelock freedom can be expressed just by forbidding the existence of unfair cycles (assuming that the initial state of the LTS can be reached from any other state, which holds for all protocols considered here). Therefore, the box modality can be dropped and the resulting formula can be expressed in LTL.

Starvation freedom. The absence of livelocks guarantees the global progress of the system, but does not ensure the access of individual processes to their critical sections. Starvation freedom is a stronger property (it implies livelock freedom), which states that each time a process is in its entry section, then *that* process will eventually execute its critical section. It can be expressed in MCL as follows:

```
[ true* . { NCS ?j:Nat } . (not { ?any ?"READ"|"WRITE" ... !j })* .
  { ?any ?"READ"|"WRITE" ... !j }
] not < (not { CS ... !j })* . { ?G:String ... ?k:Nat where G <> "CS" or k <> j } .
        (not { CS ... !j })* . { ?G:String ... !1-k where G <> "CS" or 1-k <> j }
     > @
```

The < ... > @ operator describes a cycle containing at least one action performed by each process, but no entry of process P_j in its critical section. The formula belongs to $L\mu_2$, but (a state-based version of) it can also be expressed in LTL in the same way as livelock freedom.

Bounded overtaking. Even if a mutual exclusion protocol is starvation-free, it is interesting to know, when a process P_j begins its entry section, how many times the other process P_k can access its critical section before P_j enters its own critical section. This information can be determined using EVALUATOR 4.0 by checking the following MCL formula for increasing values of max:

```
< true* . { NCS !0 } . (not { ?any ?"READ"|"WRITE" ... !0 })* .
  { ?any ?"READ"|"WRITE" ... !0 } .
  ( (not { CS ?any !0 })* . { ?G:String ... !0 where G <> "CS" } .
    (not { CS ?any !0 })* . { CS !"ENTER" !1 }
  ) { max }
> true
```

This formula expresses the existence of a sequence in which process P_0 executes its non-critical section, then the first instruction of its entry section, followed by max repetitions of a subsequence in which P_0 executes some instruction but only P_1 enters its critical section (a symmetric formula must be checked to determine the overtaking of process P_1 by P_0). For each starvation-free protocol, there exists a value of max such that the formula above holds for max and fails for $max + 1$. To minimize the number of model checking invocations, one can start with $max = 1$ and (if the formula holds for this value) keep doubling it until finding the first value max' for which the formula fails, then use a dichotomic search to reduce the size of the interval $[1, max']$ to 1.

Independent progress. A requirement formulated explicitly by Dijkstra [10] was that if a process stops (i.e., loops forever) in its *non* critical section, this must not affect the access of the other processes to their critical sections. In subsequent works, this requirement is not mentioned as a property of mutual exclusion protocols, but is often stated aside in the definition of the framework [5,2]. However, we believe that this requirement is fundamental (at least from a model checking point of view), and should be verified separately. In MCL, it can be expressed using the following formula:

```
forall j:Nat among { 0 ... 1 } .
  [ true* ] (< { NCS !1-j } > true implies < { ... !j }* . { CS ... !j } > @)
```

which states that whenever the process P_k (where $k = 1 - j$) is about to enter its non-critical section, then the other process P_j can freely execute its code. Note that this formula belongs to $L\mu_2$ and can be also expressed in ACTL* but not in LTL, because it states the existence of infinite sequences starting from several (unknown) states of the LTS. As regards expressiveness, MCL lies between the $L\mu_1$ and $L\mu_2$ fragments of the modal μ-calculus, and is strictly more expressive than LTL, whose model checking problem can be translated into the evaluation of a single < ... > @ operator that encodes the underlying Büchi automaton.

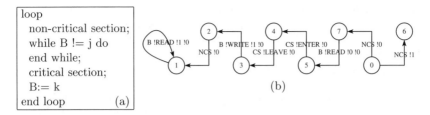

Fig. 3. (a) Trivial one-bit protocol for process P_j ($k = 1 - j$); (b) Counterexample for the independent progress of P_0 when P_1 has stopped in its non-critical section

To see that the property of independent progress is not implied by the three other properties of mutual exclusion protocols, consider the trivial one-bit protocol shown in Figure 3(a). This simple protocol satisfies mutual exclusion and starvation freedom, but does not satisfy independent progress because it forces a strict alternation between the accesses of the two processes to their critical sections. The evaluation of the formula above on the LTS of the trivial protocol using EVALUATOR 4.0 yields the counterexample shown in Figure 3(b), in which process P_0 executes its main loop once but then spins forever in its entry section because P_1 has stopped in its non-critical section. The trivial protocol should be considered an unacceptable solution to the mutual exclusion problem, since it was proven in [5] (where independent progress is part of the framework definition) that any livelock-free mutual exclusion protocol must use at least *two* shared bits.

Finally, we can remark that the independent progress property cannot be made stronger without destroying the livelock or starvation freedom of the protocols: if a process is allowed to stop (e.g., by crashing) outside its non-critical section, then the other process may spin forever without entering its critical section. For all protocols considered here, we checked that this indeed holds; Figure 2(c) shows the diagnostic produced by EVALUATOR 4.0 illustrating, for Peterson's protocol, the livelock of each process when the other one has crashed after executing the first instruction of its entry section.

Model checking results. Table 1 summarizes the model checking results for the protocols considered. The generation of the IMCs for all protocols takes about 1 minute and a half on a standard desktop computer. Because the IMCs are small, the execution of the SVL script (48 lines) implementing the model checking of all properties on all protocols takes about 10 minutes. All properties have been checked on-the-fly using LNT.OPEN and EVALUATOR 4.0.

All the protocols considered satisfy the mutual exclusion, livelock freedom, and (except the trivial) the independent progress properties stated above. As regards the overtaking of processes, all starvation-free protocols (except Szymanski's) are symmetric, the minimal (1) and maximal (4) amount of overtaking being reached by Knuth's and by Dekker's protocol, respectively. The unbounded overtaking of one process by the other one has been checked by

Table 1. Model checking results: the first column gives the name of the protocol; the second column gives the number of shared variables; the third and fourth columns give the size of the IMC; the fifth column indicates whether the protocol is only livelock- (L) or livelock- and starvation-free (S); the last two columns give the maximal number of times process P_j can overtake process P_k in accessing the critical section (P_j/P_k).

Protocol (2 processes)	Number of variables	IMC size		L/S-free	Overtaking	
		states	transitions		P_0/P_1	P_1/P_0
trivial	1	89	130	S	1	1
Burns & Lynch		259	368	L	∞	3
Szymanski		547	803	S	2	1
2b_p1	2	259	369	L	∞	1
2b_p2		271	386	L	∞	1
2b_p3		277	392	L	1	∞
Dekker		599	856	S	4	4
Knuth		917	1312	S	1	1
3b_p1		486	690	S	3	3
3b_p2	3	627	879	L	∞	1
Peterson		407	580	S	2	2
3b_c_p1		627	884	S	2	2
3b_c_p2		407	580	S	2	2
3b_c_p3		363	516	S	2	2
Lamport		1599	2274	L	∞	∞
Kessels		1073	1502	S	2	2
CLH		690	936	S	2	2
4b_p1	4	432	610	L	∞	1
4b_p2		871	1229	S	3	3
4b_c_p1		1106	1542	L	∞	1
4b_c_p2		1106	1542	L	1	∞
Dijkstra	5	899	1260	L	∞	∞
Mcs		424	612	S	2	2
B&W Bakery	7	31222	43196	S	2	2

replacing, in the bounded overtaking formula given above, the bounded iteration operator $R\{max\}$ by an infinite looping operator <...>@. All livelock-free, but not starvation-free protocols (except Dijkstra's and Lamport's) are asymmetric w.r.t. overtaking, only one process being able to overtake the other one unboundedly.

3.2 Performance Evaluation

To measure the performance of a mutual exclusion protocol, we compute the throughput of the critical section, i.e., the steady state probability of being in the critical section. All delays being equal, the higher the throughput, the more efficient the protocol, because the longer a process is in the critical section, the less time it spends executing the protocol or waiting to enter the critical section.

Performance evaluation of an IMC is based on the transformation of the IMC into a Continuous-Time Markov Chain (CTMC) extended with probabilistic choices. A first step is to transform the IMC into a stochastic LTS by renaming all actions: (1) each action not representing a delay is hidden, i.e., renamed into the invisible action (written i in LOTOS NT and CADP), and (2) each MU action is transformed into an exponential delay by associating a rate λ to it, i.e., renaming it into "rate λ". Using exponential delays reflects that we make hypotheses only about the *relations* between the mean values of the actual durations, because our model-based performance evaluation does assume neither a particular application nor a particular hardware architecture.

In all our experiments, we kept the rates for accesses to the shared variables constant: each read access has rate 3000 and each write access has rate 2000, reflecting that, on average, a write access is generally slower than a read access. For complex operations, namely *fetch-and-store* (used by the protocols CLH and MCS) and *compare-and-swap* (used by MCS), we used the same rate as for a write access. We also kept the rate for the critical section constant at 100, i.e., making the assumption that the critical section contains (on average) several read and write accesses. Hence, we varied only the delay for the non-critical section of both processes to compare the protocols in different usage scenarios.

In a second step, the stochastic LTS is minimized for stochastic branching bisimulation [22]. Unfortunately, this does not yield a CTMC, because due to the nondeterminism only some, but not all, of the i actions are eliminated. As discussed in Section 2.3, this nondeterminism is resolved by assuming an uniform scheduler. Practically, each nondeterministic choice is replaced by a uniform probabilistic choice, by renaming all i transitions into "prob 0.5".

Finally, we compute the throughput of the entries into the critical sections by both processes in the steady state using the BCG_STEADY tool [20], which is able to handle CTMCs extended with probabilistic choices. The results of our experiments are shown in Figures 4 to 6. Because these figures depend on the arbitraily chosen rates, the concrete values are, although exact up to floating point errors, less interesting than the relations and tendencies.

The performance evaluation experiments are automated by an SVL script (160 lines); computing all shown performance measures requires less than ten minutes on a standard computer.

Figure 4 shows the effect of varying the ratio "critical-section-rate / non-critical-section-rate". Concerning the global throughput, the results should not be surprising. A first observation is that the longer the non-critical section with respect to the critical section (and the accesses to the shared variables), the less the performance of the protocols differs. Conversely, the largest performance differences of the protocols are observed if the critical section is longer than the non-critical section. A second observation is that the complexity of the protocol (number of shared variables and length of entry and exit sections) impacts its performance: the most complex protocol (B&W Bakery) is the least efficient, whereas the trivial one-bit protocol is the most efficient, the second most efficient being CLH, followed by Peterson's protocol.

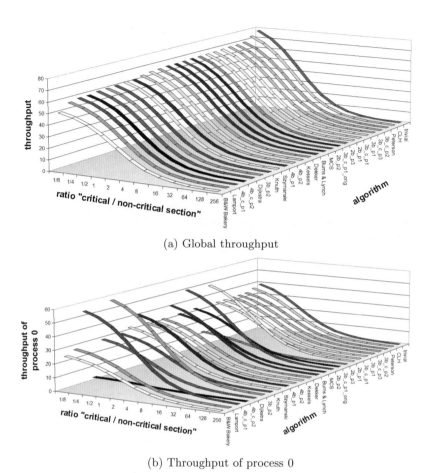

(a) Global throughput

(b) Throughput of process 0

Fig. 4. Performance when varying the ratio critial-section-rate/non-critical-section-rate

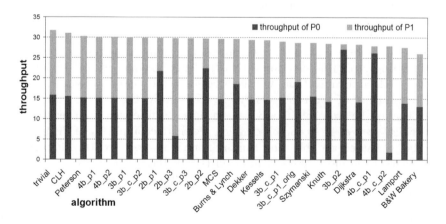

Fig. 5. Relative throughputs (ratio rate critical section/rate non-critical section = 2)

Concerning the throughput of process 0, the values are wider spread than for the global throughput. This difference is related to the symmetry concerning bounded overtaking of the protocols. For symmetric protocols, where the processes can overtake each other the same number of times, the throughput of process 0 is half the global throughput. For asymmetric protocols, the throughput of process 0 is either higher (if process 0 can overtake process 1 more often) or lower (if process 1 can overtake process 0 more often) than half the global throughput. Thus, the highest throughput for process 0 is obtained by some automatically generated asymmetric protocols (3b_p2 and 4b_c_p1).

Figure 5 shows the throughputs of all protocols, using 50 for the rate of the non-critical section (thus, the non-critical section is, on average, two times as long as the critical section). One observes significant differences in the throughputs of the two processes if and only if the protocol is asymmetric; for these protocols, the qualitative and quantitative properties are related in the sense that the process that can overtake the other has a significantly higher throughput.

We also observed that making a protocol symmetric might (slightly) improve its performance. For instance, the original version of the automatically generated protocol 3b_c_p1 as described in [3] is asymmetric: with the same rates as in Figure 5, the throughput of process 0 (14.7499) is lower than the throughput of process 1 (15.0387). However, the symmetric version (that was used throughout this paper) has a higher global throughput of 29.8854 (instead of 29.7886, i.e., an increase of 0.3%, to be compared with the 20% performance improvement between the least and most efficient protocol).

The three plots of Figure 6 show the effect of varying the ratio between the non-critical section rates of the two processes. In all three plots, for ratio 1, the rate of the non-critical section is 50 for both processes; towards the left, process 0 is slowed down (by decreasing the rate of the non-critical section of process 0); towards the right, process 1 is slowed down (by decreasing the rate of the non-critical section of process 1).

Figure 6(a) graphically justifies the name "symmetric" protocols: they are symmetric in the sense that slowing down process 0 has exactly the same effect on the global throughput as slowing down process 1: in both cases the general throughput decreases in the same way. Figure 6(b) shows that the situation is different for asymmetric protocols: slowing down the advantaged process that can overtake the other one reduces the general throughput more than slowing down the disadvantaged process that can be overtaken. This seems intuitive, because slowing down the advantaged process, slows down both processes, whereas slowing down the disadvantaged process should not impact too much the advantaged process. Figure 6(c) confirms this intuition. On the one hand, for all those asymmetric protocols where process 0 can overtake process 1 infinitely, slowing down process 1 has less impact on the throughput of process 0 than slowing down process 0. On the other hand, for the two protocols 2b_p3 and 4b_c_p2, where process 0 can be overtaken infinitely by process 1, slowing down process 1 has more impact on the throughput of process 0 than slowing down process 0.

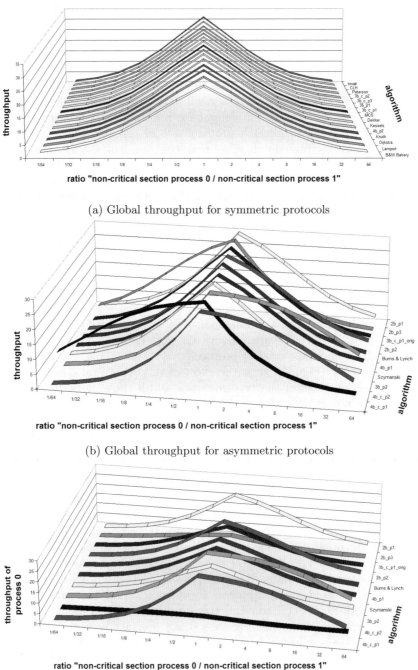

(a) Global throughput for symmetric protocols

(b) Global throughput for asymmetric protocols

(c) Throughput of process 0 for asymmetric protocols

Fig. 6. Performance when varying the ratio ncs-rate-p_0/ncs-rate-p_1

4   Conclusion and Future Work

This study aimed at assessing the applicability of model-based approaches for analyzing the functional behavior and the performance of shared-memory mutual exclusion protocols. As underlying semantic model, we used IMCs [19], which provide a uniform framework suitable both for model checking and performance evaluation. We carried out the analysis of 23 protocols using the state-of-the-art functionalities provided by the CADP toolbox [17]: formal specification using the LOTOS NT imperative-style process-algebraic language; description of functional properties using the MCL data-based temporal language; manipulation of IMCs by minimization and steady-state analysis using the BCG_MIN and BCG_STEADY tools; automation of the analysis procedures using SVL scripts.

We attempted to formulate the correctness properties of mutual exclusion protocols accurately and observed that several of them (livelock and starvation freedom, independent progress, unbounded overtaking) belong to $L\mu_2$, the μ-calculus fragment of alternation depth two; however, they can still be expressed using the infinite looping operator of PDL-Δ [39], which can be checked in linear-time [32]. Performance evaluation made it possible to compare the protocols according to their efficiency (global and individual throughput of processes) and to study the effect of varying several parameters (relative speeds of processes, ratio between the time spent in critical and non-critical sections, etc.). We observed that symmetric protocols are more robust concerning the difference in execution speed between processes, which confirms the importance of the symmetry requirement originally formulated by Dijkstra [10]. The quantitative results were corroborated by those of functional verification, in particular the presence of (asymmetric) starvation of processes, detected using temporal formulas, was clearly reflected in the steady-state behavior of the corresponding protocols.

An interesting future work direction is to continue the performance evaluation study for *adaptive* mutual exclusion protocols involving $n > 2$ processes, which so far were subject only to analytical studies [1]. Another direction would be a more detailed modeling of the underlying hardware architecture, in particular non-uniform memory access times. For instance, knowing which process accesses a variable most frequently might guide the placement of that variable to the local memory of the appropriate processor in the architecture.

References

1. Anderson, J.H., Kim, Y.-J.: Adaptive mutual exclusion with local spinning. In: Herlihy, M.P. (ed.) DISC 2000. LNCS, vol. 1914, pp. 29–43. Springer, Heidelberg (2000)
2. Anderson, J.H., Kim, Y.-J., Herman, T.: Shared-memory mutual exclusion: major research trends since 1986. Distributed Computing 16, 75–110 (2003)
3. Bar-David, Y., Taubenfeld, G.: Automatic discovery of mutual exclusion algorithms. In: Fich, F.E. (ed.) DISC 2003. LNCS, vol. 2848, pp. 136–150. Springer, Heidelberg (2003)
4. Botincan, M.: AsmL specification and verification of Lamport's bakery algorithm. J. of Computing and Information Technology 13(4), 313–319 (2005)

5. Burns, J.E., Lynch, N.A.: Mutual exclusion using indivisible reads and writes. In: Proc. of ACCCC'80, pp. 833–842 (1980)
6. Champelovier, D., Clerc, X., Garavel, H., Guerte, Y., Lang, F., Serwe, W., Smeding, G.: Reference manual of the Lotos NT to Lotos translator (Version 5.0). INRIA/VASY, 107 pages (March 2010)
7. Chehaibar, G., Zidouni, M., Mateescu, R.: Modeling multiprocessor cache protocol impact on MPI performance. In: Proc. of QuEST'09. IEEE Press, Los Alamitos (2009)
8. Craig, T.S.: Building FIFO and priority-queuing spin locks from atomic swap. Technical Report 93-02-02, University of Washington, Seattle (February 1993)
9. Delzanno, G., Podelski, A.: Model checking in CLP. In: Cleaveland, W.R. (ed.) TACAS 1999. LNCS, vol. 1579, pp. 223–239. Springer, Heidelberg (1999)
10. Dijkstra, E.W.: Solution of a problem in concurrent programming control. ACM Commun. 8(9), 569–570 (1965)
11. Dijkstra, E.W.: Co-operating sequential processes, pp. 43–112. Academic Press, New York (1968)
12. Emerson, E.A., Lei, C.-L.: Efficient model checking in fragments of the propositional mu-calculus. In: Proc. of LICS'86, pp. 267–278 (1986)
13. Fischer, M.J., Ladner, R.E.: Propositional dynamic logic of regular programs. J. Comput. Syst. Sci. 18(2), 194–211 (1979)
14. Garavel, H.: Open/Cæsar: an open software architecture for verification, simulation, and testing. In: Steffen, B. (ed.) TACAS 1998. LNCS, vol. 1384, pp. 68–84. Springer, Heidelberg (1998)
15. Garavel, H., Hermanns, H.: On combining functional verification and performance evaluation using CADP. In: Eriksson, L.-H., Lindsay, P.A. (eds.) FME 2002. LNCS, vol. 2391, pp. 410–429. Springer, Heidelberg (2002)
16. Garavel, H., Lang, F.: SVL: a scripting language for compositional verification. In: Proc. of FORTE'01, pp. 377–392 (2001)
17. Garavel, H., Lang, F., Mateescu, R., Serwe, W.: CADP 2006: a toolbox for the construction and analysis of distributed processes. In: Damm, W., Hermanns, H. (eds.) CAV 2007. LNCS, vol. 4590, pp. 158–163. Springer, Heidelberg (2007)
18. Garavel, H., Sighireanu, M.: Towards a second generation of FDTs – rationale for the design of E-LOTOS. In: Proc. of FMICS'98, pp. 187–230 (1998)
19. Hermanns, H. (ed.): Interactive Markov chains and the quest for quantified quality. LNCS, vol. 2428, p. 57. Springer, Heidelberg (2002)
20. Hermanns, H., Joubert, C.: A set of performance and dependability analysis components for CADP. In: Garavel, H., Hatcliff, J. (eds.) TACAS 2003. LNCS, vol. 2619, pp. 425–430. Springer, Heidelberg (2003)
21. Hermanns, H., Katoen, J.-P.: Performance evaluation:=(process algebra+model checking) Markov chains. In: Larsen, K.G., Nielsen, M. (eds.) CONCUR 2001. LNCS, vol. 2154, pp. 59–81. Springer, Heidelberg (2001)
22. Hermanns, H., Siegle, M.: Bisimulation algorithms for stochastic process algebras and their BDD-based implementation. In: Katoen, J.-P. (ed.) ARTS'99. LNCS, vol. 1601, pp. 244–265. Springer, Heidelberg (1999)
23. ISO/IEC. Enhancements to LOTOS (E-LOTOS). International Standard 15437:2001, International Organization for Standardization, Genève (September 2001)
24. Jensen, H.E., Lynch, N.A.: A proof of Burns N-process mutual exclusion algorithm using abstraction. In: Steffen, B. (ed.) TACAS 1998. LNCS, vol. 1384, pp. 409–423. Springer, Heidelberg (1998)

25. Kessels, J.L.W.: Arbitration without common modifiable variables. Acta Informatica 17, 135–141 (1982)
26. Knuth, D.E.: Additional comments on a problem in concurrent programming control. ACM Commun. 9(5), 321–322 (1966)
27. Lamport, L.: A fast mutual exclusion algorithm. ACM Transactions on Computer Systems 5(1), 1–11 (1987)
28. Magnusson, P.S., Landin, A., Hagersten, E.: Queue locks on cache coherent multiprocessors. In: Proc. of IPPS'94, pp. 165–171 (1994)
29. Manna, Z., Pnueli, A.: Tools and rules for the practicing verifier, pp. 125–159. ACM Press and Addison-Wesley (1991)
30. Manna, Z., Pnueli, A.: The temporal logic of reactive and concurrent systems, vol. I(specification). Springer, Heidelberg (1992)
31. Mateescu, R.: CAESAR_SOLVE: a generic library for on-the-fly resolution of alternation-free boolean equation systems. STTT 8(1), 37–56 (2006)
32. Mateescu, R., Thivolle, D.: A model checking language for concurrent value-passing systems. In: Cuellar, J., Maibaum, T., Sere, K. (eds.) FM 2008. LNCS, vol. 5014, pp. 148–164. Springer, Heidelberg (2008)
33. Mellor-Crummey, J.M., Scott, M.L.: Algorithms for scalable synchronization on shared-memory multiprocessors. ACM Transactions on Computer Systems 9(1), 21–65 (1991)
34. Nicola, R.D., Vaandrager, F.W.: Action versus state based logics for transition systems. LNCS, vol. 469, pp. 407–419. Springer, Heidelberg (1990)
35. Peterson, G.L.: Myths about the mutual exclusion problem. IPL 12(3), 115–116 (1981)
36. Puterman, M.L.: Markov decision processes: discrete stochastic dynamic programming. Wiley, Chichester (1994)
37. Raynal, M.: Algorithmique du parallélisme : le problème de l'exclusion mutuelle. Dunod-Informatique, Paris (1984)
38. Shiryaev, A.: Probability. Springer, Heidelberg (1996)
39. Streett, R.: Propositional dynamic logic of looping and converse. Information and Control (54), 121–141 (1982)
40. Szymanski, B.K.: A simple solution to Lamport's concurrent programming problem with linear wait. In: Proc. of ICSS'88, pp. 621–626 (1988)
41. Taubenfeld, G.: The black-white bakery algorithm and related bounded-space, adaptive, local-spinning and FIFO algorithms. In: Guerraoui, R. (ed.) DISC 2004. LNCS, vol. 3274, pp. 56–70. Springer, Heidelberg (2004)
42. Taubenfeld, G.: Synchronization algorithms and concurrent programming. Pearson, Prentice Hall (2006)
43. Yang, J.-H., Anderson, J.H.: A fast, scalable mutual exclusion algorithm. Distributed Computing 9(1), 51–60 (1995)
44. Zhang, L., Neuhäußer, M.R.: Model checking interactive Markov chains. In: Esparza, J., Majumdar, R. (eds.) TACAS 2010. LNCS, vol. 6015, pp. 53–68. Springer, Heidelberg (2010)
45. Zhang, X., Yan, Y., Castaneda, R.: Evaluating and designing software mutual exclusion algorithms on shared-memory multiprocessors. IEEE Parallel Distributed Technology 4(1), 25–42 (1996)

A Formal Model of Identity Mixer*

Jan Camenisch[2], Sebastian Mödersheim[1], and Dieter Sommer[2]

[1] DTU Informatics, Denmark
samo@imm.dtu.dk
[2] IBM Research – Zurich, Switzerland
{jca,dso}@zurich.ibm.com

Abstract. Identity Mixer is an anonymous credential system developed at IBM that allows users for instance to prove that they are over 18 years old without revealing their name or birthdate. This privacy-friendly technology is realized using zero-knowledge proofs. We describe a formal model of Identity Mixer that is well-suited for automated protocol verification tools in the spirit of black-box cryptography models.

1 Introduction

Due to the spreading use of electronic communication means, users increasingly disperse their personal information widely. Users have lost control over their data, as it is most often not clear who receives and stores which information and how organizations handle this information, particularly to whom they pass it on. This situation is aggravated by the increasing easiness to store, distribute, and profile these data. While on the one hand protecting users' privacy is very important, on the other hand, many transactions require authentication, authorization, and accountability. There is seemingly a partial conflict of goals of properly identifying users while protecting their privacy.

The Identity Mixer system developed by IBM Research – Zurich solves this contradiction by employing particular non-interactive zero-knowledge proofs and suitable signature and encryption schemes. For instance, using Identity Mixer to issue electronic identity credentials, a user is able to prove being at least 18 years old or living in a certain town—without revealing their name or their precise age or any other details. The system's main goal is to provide strong authentication of users and at the same time to protect the users' privacy by minimizing the amount of the users' information being revealed in an interaction.

Identity Mixer is an implementation of the Camenisch-Lysyanskaya anonymous credential system [13], extended by a number additional features aimed at enabling its use in practice. These features were put forth in a number of later publications [9,15]. The cryptography behind Identity Mixer is well understood and the basic system got proved secure [13]. However, the extended system

---

* This work was partially supported by the EU-funded projects AVANTSSAR and PrimeLife (grant agreements 216471 and 216483). The authors enjoyed discussions with Alberto Calvi, Luca Viganò, and Greg Zaverucha. Thank you!

S. Kowalewski and M. Roveri (Eds.): FMICS 2010, LNCS 6371, pp. 198–214, 2010.

as implemented has never been proved secure. Indeed, proving security of the complex and dynamic system resulting from the combination of the many cryptographic building blocks is a challenging task in general. Subtle mistakes in the design can easily lead to vulnerabilities that can be exploited without breaking the cryptography. Such mistakes are often hard to find due to the complicated behavior of distributed systems. Automated verification with model-checking methods based on perfect cryptography models can help here to discover many such mistakes and increase the confidence in systems when the verification is successful, e.g., [4,17]. The goal of this paper is provide a formal model for Identity Mixer, in particular the zero-knowledge proofs it uses, in a way feasible for automated protocol verification tools.

While a lot of verification tools exist for protocol verification, the area of zero-knowledge-proof based system has been started only recently. Backes, Maffei, and Unruh [7] provide a first attempt to integrate this "cryptographic primitive" into the verification tool ProVerif [11]. Their model considers non-interactive zero-knowledge proofs as terms and a set of function symbols representing verification operations that a verifier can apply to a received proof term. Algebraic properties ensure that the term resulting from the operations evaluate to true or false according to whether the zero-knowledge proof term indeed proves the desired statement. While this gives a highly declarative model of the zero-knowledge proofs as an abstract primitive, this is hardly feasible in automated verification tools due to the extensive use of algebraic properties. In fact, even the properties for the boolean combinations induce an undecidable unification problem, and it is no wonder that tools that allow for such properties easily run into infinite loops. As a consequence, Backes et al. [7] uses a very restricted re-encoding of the algebraic theory in ProVerif, and the authors have eventually moved to another approach altogether, namely security types [6]. While this is a valuable complementary approach, the question remains whether we cannot use at all the existing methods and tools of protocol verification that were so successful on closely related tasks.

We show that there is indeed a feasible way to model zero-knowledge proofs in standard black-box protocol verification tools. In a nutshell, the idea to avoid the difficulties that arise when employing algebraic properties to model statements that are proved is to use *pattern matching*. This applies when an honest agent receives a zero-knowledge proof term. Instead of expressing the verification of this proof by verification operations, we show how to transform the desired properties into a pattern that describes the set of zero-knowledge proof terms that the receiver will accept. This can be done by a simple matching (or unification in case of symbolic representations) without any algebraic reasoning.

Contributions. The first contribution of this paper is a model of zero-knowledge proofs that is feasible for automated verification. In fact, the specifications (except for privacy goals, which are not considered in this paper) can directly be run in existing tools without requiring extensions. The second contribution is a formalization of Identity Mixer in this abstract model, both allowing for verification, and also as an overview that abstracts from the underlying cryptography and some implementation details. The long-term vision here is to design a model that can be turned into a correct (though maybe not optimized) implementation by plugging in appropriate cryptographic tools; in fact, a first analysis suggests that this paper provides the initial step to this idea.

Outline. This paper is organized as follows. In section 2, we summarize the standard black-box cryptography models of security protocols. In section 3, we describe our black-box style model of zero-knowledge protocols. In section 4, the main section, we describe our model of Identity Mixer. In section 5 we present a concrete application scenario for Identity Mixer and the results of model checking it with the AVISPA tool. In section 6, we conclude with an overview of experiments, discuss related work, and give an outlook on future work.

2   Preliminaries

Black-Box Cryptography Models. We assume that the reader is familiar with Dolev-Yao style protocol models, see for instance [25]. We will denote deduction rules for the intruder similar to the following one for symmetric encryption:

$$\frac{k \in \mathcal{DY}(M) \quad m \in \mathcal{DY}(M)}{\{\!|m|\!\}_k \in \mathcal{DY}(M)} ,$$

This expresses that an intruder whose knowledge is characterized by a set of messages M, can take any derivable terms k and m, and derive the symmetric encryption $\{\!|m|\!\}_k$. What the intruder can derive, $\mathcal{DY}(M)$, is the least set closed under all considered deduction rules. We will later introduce further function symbols representing several operations in zero-knowledge proofs and similarly give intruder deduction rules for them. We will also make use of the following generalization to simplify the presentation. We consider a set of *public* function symbols Σ_p, containing for instance the above $\{\!| \cdot |\!\}.$, and define the generic rule (subsuming the above example):

$$\frac{t_1 \in \mathcal{DY}(M) \quad \ldots \quad t_n \in \mathcal{DY}(M)}{f(t_1, \ldots, t_n) \in \mathcal{DY}(M)} \ f \in \Sigma_p ,$$

We assume that there can be several intruders that collaborate (which can be regarded as one intruder acting under different dishonest identities). The model includes, for instance, that the machines of an actually honest organization were compromised by the intruder (which may not be immediately obvious) who can now control the organization's machines at his will. We do not consider several intruders that attack each other as (1) the overall goal is to protect and ensure the guarantees of the honest participants and (2) from that perspective the collusion of all dishonest participants is the worst case. We denote with a predicate dishonest(U) that participant U is dishonest.

It is also standard to model a communication medium that is entirely controlled by the intruder (which is again the worst case). Our model is parametrized over different types of channels that can be used, but this is mainly important for privacy properties that we do not consider in this paper.

Honest Agents and Pattern Matching. The behavior of honest agents can be described by various formalisms such as process calculi or set rewriting as in the Intermediate Format of the AVISPA platform [3]. The most common way to describe what messages an agent can receive at a particular point of the protocol execution is a pattern, i.e., a message term with variables. The variables can be substituted for an arbitrary value (possibly with a type restriction). For instance, a message transmission such as

$$A \to B : \{\!| N, \{\!| M |\!\}_{K_{AS}} |\!\}_{K_{AB}} ,$$

where K_{AB} is a shared key of A and B, K_{AS} is the shared key of A and a server S and N and M are some nonces, will have the pattern $\{\!| N, X |\!\}_{K_{AB}}$ on the receiver side for a variable X, because B does not have the shared key and cannot check the format of that part of the message.

3   Modeling Zero Knowledge

3.1   Communication

Many zero-knowledge protocols are concerned with proving authentication and they do in fact not make much sense when assuming insecure channels as it is standard in protocol analysis models. Vice versa, we also cannot assume secure channels as that would assume authentication already. One may rather think of a TLS channel without client authentication or a card in a card reader. For a formal model of such channels see [27].

Identity Mixer, in contrast, can indeed be run over insecure channels: the basic authentication properties (in terms of ownership of certain credentials) should be satisfied. This is because the proof of ownership of a credential is always bound to the knowledge of the user's master secret that even the issuing party does not know. However, when doing that, we immediately loose many of the privacy guarantees, as all actions become observable for an intruder who controls the network. While in the notation of this paper we do not bother about channels, in the formal verification we have considered both the pseudonymous-secure case and the insecure case of communication channels.

3.2   Non-interactive Zero Knowledge Proofs of Knowledge

Zero-knowledge proofs of knowledge [10] are a cryptographic building block that allow a prover to convince a verifier that he "knows" a secret value (witness) S such that $(S, P) \in \mathcal{R}$ holds for some public relation $\mathcal{R} \subseteq \{0, 1\}^* \times \{0, 1\}^*$ and a public value P. Here "knows" is defined by if the prover is able to convince the verifier then he is also able to compute S such that $(S, P) \in \mathcal{R}$. Non-interactive zero-knowledge proofs [12] are a variant where the prover sends the verifier only a single message (the proof) and thus requires no interaction. Informally, zero-knowledge means that the verifier cannot compute any information about S from the proof, P, and $\mathcal{R}$ that he could not have computed from P and $\mathcal{R}$ alone.

In practice, non-interactive zero-knowledge proofs (of knowledge) are often derived from discrete logarithm based proofs protocols (such as the well-known Schnorr protocol [28]) by applying the Fiat-Shamir heuristic. Here, the challenge is computed as (cryptographic) hash of the message sent to the verifier instead of being chosen by the verifier. They are often also called *signature of knowledge* [16] as they can also be seen as a signature scheme: by including the message m to be signed in the input to the hash function used for the Fiat-Shamir heuristic one can conclude that the entity who has constructed the proof has authorized m.

We now consider how such non-interactive zero-knowledge proofs can be integrated into our black-box cryptography model, i.e., we assume that an intruder cannot break the cryptography.

To this end, we model a non-interactive zero-knowledge proof of knowledge for a relation $\mathcal{R}$ and public input P as an abstract message term that has the following crucial properties:

1. One can compose the term (proof) for P and $\mathcal{R}$ only when "knowing" a secret S such that $(S, P) \in \mathcal{R}$.
2. Given the term, P, and $\mathcal{R}$, one can neither obtain the secret S (nor any information about it).
3. The prover can include a statement in the proof that is "signed" by the proof, i.e., the verifier has (transferable) evidence that the person who performed the zero-knowledge proof authorized the statement.
4. The term identifies what exactly is proved about the secret (and some public values).
5. The term "behaves" like any other message term, in particular, when the intruder sees a zero-knowledge proof, he is able to replay or forward that term arbitrarily.

The Properties 1 and 2 model the cryptographic properties of "proof of knowledge" and "zero-knowledge". Property 3 models the signature-scheme nature of the Fiat-Shamir heuristic. Property 4 models that the proof unambiguously identifies the relation $\mathcal{R}$ that is being proved (about the given public P and the secret S). This is crucial for the model of both honest and dishonest verifiers that we will discuss shortly. For Property 5 is models the fact that NIZK in the end are just strings that can be used out of context. We discuss this in more detail below as well.

Black-Box Model. As in the case of other cryptographic primitives, we use an "uninterpreted" function symbol representing the operation of performing a zero-knowledge proof, namely the 4-ary symbol spk (for "signature of knowledge"); this was inspired by the notation of [16]). In the proof term $\mathsf{spk}(S; P; \phi; Stmt)$, S is a list of secret values that the prover knows, P is a list of public values about which something is proved, ϕ is (an identifier of) the relation $\mathcal{R}$ and $Stmt$ is an arbitrary string being signed by the proof.

As an example, let us consider a classical application of zero-knowledge proofs: a user has a secret S (may be considered a private key) and a server knows a corresponding value $f(S)$ for a public function f. The user authenticates itself by proving the knowledge of S without revealing S. This proof is modeled by the term

$$\mathsf{spk}(S; f(S); \phi; Stmt) \ ,$$

where ϕ is an identifier for the relation $\mathcal{R} = \{(S, P) : P = f(S) \wedge S \in \{0, 1\}^*\}$, i.e., the proof proves knowledge of an S that is a pre-image of $P = f(S)$. We discuss below the precise role of this identifier. For now it suffices that every proof that occurs in a system specification has a unique identifier. The $Stmt$ can be an arbitrary message term that is used together with the protocol, however, as we discuss below, it should contain certain items.

Honest Provers and Verifiers. As the next part of our model, we need to define how honest agents deal with spk terms during proving and verifying proofs. As this is basically sending and receiving a message, respectively, let us consider again how this is done in standard black-box models for, e.g., symmetric cryptography. Basically, since honest agents always execute the protocol to the best of their knowledge, the terms that they send and receive reflect the ideal protocol run except for subterms that they cannot control. In particular, receiving is expressed by a pattern that describes the set of acceptable messages, where each variable of the pattern can be replaced by an arbitrary message.

Using pattern matching is in fact one of the key ideas of our formal model of zero-knowledge proofs. In contrast, the previous formal model of Backes et al. [7] uses algebraic properties to express, roughly speaking, that applying an abstract verification operator to a proof reduces to valid iff the proof is valid. This algebraic reasoning makes automated verification difficult, at least for a large variety of analysis methods including those used by OFMC and ProVerif, and we see the main advantage of our model in entirely avoiding the algebraic reasoning by using pattern matching. We note that in the formal modeling of ordinary encryption/decryption we have a similar situation: one may either describe decryption as receipt of terms by an appropriate pattern or instead use algebraic properties stating that decryption and encryption cancel each other out; the latter model is usually more complicated to handle and incompatible with many approaches while all verification tools can easily support pattern matching.

For each zero-knowledge proof we define a *proof pattern*, i.e., an spk term with variables that describes the "correct" proofs that an honest verifier accepts. For the above example of proving the knowledge of a secret S, this pattern can be

$$\mathsf{spk}(\mathcal{X}; f(\mathcal{X}); \phi; Stmt) \ ,$$

where $\mathcal{X}$ is a variable of the pattern that represents a term that the verifier does not see; here, and in the following, we will use the convention to use calligraphic variable names for such secrets.

We thus define the "view" of the verifier, describing which aspects of the message it can observe (and which it cannot). Thus, the verifier's pattern is the crucial part in our model of zero-knowledge proofs. We describe a system based on zero-knowledge proofs in a simple graphical notation close to Alice and Bob

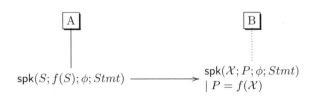

Fig. 1. An example of our notation for zero-knowledge protocols

notation; Figure 1 shows the message sequence chart for the above identification example, making explicit the terms sent and received. In this example, the receiver B initially knows P, and will thus accept only a zero-knowledge proof for knowing a corresponding secret S (i.e., such that $f(S) = P$).

More generally, we write $s \rightarrow t$ where s is in the column of role A and t is in the column of role B to denote the following: A constructs and sends the message s and B will accept any message that has the form t. This is similar to a classical notation due to Lowe and used in [24]. We also abbreviate the patterns using equations, e.g., we may write $t \mid X = t'$ meaning the substitution of all occurrences of X in t by t'. We also note that every column represents a variable scope of its own; each agent can only see the values in its own scope that are not calligraphic. If the same variable name occurs in two scopes then the protocol intends them to be the same, but it does not assume that, i.e., we do not a priori exclude that (due to an attack) there may be a mismatch. However, all occurrences of a particular variable in one column (*role* of the protocol) always shall be the same value.

Dishonest Provers and Verifiers. It is crucial that an intruder (or several dishonest agents controlled by the intruder) can act as a normal participant and perform zero-knowledge proofs about its knowledge, or act as a dishonest server, accepting proofs. As it is standard in black-box cryptography models, the intruder is characterized by a set of rules that express what new messages he can derive from a given set of messages. For the zero-knowledge proofs we have the following two rules:

$$\frac{\mathsf{spk}(S; P; \phi; Stmt) \in \mathcal{DY}(M)}{\langle P, \phi, Stmt \rangle \in \mathcal{DY}(M)} \quad \text{and} \quad \frac{\langle S, P, \phi, Stmt \rangle \in \mathcal{DY}(M)}{\mathsf{spk}(S; P; \phi; Stmt) \in \mathcal{DY}(M)},$$

The first rule tells us that from seeing a zero-knowledge proof, the intruder can learn the public values, the property proved, and the statement signed—but not the secret values, of course. Note that we do not need to consider proof verification for the intruder, since honest agents perform only correct proofs, and since dishonest agents in our model collaborate and do not try to cheat each other.

The second rule tells us that the intruder can construct spk terms for any subterms that he knows. This includes many terms that do not make up valid zero-knowledge proofs, i.e., when the claimed property ϕ does not hold for the secret and public values involved. In reality, this corresponds to the intruder sending nonsensical terms instead of a zero-knowledge proof, that have the correct basic format, but on which the verification will fail. One may rule out such terms from our model by specializing the intruder rules, but in fact they do not hurt because honest agents only accept valid zero-knowledge proofs (and dishonest agents do not need to be convinced).

Proof Identifiers. The proof identifiers ϕ in the zero-knowledge proofs play the role of identifying the relation that is being proved. While of course the secret and public values the prover holds might also satisfy other relations (or properties), the cryptographic properties of the implementation of a proof hold only for the specified relation. This becomes also clear in our abstraction, as the following simple example shows. In Identity Mixer, a user may show for instance that he or she is over 18 years old. Another service of a deployed system may give a reduction on an entry fee if one proves to be over 65. Consider a user U who has shown to be over 18 and who is in fact 70. Obviously, the credential of U in this proof can also be used to prove that U is over 65. So the over-18 proof must carry the information that it proves only the over-18 property, not the stronger over-65 property. Otherwise there would be the danger to misuse proof terms for getting more information about a person than actually revealed.

Mafia Attacks. A Mafia Attack is a classical man-in-the-middle attack against zero-knowledge proofs for authentication, where a dishonest verifier I tries to use the identity of the prover P towards another (honest) verifier V, by forwarding every message from P to V and vice-versa. In the non-interactive zero-knowledge world, I can simply forward the entire proof term from P to any V at any time. A simple way to prevent this attack is to include in the signed statement *Stmt* of an spk term the name of the intended verifier. In fact, in Identity Mixer all proofs implicitly contain the name of the intended verifier.

Replay Attacks. Also, when an intruder has seen a zero-knowledge proof, he can replay it (to the intended verifier) any number of times. Usually, the concrete application will insert into the proved statements also some mechanisms to prevent replay, e.g., include context information in the message *Stmt*, so an anonymous electronic order may contain an order number (and timestamp).

4   Identity Mixer Components

We now describe step-by-step the components of Identity Mixer along with our formalization. We proceed bottom up, from the smallest units of Identity Mixer to the largest. In the next section, we then show how these components are used in concrete example protocols.

The Identity Mixer system defines two kinds of parties: *users* and creates a *master secret*, which it never reveals to any other party.

Users are known to organizations under *pseudonyms* and organizations make statements about users by issuing *credentials* to the users. Each credential is bound to the master secret of the user that it is issued to (without the issuer learning that master secret).

Master Secret. Every user U has a master secret that we denote x_U. This master secret is crucial because each pseudonym and credential in Identity Mixer is based on a master secret and we define the ownership of pseudonyms and credentials as knowledge of their master secrets. We can model $x_{.}$ as a private function (i.e., the intruder cannot obtain the master secret of a known user). Note, however, that the function is not a cryptographic operation, but just a mapping from users to their respective master secrets. (This also reflects the assumption that every user can have only one master secret.)

Pseudonyms and Domain Pseudonyms. Users interact with organizations under pseudonyms. We assume that by default users create a fresh pseudonym for every separate interaction with an organization, so that different interactions cannot be linked. A pseudonym is related to the master secret of the user. A pseudonym has the form:

$$p(x_U, R) \ ,$$

where R is a random value created by the user (without R, all pseudonyms of a user would be the same). This allows every user to establish as many different pseudonyms with an organization as it wishes. There are cases where this is not desirable and a user should have only one pseudonym for a given domain (e.g., a set of organizations, identified by a string) so that the user can be anonymous but not acting under different pseudonyms. This is useful for instance for petitions where users should state their opinion only once. For this, we use a *domain pseudonym* which has the form:

$$pd(x_U, domain) \ ,$$

where *domain* is a string specifying the domain.

Both the functions are public (see section 2), so the intruder can form his own pseudonyms and domain pseudonyms, but there is no further rule, in particular one cannot obtain x_U from a known pseudonym.

Commitments. In several transactions, we need commitments of the form

$$commit(R, V) \ ,$$

where V is a value that is committed to, and R is a random number. Also this function is public, i.e., the intruder can build commitments, but from the commitment one cannot obtain the committed value V (nor R). Commitments will be used for dealing with values in a credential that the issuing organization does not see while proofs have to be made about these values.

Credentials. Roughly speaking, a credential is a list of attributes signed by the issuing organization O. We assume, for simplicity, that every organization issues only one *type* of credentials. We assume that the public keys of each organization O, along with a description of the credential type that O issues, are publicly known. This may include (informal or formal) descriptions of the meaning of the attributes. In the implementation, all attributes are represented as integers (or fixed-length sequences of integers), so we shall not distinguish the different attribute types (like *date* or *string*) here, but assume that they are understood from the credential type (which is determined by the signature of O). Also, a credential is relative to the master secret x_U of a user U, and the ownership of a credential is defined by the knowledge of the underlying master secret. Thus, a credential has the form

$$cred_O^{x_U}(V_1, \ldots, V_{k_O}) .$$

Here, the V_i are the values of the attributes and k_O is the number of attributes contained in credentials issued by O.

The function symbol *cred* is characterized by two intruder rules. First, from a credential, the intruder can derive its attributes (but not the master secret):

$$\frac{cred_O^{x_U}(A) \in \mathcal{DY}(M)}{A \in \mathcal{DY}(M)} ,$$

where A is any list (a concatenation) of attributes. Second, for every dishonest organization O the intruder can issue credentials given a commitment by the user on its master secret.

$$\frac{A \in \mathcal{DY}(M) \quad commit(R, x_U) \in \mathcal{DY}(M)}{cred_O^{x_U}(A) \in \mathcal{DY}(M)} \text{ dishonest}(O) ,$$

Relations on Attributes. When using credentials to prove properties about one-self, Identity Mixer allows the user to hide the attribute and to prove only a statement about it. For instance, the user could prove to be over 18 years old according to an electronic passport. More concretely, suppose we have a passport $cred_O^{x_U}(name, bd, \ldots)$ where *name* is the bearer's name, *bd* is the birthdate etc. We want to show $plusYears(bd, 18) \leq today$ where *plusYears* adds to a date a given number of years and *today* is the date of the verification, and $\leq$ is the comparison on dates.

This is problematic in two regards. First, if we commit to using concrete numbers, e.g., setting a birthdate to a concrete date in a scenario, then the verification result only applies to that particular birthdate which is clearly not very helpful. Second, we get the problem of dealing with arithmetic in general (e.g., that from $bd_1 \leq bd_2$ and $bd_2 \leq bd_3$ it immediately needs to follow that $bd_1 \leq bd_3$ without further proof).

To avoid both problems, we consider only unary relations $R(x)$, e.g., R can be the "over-18" property of birthdates. (This excludes for instance the proof that one birthdate is greater than another.) Let $R_1, \ldots, R_n$ be the set of relations that can occur in all zero-knowledge protocols of our verification task. We consider the 2^n equivalence classes of data (recall that we assume just one data type for attributes), denoted as $D_{0,\dots,0}, \dots, D_{1,\dots,1}$, where

$$D_{b_1,\dots,b_n} = \{x \mid R_1(x) \iff b_1 \wedge \dots \wedge R_n(x) \iff b_n\} \ .$$

We do not exclude that one relation may imply another, e.g., R_1 may be "over-18" and R_2 may be "over-21"; in this case the equivalence classes $D_{0,1,\dots}$ are simply empty.

For the encoding of concrete credential attribute values such as names, dates, and so on, we use terms of the form $val(c, b_1, \dots, b_n)$ where val stands for an abstract value, c is an ordinary constant (so we can have several abstract values that belong to the same equivalence class) and $b_1, \dots, b_n$ is the list of booleans that characterizes the concrete equivalence class.

Let us assume for the concrete age example that there is only one relation "over-18" and we consider the concrete scenario with the certificate

$$cred_O^{x_U}(val(alice, 0), val(aliceBirthday, 1)) \ ,$$

i.e., where the name $alice$ does not satisfy "over-18", but the date of birth does. (Note that there is only one other reasonable case, namely with $val(aliceBirthday, 0)$ where alice is a minor.)

Verifiable Encryption. Our model of verifiable encryption does differ somewhat from standard public-key encryption, namely we will use so-called *labels*. A label is a public string that can be attached to a ciphertext when generating it. The label has the property that (1) a ciphertext cannot be decrypted without the correct label and (2) the label cannot be modified. Labels are useful for instance to bind the context to a ciphertext or a policy defining under what circumstances the third party is expected to decrypt. To model this encryption primitive, we use terms of the form $\mathsf{crypt}(k; m; l)$ where k is the public key of the recipient (usually a trusted party) m is the encrypted message and l is the encryption label. The symbol is characterized by three intruder deduction rules. First, $crypt$ is again a public symbol; the other two are:

$$\frac{\mathsf{crypt}(k; m; l) \in \mathcal{DY}(M)}{l \in \mathcal{DY}(M)} \quad \text{and} \quad \frac{\mathsf{crypt}(k; m; l) \in \mathcal{DY}(M) \quad \mathsf{inv}(k) \in \mathcal{DY}(M)}{m \in \mathcal{DY}(M)} \ ,$$

These rules express that the intruder can see the label from any encryption, and that he can decrypt the message if he knows the private key $\mathsf{inv}(k)$.

Another difference with respect to the standard model of encryption is that we will use the term in zero-knowledge proofs, e.g., that the encryption indeed has the form $\mathsf{crypt}(T; M; L)$ for the trusted third party T that an organization wants to use and M is, for instance, the attributes of a particular credential.

5   Identity Mixer Protocols in Concrete Scenarios

The components introduced in the previous section can be put together in many different ways, depending on what scenario shall be addressed. The resulting protocols can then be analyzed using automated formal verification tools such as OFMC [26]. In this section we give an example protocol that uses Identity Mixer.

We consider a scenario where a user U wants to buy some wine at an online winery without revealing its personal information. For that, U needs to prove to the wineshop that it is over 18 years old according to a passport that was issued by organization I. The passport credential shall have the format (omitting a lot of common passport fields for simplicity):

$$cred_I^{x_U}(Surname, Prename, DateOfBirth) \ .$$

We model a statement about an attribute by a relation R indicating the "over-18" property, so the date of birth of an adult will simply be $val(c, 1)$ where c is an individual constant (i.e., the birthdate). For instance, U may have the following concrete credential in its possession:

$$cred_I^{x_U}(Smith, Alice, val(c, 1)) \ .$$

The online winery O and the user run a protocol, shown in Figure 2, that requires the user to prove (1) the possession of a credential C that was issued by I and has $val(\mathcal{B}, 1)$ in the birthdate field; (2) the knowledge of its master secret $\mathcal{X}$ to which C is bound (recall that all expressions that the receiver does not learn from the zero-knowledge proof are set in calligraphic font); and (3) that the pseudonym $p(\mathcal{X}, \mathcal{R})$ by which the user introduces itself also contains its master secret. We denote this proof statement by *wine*. With the zero-knowledge proof, the user also signs an order description ORD; we assume that this order contains a unique order ID that is assigned when U has browsed the offers of the winery and selected "order". Such a unique ID (and also a timestamp) trivially prevent all problems with multiple processing of the same order (due to replay of the intruder or honest mistakes).

Finally, O also requires a verifiable encryption of the surname and prename attributes of C for the trusted third party T. This includes an encryption label LO that identifies the purpose of the verifiable encryption and specifies a condition under which the encryption may be opened. In this scenario, the label should include an opening date if the customer did not pay. In case that A never pays for the order, O can forward the entire zero-knowledge proof and the verifiable encryption to T. Now T checks whether O's claim is valid: first it verifies the zero-knowledge proof and whether the payment conditions (as stated in LO) were indeed not met by the user (how this is verified is not part of our scenario). If these checks are successful, T decrypts the verifiable encryption using the label LO. Hence, according to our convention, the attributes S and P are set here in italic and not in calligraphic font. The same holds for these two attributes within the shown credential—because T can also check the zero-knowledge proof. Thus T can infer the real name of the spk-signer of ORD. Note, however, that T does not learn any more information than what was intentionally revealed by U, namely it does not learn the master secret $\mathcal{X}$, the credential C, or the contained concrete date of birth $\mathcal{B}$.

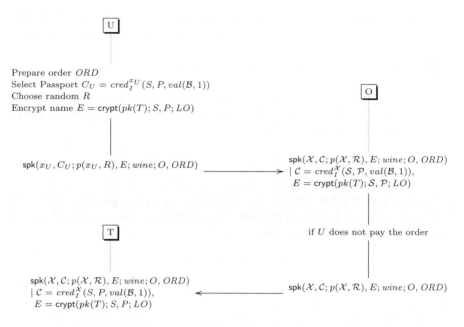

Fig. 2. First scene of the online shopping scenario

In this scene, we have omitted the delivery and payment processes. There are several possible ways to implement them. One can use verifiably encrypted orders to a payment organization (like U's credit card organization) and a delivery company. But one can alternatively use anonymous payment (which can be realized again using Identity Mixer) and anonymous pickup (which is offered, e.g., by gas stations in which case a delivery code could be verifiably encrypted for it).

Verification Goals. We omit here the details of special events that are used in the formal specification to allow for a declarative specification of the goals, and just give an informal account of them:

Correct presentation of credentials. First, if an honest O appears to have received a well-formed order, then there indeed exists a user U (not necessarily honest) who owns the required credential and has submitted the order. Second, if the honest judge T is convinced that a particular user has submitted an order, then this is indeed the case, even if O is not honest.

Privacy. Here we consider only some secrecy goals (i.e., safety properties), not indistinguishability of traces. First, the intruder knows x_U iff U is dishonest. Nobody ever learns other agents' credentials or contents that are not intentionally revealed.

Accountability. After a shop has received an order, there is enough evidence from which, with the help of T, the identity of the ordering user can be obtained in case no payment is made.

Formal Verification Results. All the goals just stated have been formulated and checked to hold for the given scene with the OFMC tool [26] for at least two symbolic sessions. Here, a session means that each role like U and O is instantiated with one individual agent (honest or dishonest) who wants to execute the protocol and symbolic means that we do not specify a concrete instantiation, but let OFMC consider every possible instantiation of the role names with agent names. As a result, we can be sure that there is no attack in any scenario with two sessions. More complicated attacks are thus those that necessarily relate to at least three individual sessions, for which, besides contrived examples, we have only examples in parametrized protocols. A major goal of Identity Mixer is that one cannot observe more information about users than they deliberately released, including that the different transactions of a user cannot be linked. These privacy goals are quite difficult to formalize since they are not properties of single execution traces but rather based on the question whether the intruder can observe a difference between certain pairs of traces. In the automated protocol verification, there are only few approaches that address privacy properties [19]. We therefore do not consider privacy properties formally and just give an informal account. All an intruder is able to learn from the zero-knowledge proof

$$\mathsf{spk}(\mathcal{S}; P; \phi; Stmt) \ ,$$

are the public values P, the signed statement $Stmt$, and the fact that the proved property ϕ holds on $\mathcal{S}$ and P. The idea is thus that the intruder cannot distinguish two such terms that differ only in the $\mathcal{S}$ part and this would reflect that the intruder can only observe those properties that are deliberately released by the respective participant. Things are indeed tricky, however. Note that throughout our formalization, for simplicity, we have used deterministic functions, i.e., when a user performs several times the same zero-knowledge proof or verifiable encryption with exactly the same arguments, the result will exactly be the same—and this can indeed be observed. It is not difficult to include a fresh random value into every relevant function as an additional argument, and this correctly models the non-deterministic behavior of the real operations. Given non-deterministic functions, one can indeed formally define what it means that two terms are unequal but not distinguishable for the intruder and based on that prove the privacy. Unfortunately, this is beyond the scope of the current automated verification tools.

6   Conclusions

Experimental Results. The goal of our formalization is a model that is well suited for automated protocol verification tools. We have developed this model in interaction with experiments on the tool OFMC [26]. However, our formalization does not dependend on OFMC and we have initial results also with other tools of the AVIPSA/AVANTSSAR platform [3] (into which OFMC is integrated) and that share with OFMC the common input languages IF and ASLan. We have modeled an e-Commerce scenario that uses Identity Mixer protocols as building blocks as described in Section 5. The tools of the AVISPA platform can verify this scenario within minutes. Also, for the variant that ommits the intended verifier in zero-knowledge proofs the tools can detect the classical Mafia-attack (cf. Section 3) within seconds.

Related Work. The SPK notation that we have used in this paper was inspired by the notation for the cryptographic protocols of Camenisch and Stadler [16]. We have slightly adapted the use here, explicitly denoting the values that are revealed and moreover denoting only those secret values that one must prove to posses. Another difference is the use of a proof identifier rather than a proof statement; this is to enable that we can exploit pattern matching in tools. In fact, one may use as the proof identifier a term that encodes the proof statement in some way, but the tools cannot interpret these terms (and only check for equality of these terms). Related to the original notation, Bangerter et al. [8] show how to derive automated zero-knowledge proofs from this. The modeling of non-interactive zero-knowledge proofs has independently been studied by Backes et al. [7]. Their approach is mainly based on algebraic properties: they use explicit verify-operations that can be applied by the receiver to the received proof terms and that explicitly check for certain conditions. This algebraic formalization is very involved and easily leads to non-termination of the verification tool, ProVerif [11], that they use. To avoid the non-termination, the algebraic theory has to be carefully adapted and to make this encoding still manageable, it is generated by a special compiler. For all these difficulties, the authors have turned to a type-system approach [6].

Li, Zhang, and Deng [23] give a similar formalization of an old version of Identity Mixer that seems to work fine in ProVerif. Indeed, their model works at a deeper level of cryptographic detail than that of Backes et al. [7]—which requires an even more complex algebraic theory. However, Li el al. [23] has a fundamental mistake in the handling of algebraic properties in verification tools: implicitly, all function symbols are interpreted in the free algebra in ProVerif and even encoding just those properties of exponentiation that are needed for Diffie-Hellman is far from trivial [22]. For this reason, Li et al. [23] accidentally arrive at a model that cannot make any progress at all—on which all kinds of safety and privacy properties trivially hold.

From all this, one may get the wrong impression that algebraic properties in general thwart practical protocol verification. In fact the noted tools OFMC and ProVerif can handle algebraic properties and with Maude-NPA there is even a protocol verifier based on the algebraic specification framework Maude [21]. However, a declarative formalization of zero-knowledge proofs does not fall into the fragments of algebraic reasoning that can be handled well (such as convergent rewrite theories), and therefore require a quite technical encoding [7].

Resumee. We thus see as our main contribution to define a model of zero-knowledge proofs that does not require algebraic properties at all. This is of big advantage when using the two most successful methods in protocol verification: the constraint-based approach [2] implemented in tools like OFMC and the stateless over-approximation approach of tools like ProVerif. Moreover it enables the use of successful tools like SATMC [5] that do not support algebraic properties at all.

The key idea to achieve that is to use pattern matching to describe the receiving of zero-knowledge protocols. This is analogous to the problem of modeling decryption in a Dolev-Yao style black-box model of cryptography: instead of a property that says that encryption and decryption cancel each other out, we use pattern matching for decryption, i.e. honest agents accept only messages that are encrypted with the expected key (plus an appropriate intruder deduction rule for decrypting messages). We thus obtain a formal model of zero-knowledge proofs that is both declarative and efficient. This enables us to use zero-knowledge proofs as a primitive of security protocols in formal verification just like any other standard cryptographic primitive such as symmetric encryption.

This is practically illustrated by our verification of two scenarios based on Identity Mixer. In fact, it is a further contribution that we provide a formal model of Identity Mixer which itself is a building-block for complex applications, e.g. in e-Commerce and e-Government. This model provides an important intermediate step between very high-level, technology-neutral specifications such as CARL [14] and the cryptographic details of the actual Identity Mixer implementation.

We finally note that there have been several proposals for formalizing privacy goals in the black-box model, see for instance Abadi and Fournet [1]. These models are quite difficult for automated analysis, though there are some new ideas [20,19]. Further investigation is left for future work.

References

1. Abadi, M., Fournet, C.: Private authentication. Theoretical Computer Science 322(3), 427–476 (2004)
2. Amadio, R., Lugiez, D.: On the reachability problem in cryptographic protocols. In: Palamidessi, C. (ed.) CONCUR 2000. LNCS, vol. 1877, pp. 380–394. Springer, Heidelberg (2000)
3. Armando, A., Basin, D.A., Boichut, Y., Chevalier, Y., Compagna, L., Cuéllar, J., Drielsma, P.H., Héam, P.-C., Kouchnarenko, O., Mantovani, J., Mödersheim, S., von Oheimb, D., Rusinowitch, M., Santiago, J., Turuani, M., Viganò, L., Vigneron, L.: The AVISPA Tool for the Automated Validation of Internet Security Protocols and Applications. In: Etessami, K., Rajamani, S.K. (eds.) CAV 2005. LNCS, vol. 3576, pp. 281–285. Springer, Heidelberg (2005)
4. Armando, A., Carbone, R., Compagna, L., Cuellar, J., Abad, L.T.: Formal Analysis of SAML 2.0 Web Browser Single Sign-On: Breaking the SAML-based Single Sign-On for Google Apps. In: FMSE 2008. ACM Press, New York (2008)
5. Armando, A., Compagna, L.: SAT-based Model-Checking for Security Protocols Analysis. International Journal of Information Security 7(1), 3–32 (2008)
6. Backes, M., Hritcu, C., Maffei, M.: Type-checking zero-knowledge. In: ACM Conference on Computer and Communications Security, pp. 357–370 (2008)
7. Backes, M., Maffei, M., Unruh, D.: Zero-knowledge in the applied pi-calculus and automated verification of the direct anonymous attestation protocol. In: IEEE Symposium on Security and Privacy, pp. 202–215 (2008)
8. Bangerter, E., Camenisch, J., Krenn, S., Sadeghi, A.-R., Schneider, T.: Automatic generation of sound zero-knowledge protocols. Cryptology ePrint Archive (2008)

9. Bangerter, E., Camenisch, J., Lysyanskaya, A.: A Cryptographic Framework for the Controlled Release Of Certified Data. In: Christianson, B., Crispo, B., Malcolm, J.A., Roe, M. (eds.) Security Protocols 2004. LNCS, vol. 3957, pp. 43–50. Springer, Heidelberg (2006)
10. Bellare, M., Goldreich, O.: On defining proofs of knowledge. In: Brickell, E.F. (ed.) CRYPTO 1992. LNCS, vol. 740, pp. 390–420. Springer, Heidelberg (1993)
11. Blanchet, B.: An efficient cryptographic protocol verifier based on Prolog rules. In: CSFW 2001, pp. 82–96. IEEECOSO (2001)
12. Blum, M., Feldman, P., Micali, S.: Non-interactive zero-knowledge and its applications (extended abstract). In: STOC, pp. 103–112 (1988)
13. Camenisch, J., Lysyanskaya, A.: An efficient system for non-transferable anonymous credentials with optional anonymity revocation. In: Pfitzmann, B. (ed.) EUROCRYPT 2001. LNCS, vol. 2045, p. 93. Springer, Heidelberg (2001)
14. Camenisch, J., Mödersheim, S., Neven, G., Preiss, F.-S., Sommer, D.: A card requirements language enabling privacy-preserving access control. In: SACMAT, pp. 119–128. ACM Press, New York (2010)
15. Camenisch, J., Sommer, D., Zimmermann, R.: A general certification framework with application to privacy-enhancing certificate infrastructures. In: SEC (2006)
16. Camenisch, J., Stadler, M.: Efficient group signature schemes for large groups. In: Kaliski Jr., B.S. (ed.) CRYPTO 1997. LNCS, vol. 1294, pp. 410–424. Springer, Heidelberg (1997)
17. Cervesato, I., Jaggard, A.D., Scedrov, A., Tsay, J.-K., Walstad, C.: Breaking and fixing public-key Kerberos. Information and Computation 206(2-4) (2008)
18. Chaum, D.: Blind signatures for untraceable payments. In: Advances in Cryptology - Crypto '82, pp. 199–203. Springer, Heidelberg (1983)
19. Cheval, V., Comon-Lundh, H., Delaune, S.: Automating security analysis: symbolic equivalence of constraint systems. In: Giesl, J., Hähnle, R. (eds.) IJCAR'10. LNCS (LNAI), vol. 6173, pp. 412–426. Springer, Heidelberg (2010)
20. Cortier, V., Rusinowitch, M., Zalinescu, E.: Relating two standard notions of secrecy. In: Ésik, Z. (ed.) CSL 2006. LNCS, vol. 4207, pp. 303–318. Springer, Heidelberg (2006)
21. Escobar, S., Meadows, C., Meseguer, J.: A rewriting-based inference system for the NRL protocol analyzer and its meta-logical properties. Theoretical Computer Science 367(1-2), 162–202 (2006)
22. Küsters, R., Truderung, T.: Using proverif to analyze protocols with diffie-hellman exponentiation. IEEE CSF, 157–171 (2009)
23. Li, X., Zhang, Y., Deng, Y.: Verifying anonymous credential systems in applied pi calculus. In: Garay, J.A., Miyaji, A., Otsuka, A. (eds.) CANS 2009. LNCS, vol. 5888, pp. 209–225. Springer, Heidelberg (2009)
24. Millen, J.K., Denker, G.: Capsl and mucapsl. Journal of Telecommunications and Information Technology 4, 16–27 (2002)
25. Mödersheim, S.: Models and Methods for the Automated Analysis of Security Protocols. PhD-thesis, ETH Zürich (2007)
26. Mödersheim, S., Viganò, L.: The open-source fixed-point model checker for symbolic analysis of security protocols. In: Fosad 2007–2008–2009. LNCS. Springer, Heidelberg (2009)
27. Mödersheim, S., Viganò, L.: Secure Pseudonymous Channels. In: Backes, M., Ning, P. (eds.) ESORICS 2009. LNCS, vol. 5789, pp. 337–354. Springer, Heidelberg (2009)
28. Schnorr, C.P.: Efficient signature generation for smart cards. Journal of Cryptology 4(3), 239–252 (1991)

Automatic Structure-Based Code Generation from Coloured Petri Nets: A Proof of Concept

Lars Michael Kristensen[1] and Michael Westergaard[2]

[1] Department of Computer Engineering, Bergen University College, Norway
lmkr@hib.no
[2] Department of Mathematics and Computer Science,
Eindhoven University of Technology, The Netherlands
m.westergaard@tue.nl

Abstract. Automatic code generation based on Coloured Petri Net (CPN) models is challenging because CPNs allow for the construction of abstract models that intermix control flow and data processing, making translation into conventional programming constructs difficult. We introduce Process-Partitioned CPNs (PP-CPNs) which is a subclass of CPNs equipped with an explicit separation of process control flow, message passing, and access to shared and local data. We show how PP-CPNs caters for a four phase structure-based automatic code generation process directed by the control flow of processes. The viability of our approach is demonstrated by applying it to automatically generate an Erlang implementation of the Dynamic MANET On-demand (DYMO) routing protocol specified by the Internet Engineering Task Force (IETF).

1 Introduction

The development of concurrent software systems is complex due to the rich behaviour introduced by concurrency, communication, and non-determinism. Coloured Petri Nets (CPNs) [9] and CPN Tools [2] (and formal modelling in general) have been widely used to address these challenges and construct formal and executable models of system designs with the aim of validating functional and performance properties prior to implementation [7]. Constructing a formal model yields important insight into the system design, and is a very helpful reference artefact when conducting a manual implementation of a software design. Even so, manual implementation is error-prone and time-consuming, making automatic code generation [8, Chap. 21] preferable in order to reduce the risk of introducing errors and to exploit the resources invested in model construction.

Despite the wide use of CPNs and high-level Petri Nets for modelling and design validation, we are aware of relatively few examples where CPNs have been used to automatically obtain an implementation of the final software system. This is in contrast to, e.g., the area of hardware design, where low-level Petri nets have been widely used to synthesise hardware circuits [17]. A *simulation-based approach* to automatic code generation from CPNs has been used in the projects reported in [13] and [10]. Here, the simulation code for the CPN model

S. Kowalewski and M. Roveri (Eds.): FMICS 2010, LNCS 6371, pp. 215–230, 2010.

generated by CPN Tools is extracted, and after undergoing automatic modifications, e.g., linking the code to external libraries, the generated simulation code is used as the system implementation. A simulation-based approach is also used in [14] to generate Java code from a high-level Petri net. The idea of [14] is to make a class diagram which outlines the classes and method signatures of the program. From this diagram, classes are generated where the method bodies are filled with simulator code. The advantage of a simulation-based approach is that it does not put any additional limitations on the class of models for which code can be generated. Furthermore, the direct use of the simulation code automatically ensures that the implementation is behaviourally equivalent to the underlying model. A main disadvantage is performance. Firstly, the execution speed is affected because each step in the execution of the program involves the computation and execution of enabled transitions (as done by a simulator) in order to determine the next state. Secondly, the approach ties the target platform to that of the simulator which may make the approach impractical for certain application domains due to resource consumption. As an example, the SML/NJ compiler used for the simulator in CPN Tools has a large memory footprint making it ill-suited for the domain of embedded systems. These disadvantages can to some extent be overcome using a *state-based approach*. Here, the state space of the model is used to control the execution of the program and determine the next state. This approach assumes that the state space is finite and small.

The disadvantages of simulation- and state-based approaches to code generation motivate our work on a *structure-based approach*. The key idea is to exploit *structure* in the CPN model, which can be naturally mapped to conventional programming language constructs. This has the advantage that the structure of the CPN model becomes clearly recognisable in the generated code, and that the generated code has a structure closer to code written by a human programmer. Furthermore, the code generated using a structure-based approach contains no simulator scheduler to control the execution, thereby improving performance, and the approach can be made target language independent. Exploiting structure in CPNs for code generation purposes is challenging since CPNs makes it possible to model control flow structures, message passing, and data access more abstractly than supported directly in most programming languages.

To address this, we introduce *Process-Partitioned CPNs* (PP-CPNs) which constitute a subclass of CPNs. PP-CPNs contain additional syntactical information and semantic restrictions that provide an explicit separation of process control flow, message passing, and access to data. This is used in a four phase code generation approach, where the choice of target language is deferred to the last two phases. Figure 1 shows the four phases in our structure-based code generation approach for translating a PP-CPN model into code in a target programming language. The first phase (**1**) translates a PP-CPN into a control flow graph (CFG) for each process subnet, extracting the control flow from the model. Nodes in a CFG represent statements and directed edges represent jumps in the control flow. The CFG may also be subject to static analysis, e.g., dead code elimination. In the second phase (**2**) the CFG is translated into an abstract

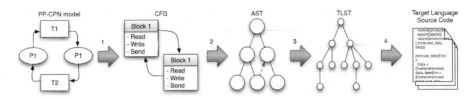

Fig. 1. Structure-based code generation phases

syntax tree (AST) for a simple intermediate language designed to be abstract enough that it can be translated into most programming languages (see [4] for details), and such that it can capture the assumptions made on the target language in a generic way. The AST can also be used to recognise common control structures such as while loops and if-statements. In the third phase **(3)**, the AST is translated into a syntax tree for the target language (TLST). Finally, in phase four **(4)** the TLST is traversed and the target language source code is produced. The first two phases are target language independent.

To validate our automatic code generation approach, we have implemented it in a computer tool where Erlang [3] is used as the target language. Erlang is a concurrency-oriented language developed at Ericsson for reliable and fault-tolerant concurrent software in telecommunication switches. We report on the use of the developed approach and supporting computer tool to automatically obtain an implementation of the Dynamic MANET On-demand (DYMO) protocol [1]. Being able to model an industrial protocol like DYMO demonstrates that PP-CPNs are sufficiently expressive to model systems occurring in practice. The definition of PP-CPNs is inspired by [11], where a process-oriented subclass of CPNs was defined to facilitate partial-order state space reduction.

Outline. Section 2 introduces the basic concepts of PP-CPNs and the associated syntactical and semantical restrictions. Section 3 formally defines syntactical PP-CPNs that statically ensures the restrictions introduced in Sect. 2. Section 4 illustrates the four phases of the translation process using an example. In Sect. 5 we explain how our code generation approach has been used to obtain an implementation of the DYMO protocol [1]. We sum up our conclusions in Sect. 6. This paper is partly based on the thesis [4] (supervised by the authors of this paper), and an early version has appeared in the technical report [6]. The reader is assumed to be familiar with the basic notions of high-level Petri nets, i.e., the combination of Petri nets and a programming language.

Definitions and notation. The formal definition of PP-CPNs use the definitions and notation of CPNs from [9, Chap. 4] as a basis. Let V be a set of variables and $EXPR$ a set of expressions. Then for $v \in V$, $Type(v)$ is the *type* of the variable v, for $e \in EXPR$, $Var(e)$ is the set of *free variables* of e, $Type(e)$ is the *type* of the expression e, and $EXPR_V$ is the set of expressions with free variables contained in V. For a set S, we denote by $\mathbf{N}^S$ the multi-set type over S, i.e., the set of all multi-sets (bags) over S. We define $\cup$, $\cap$, $-$, $=$, $|\cdot|$, and

$\subseteq$ (union, intersection, difference, equality, size, and subset) as normal for multi-sets, and use a notation, where $m = n'a$ is the multi-set with $m(a) = n$ and $m(b) = 0$ for $b \neq a$, and use $++$ for union as an alternative symbol.

Definition 1 (Coloured Petri net). *A **coloured Petri net** CPN is a tuple* $CPN = (P, T, \Sigma, V, C, G, E, I)$ *where:*

1. *P is a finite set of **places** (by convention drawn as ellipses), and T is a finite set of **transitions** (by convention drawn as rectangles),*
2. *Σ is a set of non-empty **colour sets** (types), and V is a set of **typed variables** such that $Type(V) \subseteq \Sigma$,*
3. *$C : P \rightarrow \Sigma$ is a **colour set function** that assigns a colour set to each place,*
4. *$G : T \rightarrow EXPR_V$ is a **guard function** that assigns a guard (by convention written in square brackets) to each transition t such that $Type(G(t)) = Bool$,*
5. *$E : P \times T \cup T \times P \rightarrow EXPR_V$ is an **arc expression function** with $Type(E(p, t)) = \mathbf{N}^{C(p)}$ and $Type(E(t, p)) = \mathbf{N}^{C(p)}$,*
6. *$I : P \rightarrow EXPR_\emptyset$ is an **initialisation function** that assigns an initialisation expression to each place p such that $Type(I(p)) = \mathbf{N}^{C(p)}$.* $\square$

A *binding* of a set of variables V is a function that maps each variable $v \in V$ to an element (value) of $Type(v)$. An expression $e \in EXPR_V$ evaluated in a binding b over V (denoted $e\langle b\rangle$) is the value obtained by replacing all free occurrences of v in e by $b(v)$. A binding of a transition t is a binding over the variables $Var(t)$ of t, and $B(t)$ denotes the set of all bindings for a transition t.

2   Process-Partitioned CPNs and Process Subnets

To introduce and motivate the constructs of PP-CPNs, we use the producer-consumer system shown in Fig. 2. The figure depicts the initial marking of a producer-consumer system with two producers (identified using the colours (values) P(1) and P(2)) and two consumers (identified using the colours C(1) and C(2)). Data items produced and consumed are modelled as integer values.

A PP-CPN is a union of *process subnets* each describing the program code executed by one or more processes. The producer-consumer system consists of two process subnets: one process subnet (left) modelling the producer, and one process-subnet (right) modelling the consumer. The transitions of a process subnet model the actions of processes, and the *process places* P_{pr} model control flow locations. The transitions and the process places of a process subnet make the control flow of processes explicit in the model, and from the current marking (token distribution) it is easy to determine where a process is in its control flow. The consumer process subnet (right) has three transitions ReceivedData, ConsumeEven, and ConsumeOdd modelling the actions of consumer processes, and process places ConsumerIdle and ConsumerWaiting modelling control flow locations. ReceivedData is a local place (see below) used by consumers to locally store a received data item before it is consumed. We have modelled the consumption of data items using the two transitions ConsumeOdd and ConsumeEven in order to illustrate how our approach handles branches in the control flow of processes.

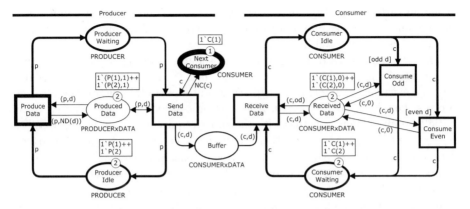

Fig. 2. The producer-consumer PP-CPN model

We introduce a special *process colour set* (type) τ, and a *process variable function PV*. The process variable function provides for each transition a *process variable* of type τ which in an occurrence of the transition identifies the process executing the statement represented by the transition. The variable p of the colour set PRODUCER used on the arcs connecting process places and transitions is a *process variable* which in an occurrence of a binding of a transition identifies the process executing the action modelled by the transition.

A process subnet has a set of *local places* P_{loc} that make explicit data which is local to a process. The place ProducedData is a *local place* (representing data local to a single producer) used to locally store produced data before it is sent to the consumer. The function ND is used to determine the produced data item. A process subnet also consists of a set of *shared places* P_{shr} and a set of *buffer places* P_{buf}. Buffer places and shared places constitute the mechanism provided in PP-CPNs for connecting process subnets and make synchronisation points explicit. Buffer places correspond to communication channels between processes, whereas shared places represent memory shared between processes. The place NextConsumer is a *shared place* representing shared data between the producer processes. The colour of the token on the place NextConsumer identifies the consumer to which a given data item will be sent. The function NC is used to determine the consumer that will receive the next data item. The place Buffer is a *buffer place* connecting the producer process subnet and the consumer process subnet. It models a buffer for the transmission of data items from producers to a specific consumer. We define a set of *process identification functions PrId* = $\{PrId_p\}$ on the set of process-, local-, and buffer places that projects multi-sets of structured types onto the process type, allowing us to project onto the *process identity* of tokens on process, local, and buffer places. We refer to tokens residing on process places as *process tokens*.

Next, we introduce semantical restrictions on the initial marking and arc expressions to make local places behave as local variables, shared places behave as global variables, and buffer places behave as unordered unicast communication channels. These semantical requirements are central to our code generation approach to be presented in Sect. 4.

The first semantical restriction concerns the initial marking. We require that all processes represented by the subnet start in the same location. This translates into the existence of single process place p_I initially containing a token for each process, i.e., $PrId_p(I(p_I)\langle\rangle) = \tau$. All other process places p are required to be initially empty which (together with the above requirement) can be expressed as $\sum_{p \in P_{pr}} PrId_p(I(p)) = \tau$. The other requirements concerning the initial marking is that each local place p initially has a token for each process, i.e., $PrId_p(I(p)) = \tau$; a shared place p holds exactly one token, i.e., $|I(p)\langle\rangle| = 1$; and each buffer place p is initially empty, i.e., $I(p)\langle\rangle = \emptyset$. The requirement on local places reflects that tokens on such a place represent the current value of a local variable (one for each process). The requirement on a shared place reflects that the single token represents the current value of a global variable.

The next requirement concerns the arc expression functions. We require that the occurrence of transitions preserve the control flow of processes, i.e., that the tokens removed from process places (when projected to process identities) by a transition t in a binding b ($\sum_{p \in P_{pr}} PrId_p(E(p,t)\langle b\rangle)$) is equal to the tokens added ($\sum_{p \in P_{pr}} PrId_p(E(t,p)\langle b\rangle)$) when projected to process identities, and that this equals $1`b(PV(t))$, i.e., exactly one process token corresponding to the process variable $PV(t)$ of the transition. For a local place, we require that each transition removes exactly one token from such a place, and that each transition adds exactly one token (or removes/adds zero tokens in case the transition is not connected to the place). Also, we require that the process identities of the tokens added and removed match the binding of the process variable of the transition. For shared places, we only require that each transition removes exactly one token and adds exactly one token (or removes/adds zero tokens in case the transition is not connected to the place). Finally, if a transition t removes tokens from a buffer place p in binding b (i.e., receives an item from the channel represented by p), then a single token is removed, and the process identity of the token removed ($PrId_p(E(p,t)\langle b\rangle)$) matches the value $b(PV(t))$ assigned to the process variable.

Finally, we have a requirement for shared and buffer places. The requirement allows us to calculate enabling for transitions (i.e., execute statements of processes) without taking special care of the race conditions that could arise when accessing buffer and shared places (which can also be accessed by other processes). The requirement is that if we have found a binding b of a transition t that satisfies the enabling condition with respect to local and process places (i.e., required tokens are available and the guard $G(t)$ of t is satisfied), then for all shared and buffer places p and colours (tokens) $c \in C(p)$, we can find a new binding b' such that the token removed from p is c, the guard $G(t)$ of t is satisfied, and the tokens removed from all other places p' ($E(p',t)\langle b'\rangle$) is equal to those removed in the original binding $E(p',t)\langle b\rangle$. The following definition summarises the definition of process subnets based on the description above.

Definition 2 (Process Subnet). *A **process subnet** is a tuple*
$(CPN, P_{pr}, P_{loc}, P_{shr}, P_{buf}, \tau, PV, PrId)$, *where:*

1. $CPN = (P_{pr} \cup P_{loc} \cup P_{shr} \cup P_{buf}, T, \Sigma, V, C, G, E, I)$ *is a CPN cf. Def. 1,*
2. P_{pr} *is a set of **process places**,* P_{loc} *is a set of **local places**,* P_{shr} *is a set of **shared places**, and* P_{buf} *is a set of **buffer places** such that* P_{pr}, P_{loc}, P_{shr}, *and* P_{buf} *are mutually disjoint,*
3. $\tau \in \Sigma$ *is a **process colour set**,*
4. $PV : T \rightarrow V$ *is a **process variable function** that assigns a process variable to each transition t such that* $Type(PV(t)) = \tau$,
5. $PrId = \{PrId_p : \mathbf{N}^{C(p)} \rightarrow \mathbf{N}^\tau\}_{p \in P_{pr} \cup P_{loc} \cup P_{buf}}$ *is a set of linear **process identification functions** that maps multi-sets over $C(p)$ into multi-sets over τ for each place $p \in P_{pr} \cup P_{loc} \cup P_{buf}$,*
6. *The initialisation function I additionally satisfies:*

   6a. *There exists a process place $p_I \in P_{pr}$ such that $PrId_p(I(p_I)\langle\rangle) = \tau$ and* $\sum_{p \in P_{pr}} PrId_p(I(p)) = \tau$,
   6b. *For all $p \in P_{loc} : PrId_p(I(p)) = \tau$, for all $p \in P_{shr} : |I(p)\langle\rangle| = 1$, and for all $p \in P_{buf} : I(p)\langle\rangle = \emptyset$,*

7. *The arc expression function E additionally satisfies:*

   7a. *For all $t \in T$, $b \in B(t)$:*
   $\sum_{p \in P_{pr}} PrId_p(E(p,t)\langle b\rangle) = \sum_{p \in P_{pr}} PrId_p(E(t,p)\langle b\rangle) = 1`(b(PV(t)))$,
   7b. *For all $p \in P_{loc}$, $t \in T$, and $b \in B(t)$:*
   $PrId_p(E(p,t)\langle b\rangle) = PrId_p(E(t,p)\langle b\rangle) \subseteq 1`(b(PV(t)))$,
   7c. *For all $p \in P_{shr}$, $t \in T$, and $b \in B(t)$: $|E(p,t)\langle b\rangle| = |E(t,p)\langle b\rangle| \leq 1$,*
   7d. *For all $p \in P_{buf}$, $t \in T$ and $b \in B(t)$: $PrId_p(E(p,t)\langle b\rangle) \subseteq 1`(b(PV(t)))$,*

8. *Shared places and buffer places are neutral with respect to enabling: Let $t \in T$, $b \in B(t)$ be such that $G(t)\langle b\rangle = $ true. Then for all $p \in P_{shr} \cup P_{buf}, c \in C(p)$ there exists a binding $b' \in B(t)$ such that:*

   8a. $E(p,t)\langle b'\rangle = 1`c$ *and $G(t)\langle b'\rangle = $ true*
   8b. *For all $p' \in P - \{p\} : E(p,t)\langle b\rangle = E(p,t)\langle b'\rangle$* □

Items (7) and (8) are central to our approach as it allows checking the enabling of a transition in a process subnet by checking a) if the transition is enabled when we ignore all arcs from shared and buffer places, and b) if there are tokens on all incoming buffer places. Hence, enabling becomes monotone, i.e., as soon as both a) and b) hold for a transition $t \in T$ in a binding $b \in B(t)$ with $b(PV(t)) = pid$, it can only stop holding for t and b if a transition $t' \in T$ is executed in a binding $b' \in B(t')$ for which $b'(PV(t')) = pid$, i.e., if another transition is executed for the same process identity. This is shown by applying (7a), (7b) and (7d) to the requirements. Relaxing (8), i.e., allowing variables in arc expressions from shared places to affect the enabling of the transition, would introduce dependency on the value of the token on the shared place, which can be modified by any other process. Allowing values from buffer places to affect the enabling of transitions would make enabling no longer dependent only on presence but also on the received value. Requirement (7d) is necessary as it is otherwise possible for a transition with another binding of the process variable to consume a value deemed available from a buffer.

A PP-CPN is a union of process subnets only intersecting on buffer and shared places. We do not formally define this union here as it can be obtained by using the above definition of process subnets in Def. 6 of [11].

3   Syntactical Process Subnets

In general, it is undecidable whether requirements (7) and (8) of Def. 2 are satisfied since they depend on all possible bindings for a transition (and the inscription language of CPNs is Turing complete). Hence, for implementation purposes we introduce sufficient syntactical requirements (which can be statically checked) that imply that the semantical requirements in Def. 2 are satisfied.

We restrict the colour sets of process places to be equal to the process colour set τ, and the colour sets of local places P_{pr} and buffer places P_{bufin} are required to be a cartesian product $\tau \times \sigma$ of the process colour set and some colour set σ. This means that the process identity function on process places becomes the identity function, and for local and buffer places it projects into the first component. As a consequence, we require arc expressions to/from process places of a transition t to have the form $1`PV(t)$.[1] Also, all variables of a transition must be bound via input arcs or in the guard, and all dependencies between variables (except the process variable) must be expressed in the guard. We denote by $InVar(t)$ the set of free variables appearing on input arcs and guards of a transition t. We require input arc expressions from local and input buffer places p to have the form $1`(PV(t), v(t)(p))$ and input arc expression from shared places to have the form $1`v(t)(p)$, where $v : T \to P_{loc} \cup P_{bufin} \cup P_{shr} \to V \cup \{\bot\}$ is a function that assigns a unique non-process variable to be used in the arc expression from p to t. We define $v(t)(p) = \bot$ in case p is not connected to t. Output arc expressions to local places are required to have the form $1`(PV(t), e(t, p))$ where $e(t, p)$ is an expression over free variables from input arc expressions and guards, i.e., $e(t, p) \in EXPR_{InVar(t)}$. For output arc expressions to shared and output buffer places we have the same requirement concerning free variables. Finally, non-process variables in arc expressions from shared places and from input buffer places cannot be referred to in the guard. Our precise requirements are given in the following definition.

Definition 3 (Syntactical Process Subnet). *A* **syntactical process subnet** *is a tuple* $(CPN, P_{pr}, P_{loc}, P_{shr}, P_{buf}, \tau, PV, PrId)$, *satisfying:*

1. $CPN, P_{pr}, P_{loc}, P_{shr}, P_{buf}, \tau, PV, PrId)$ *are as defined in items (1)-(6) of Def. 2, $P_{bufin} \subseteq P_{buf}$ denotes the set of input buffer places, and $P_{bufout} \subseteq P_{buf}$ denotes the set of output buffer places,*

---

[1] For the PP-CPN model in Fig. 2 there is not an explicit $1`$ (coefficient) in front of arc expressions that evaluates to single token as is convention in CPN Tools.

2. *The colour set function C is defined such that:*

$$C(p) = \begin{cases} \tau & \text{for } p \in P_{pr}, \\ \tau \times \sigma & \text{for } p \in P_{loc} \cup P_{bufin} \text{ and some } \sigma \text{ such that } \tau \times \sigma \in \Sigma, \\ \sigma & \text{for } p \in (P_{bufout} - P_{bufin}) \cup P_{shr} \text{ for some } \sigma \in \Sigma, \end{cases}$$

3. *The process functions $PrId = \{PrId_p : \mathbf{N}^{C(p)} \to \mathbf{N}^\tau\}_{p \in P_{pr} \cup P_{loc} \cup P_{buf}}$ are defined such that that $PrId_p$ is the identity function for $p \in P_{pr}$, and $PrId_p$ projects onto the first component for $p \in P_{loc} \cup P_{buf}$,*

4. *There exists a function $pre : T \to P_{pr}$ mapping transitions to input process places and a function $v : T \to P_{loc} \cup P_{bufin} \cup P_{shr} \to V \cup \{\bot\}$ with $v(t)(p) \neq v(t)(p')$ or $v(t)(p) = v(t)(p') = \bot$ if $p \neq p'$, assigning unique non-process variables to all non-process input places such that:*

$$E(p, t) = \begin{cases} 1'(PV(t)) & \text{for } p = pre(t), \\ 1'(PV(t), v(t)(p)) & \text{for } p \in P_{loc} \cup P_{bufin} \text{ and } v(t)(p) \neq \bot, \\ 1'(v(t)(p)) & \text{for } p \in P_{shr} \text{ and } v(t)(p) \neq \bot, \\ \emptyset & \text{otherwise} \end{cases}$$

5. *There exists a function $succ : T \to P_{pr}$ mapping transitions to output process places and expressions $e(t, p) \in EXPR_{InVar(t)}$ of correct type such that:*

$$E(t, p) = \begin{cases} 1'(PV(t)) & \text{for } p = succ(t), \\ 1'(PV(t), e(t, p)) & \text{for } p \in P_{loc} \text{ with } v(t)(p) \neq \bot, \\ 1'(e(t, p)) & \text{for } p \in P_{shr} \text{ with } v(t)(p) \neq \bot, \\ e(t, p) & \text{for } p \in P_{bufout}, \\ \emptyset & \text{otherwise} \end{cases}$$

6. *The guard function additionally satisfies that for all $p \in P_{bufin} \cup P_{shr}$ and transitions t: $Var(E(p, t)) \cap (Var(G(t)) - \{PV(t)\}) = \emptyset$.* □

We have that a syntactical process subnet also is a process subnet. Requirements (1)-(6) in Def. 2 are shared via (1) of Def. 3. Items (2) and (3) of Def. 3 comply with the requirement to the process colour set and the process identification function in items (3) and (5) of Def. 2. Items (4) and (5) in Def. 3 implies (7a)-(7d) in Def. 2. Items (4) and (6) in Def. 3 ensures that (8) in Def. 2 holds as all tokens are consumed using distinct variables that are only made dependent in the guard, and as the guard cannot include variables bound on arcs from shared or buffer places, we get the desired result.

4   Translation Process and Phases

We assume that the target language considered has a notion of processes (or threads) and that it allows for message passing between processes. We do not assume direct support for shared memory as it can be implemented using a separate process and message passing. In addition, we assume that the target language has conditional jumps and a means for storing data local to a process. The Erlang programming language (which we shall concentrate on in this paper as the target language) satisfies these requirements. We assume that the model consists of syntactical process subnets as defined in Sect. 3).

4.1   Phase 1: Translating the PP-CPN Model to a CFG

The main purpose of this phase is to extract the control flow from the PP-CPN model and represent it explicitly in a CFG. A CFG is a directed graph in which arcs correspond to jumps in the control flow and nodes correspond to sequences of statements to be executed. A CFG is constructed for all process subnets in the PP-CPN model. In the producer-consumer system two CFGs are generated: one for the producer process subnet and one for the consumer process subnet. Figure 3 shows the translated CFG for the consumer process subnet. Transitions are translated into *basic blocks*, the nodes in the CFG, yielding three basic blocks for the producer-consumer system and a special basic block, start, that indicates where the process starts.

The content of basic blocks depends on connected non-process places. Basically, arcs from a non-process place correspond to reading a local or shared variable, or receiving a value from a buffer, and arcs to a non-process place correspond to writing and sending. As all arcs from non-process places are of the form 1'(pid, c) or 1'c where pid is the process variable and c a variable of the correct type ((4) in Def. 3) and each input arc has a unique variable (also (4) in Def. 3) an input arc is translated to a Read local (for arcs from local places), Read shared (for arcs from shared places), or Receive statements (for arcs from buffer places). Each statement contains the name of the place and a temporary variable to read the value into. The name of the temporary variable corresponds to the name of the variable from the PP-CPN model. In Fig. 3, the basic block ReceiveData contains a statement reading the local variable ReceivedData into the temporary variable od and a statement receiving a value from Buffer into the variable d. Analogously, arcs to non-process places are translated into Write local, Write shared, and Send statements that update variables or transmit values according to the expressions in the PP-CPN model. In Fig. 3, the basic block ReceiveData updates the variable ReceivedData with the value of the variable d.

Process places in the PP-CPN model are represented as arcs between basic blocks. This is possible as we assume that each transition has a unique predecessor

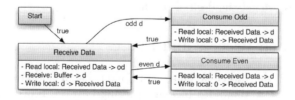

Fig. 3. The CFG of the consumer process

and successor process place ((4) and (5) in Def. 3), so we create an arc from t to t' if $succ(t) = pre(t')$. The process place with the initial marking τ (from (6a) in Def. 2) can be considered having an arc from a special transition start adding all the initial process tokens. In Fig. 3, the basic block ConsumeEven has an arc to ReceiveData signifying that after executing ConsumeEven, control should flow to the basic block ReceiveData, and after ReceiveData the program continues to either ConsumeOdd or ConsumeEven. Arcs of a CFG have a condition indicating when control can flow via an arc. The arc condition is extracted from the guard of the destination transition, using true for the absense of a guard. In Fig. 3, the arc from ConsumeEven to ReceiveData has condition true whereas the arc in the opposite direction has arc condition even d. We note that the guards should be evaluated with values of non-process places of the target node, not of the source node, but because of (4) and (6) in Def. 3 (or, equivalently, (8) from Def. 2), stating that guards can only depend on values on local places, this evaluation can be done already at the source node.

4.2   Phase 2: Translating the CFG to an AST

The main purpose of this phase is to translate the CFG into a tree form consisting of nodes representing common programming constructs such as read/write statements and jump statements. We also parse expressions used in the write statements and guards into abstract syntax, making subsequent steps independent of the inscription language used in the PP-CPN model.

Figure 4 shows a sub-tree of the AST for the producer-consumer example where only the nodes from the ReceiveData block of the Consumer have been fully expanded. When building the AST, a process is created for each CFG process. Figure 4 shows that the program contains two processes (Producer and Consumer) and a node for the global variable NextConsumer corresponding to the shared variable NextConsumer. Local variables and buffers are translated into nodes of the processes (processes can only transmit to a single process subnet because of (7) in Def. 2 and the fact that process types are unique to process subnets). In Fig. 4, the buffer place Buffer and the local place ReceivedData are translated into Buffer and Local variable sub-nodes of the Consumer process.

Each basic block is translated into a subtree of the AST, and the contents of basic blocks are translated into statements that correspond to the statements from the basic blocks, except that expressions are parsed into trees. For example, the Write local expression of the basic block ReceiveData in Fig. 3 is translated into Write local in the ReceiveData block in the AST in Fig. 4. The actual value to write (in the CFG just represented as the string d) is parsed into an expression consisting of the variable d in the AST. Arcs in the CFG are translated into conditional or unconditional jump statements in the AST. The conditions are also parsed, as can be seen in the conditional jump from ReceiveData to ConsumeOdd. The jump destinations are expressed using pointers rather than names because variables used in the conditions are in the scope of the destination, and to keep the flow of control explicit in the AST.

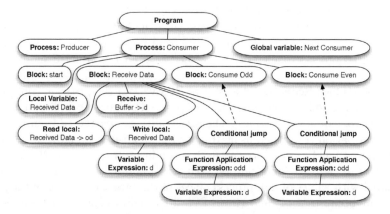

Fig. 4. The AST for the Receive Data block of the consumer

4.3   Phases 3 and 4: Translating the AST via TLST to Target Code

Phase 3 generates a syntax tree for a concrete target language based on an AST and phase 4 produces the actual target language code. Figure 5 shows part of the TLST produced for Erlang from the AST in Fig. 4. We will not go into details about the constructs, but only discuss some of the higher level concepts to give an impression of how the AST can be mapped into a TLST. We map each process into a module in Erlang, which is the primitive for code separation and processes. In addition to the processes directly represented in the AST in Fig. 4, we have added three other modules: system, buffer, and shared. The system module is responsible for setting up the system, instantiating processes, and making sure that processes have access to shared variables and buffers. The buffer module is added if a model contains a buffer place, and implements buffers using Erlang channels in order to be able to check if a buffer has any values available. The shared module uses processes to implement shared variables on top of the functional language Erlang. We represent jumps by function application, and generate a function for each block in the AST. Additionally, we introduce an environment record for each process to keep track of local variables and buffers. The environment is created by the start function and is modified and passed on by each function. Examples of Erlang code are not contained in this paper due to space limitations. The reader is referred to [4, 6] for examples.

5   Application to the DYMO Protocol

We have implemented our approach in a prototype in Java using the Access/CPN framework [16]. In addition to evaluate the prototype on smaller examples (such as the producer-consumer system), we have applied it to a PP-CPN model of the Dynamic On-demand MANET routing protocol (DYMO) [1]. The protocol is developed by the Internet Engineering Task Force and is intended for establishing routes in a *mobile ad-hoc network* (MANET). The protocol establishes routes

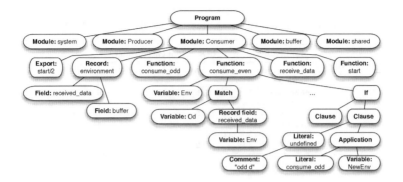

Fig. 5. Partial TLST for generated Erlang target code

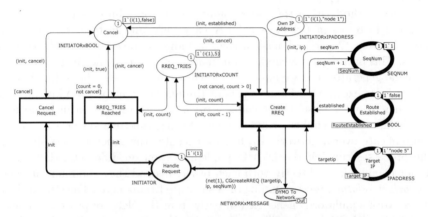

Fig. 6. The Initiator module of the PP-CPN DYMO model

on-demand, i.e., when they are actually needed. The model specifies the *route discovery* and *route maintenance* procedures of DYMO. Route discovery establishes routes by forwarding and multi-casting of *route request* messages. Route maintenance monitors links and uses timeouts to discover loss of connection, which causes *route errors* to be multi-casted to all neighbours.

The CPN model of the DYMO protocol [5] was constructed before starting our work on code generation, and were used to identify and resolve problems in the protocol specification. The complete PP-CPN model of DYMO consists of 8 modules, 49 places, and 18 transitions, and is thus fairly complex. Figure 6 shows an example module of the PP-CPN model for procedures initiating route discovery. The module can create a new route request (RREQ) or cancel the request when the retransmission limit is reached. A detailed description of the DYMO CPN model can be found in [5].

Generating Erlang code from the DYMO model yields the modules listed in Table 1. We have listed lines of code (LOC) for each module – in total we generate 563 lines of code. Since we do not support automatic translation of sequential

Table 1. Generated Erlang modules for the DYMO Protocol

Module name	LOC	Sequential functions
system.erl	20	0
buffer.erl	36	0
shared.erl	16	0
initiator.erl	116	1
receiver.erl	116	7
processer.erl	111	4
establishchecker.erl	126	0
network.erl	22	0
Total	563	12

SML to Erlang, we have to manually implement various Erlang expressions and functions on the basis of the corresponding SML code. Implementing the functions (12 in total) in Erlang is a fairly easy task, and in total we only spent approximately 12 person-hours on this, including removal of unused extracted values. This part could be handled automatically by an off-the-shelf SML parser and code generator, but we have considered it outside the scope of this paper.

In order to execute more than one node running the generated DYMO protocol implementation, we use a *distributed Erlang system* which is a mechanism in Erlang allowing a number of independent Erlang run-time systems (nodes) to communicate over a network. Each node executes the generated DYMO code. The processes running the DYMO implementation on different Erlang nodes do not communicate directly with each other. Instead they communicate via a *network simulator* process running on a separate Erlang node. The stub code for the network simulator is generated directly from the Network process subnet of the DYMO PP-CPN model. The network simulator process implements a simple MANET where both unicast and multicast is supported.

To monitor the behaviour of the program, each node prints its own routing table, which can be inspected to verify that the expected routes were established. To ensure that all parts of the generated code have been executed, we have tested the generated DYMO implementation with several different MANET configurations designed to exercise all parts of the code. The generated code established the correct routes in all cases, which provides confidence in the generated code and a proof-of-concept of our code generation approach.

6   Conclusions and Future Work

We have introduced the PP-CPN sub-class of CPNs, which forms the basis for a structure-based approach to automatically generate (Erlang) code from CPN models. The approach first extracts a control flow graph from the model, and from the control flow graph constructs an abstract syntax tree for an intermediate language. From the abstract syntax tree, we generate a syntax tree specific to the target language, translating generic control structures into language specific control structures. Furthermore, we have validated that our approach applies to real-life examples by applying it to a PP-CPN model of the DYMO protocol consisting of 8 modules, 49 places, and 18 transitions. Using manual inspection and logging, we have validated that traces in the generated code can be reproduced in the model and that the calculated routes are correct.

A structural approach to code generation in high-level Petri nets is also applied in [8]. The focus of [8] is on identifying processes in a Petri net, i.e., parts of the model that work independently of each other or only have few synchronisation points. Afterwards local variables (i.e., information only used by one process) and communication channels are found. In comparison, we provide this information explicitly in the form of the PP-CPN model. In [15], a class of CP-nets is translated into BPEL (Business Process Execution Language) which is an XML-based workflow implementation language. In contrast to our work, [15] focus on the flow of data and not on data processing and the BPEL language is not aimed at general application development. [12] improves on this by translating directly to Java by adding a data processing component, but it is very restricted and does not allow the use of general functions in the data processing part. Also, the approach [12] is limited to producing Java code, whereas our approach is target language independent.

One area of future work concerns extending the PP-CPN subclass. One direction is to allow using variables from buffer or shared places in guards. This complicates the calculation of guards, as the value may change as other process instances modify/receive values, requiring introduction of a locking mechanism for shared places. We can easily allow dependence on values from buffer places as long as all branches from any process place consume the same number of tokens from all buffer places, as we can just read all values and dispatch accordingly, allowing us to receive and dispatch a value from a buffer in a single step as opposed to the two steps required now. Allowing dependencies on input arcs, at least on arcs from local places, would make the allowed PP-CPN models more natural. It would also be interesting to look at dynamic instantiation of processes, which is not overly difficult since we already instantiate processes in our generated code. This could either be done using a language extension to PP-CPNs or simply allowing creation of new tokens on process places.

Currently, we do not perform static analysis in phase 1 in our prototype, making the generated code more verbose than needed and neither do we perform control structure recognition, which also makes the generated code a bit unnatural. It would be interesting to see how the generated code would be affected by actually conducting these steps. We have considered code generation for Erlang, but all steps until the generation of the target language dependent syntax tree are target language independent, and it would be interesting to also experiment with other target languages. A limitation of the current implementation is that the validation is done in an ad-hoc manner. Future work also includes formally proving correctness of the translation is correct by, e.g., formally defining our abstract language as represented by ASTs and proving that the generated abstract code is behaviourally equivalent to the PP-CPN model.

Acknowledgements. The authors acknowledges the work of K.L. Espensen and M.K. Kjeldsen on which this paper is partly based.

References

1. Chakeres, I.D., Perkins, C.E.: Dynamic MANET On-demand (DYMO) Routing, version 14, Internet-Draft. Work in Progress (June 2008)
2. CPN Tools webpage, http://www.cs.au.dk/CPNTools/
3. The Erlang programming language, http://www.erlang.org/doc.html
4. Espensen, K.E., Kjendsen, M.K.: Automatic Code Generation from Process-Partitioned Coloured Petri Net Models. Master's thesis, Dept. of Computer Science, Aarhus University (2008)
5. Espensen, K.L., Kjeldsen, M.K., Kristensen, L.M.: Modelling and Initial Validation of the DYMO Routing Protocol for Mobile Ad-Hoc Networks. In: van Hee, K.M., Valk, R. (eds.) ATPN'08. LNCS, vol. 5062, pp. 152–170. Springer, Heidelberg (2008)
6. Espensen, K.L., Kjeldsen, M.K., Kristensen, L.M., Westergaard, M.: Towards Automatic Code Generation from Process-Partitioned Coloured Petri Nets. In: Proc. of 10th CPN Workshop, pp. 41–60. Aarhus University (2009)
7. Examples of Industrial Use of CP-nets,
   http://www.cs.au.dk/CPnets/intro/example/indu.html
8. Girault, C., Valk, R.: Petri Nets for System Engineering: A Guide to Modeling, Verification, and Applications. Springer, Heidelberg (2003)
9. Jensen, K., Kristensen, L.M.: Coloured Petri Nets – Modelling and Validation of Concurrent Systems. Springer, Heidelberg (2009)
10. Kristensen, L.M., Mechlenborg, P., Zhang, L., Mitchell, B., Gallasch, G.E.: Model-based Development of COAST. STTT 10(1), 5–14 (2007)
11. Kristensen, L.M., Valmari, A.: Finding Stubborn Sets of Coloured Petri Nets Without Unfolding. In: Desel, J., Silva, M. (eds.) ICATPN 1998. LNCS, vol. 1420, pp. 104–123. Springer, Heidelberg (1998)
12. Lassen, K.B., Tjell, S.: Translating Colored Control Flow Nets into Readable Java via Annotated Java Workflow Nets. In: Proc. of 8th CPN Workshop. DAIMI-PB, vol. 584, pp. 127–146 (2007)
13. Mortensen, K.H.: Automatic Code Generation Method Based on Coloured Petri Net Models Applied on an Access Control System. In: Nielsen, M., Simpson, D. (eds.) ATPN'00. LNCS, vol. 1825, pp. 367–386. Springer, Heidelberg (2000)
14. Philippi, S.: Automatic code generation from high-level Petri-Nets for model driven systems engineering. Journal of Systems and Software 79(10), 1444–1455 (2006)
15. van der Aalst, W.M.P., Jørgensen, J.B., Lassen, K.B.: Let's Go All the Way: From Requirements Via Colored Workflow Nets to a BPEL Implementation of a New Bank System. In: Meersman, R., Tari, Z. (eds.) OTM 2005. LNCS, vol. 3760, pp. 22–39. Springer, Heidelberg (2005)
16. Westergaard, M., Kristensen, L.M.: The Access/CPN Framework: A Tool for Interacting With the CPN Tools Simulator. In: Franceschinis, G., Wolf, K. (eds.) ATPN 2009. LNCS, vol. 5606, pp. 313–322. Springer, Heidelberg (2009)
17. Yakovlev, A., Gomes, L., Lavagno, L.: Hardware Design and Petri Nets. Kluwer Academic Publishers, Dordrecht (2000)

Author Index

Printing: Mercedes-Druck, Berlin
Binding: Stein+Lehmann, Berlin